This book is dedicated to
My dear wife, Surie
My daughter, Esther
and
My son, Avrohom

Without their patience and love,
the writing of this book would not have been possible

SCHAUM'S OUTLINE OF

THEORY AND PROBLEMS

OF

INTERMEDIATE ACCOUNTING II

•

Assistant Professor of
Accounting and Computer Science
The College of Staten Island
The City University of New York

SCHAUM'S OUTLINE SERIES

McGRAW-HILL

New York   San Francisco   Washington, D.C.   Auckland   Bogotá   Caracas   Lisbon
London   Madrid   Mexico City   Milan   Montreal   New Dehli
San Juan   Singapore   Sydney   Tokyo   Toronto

About the author:

BARUCH ENGLARD, M.S., M.B.A., CPA is Assistant Professor of Accounting and Computer Science at The College of Staten Island of The City University of New York. He holds Masters' degrees in both accounting and computer science.

Professor Englard is a coauthor of *Intermediate Accounting I* in the Schaum's Outline Series and has published numerous articles on accounting and computer topics in professional accounting journals. He has participated in the grading of the CPA examination and has also lectured at Fordham University.

Schaum's Outline of Theory and Problems of
INTERMEDIATE ACCOUNTING II

6 7 8 9 10 11 12 13 14 15 16 17 18 19 20 PRS PRS 9 8

ISBN   0-07-019483-1

Sponsoring Editor, John Aliano
Production Supervisor, Rich Ausburn
Project Supervision, The Total Book

Library of Congress Cataloging-in-Publication Data

Englard, Baruch.
    Schaum's outline of intermediate accounting II / Baruch Englard.

    p.   cm.--(Schaum's outline series)
    Includes index.
    ISBN 0-07-019483-1
    1. Accounting.   I. Title.   II. Title: Schaum's outline of
intermediate accounting 2.
    HF5635.E55   1992
    657'.044--dc20   91-31252
                                                      CIP

McGraw-Hill

A Division of The McGraw-Hill Companies

PREFACE TO THE TEACHER AND STUDENT

This book may be used as a *complete stand-alone* text for the classroom, or as a supplement to a standard intermediate accounting textbook. I have used it as a stand-alone text in my classes and the students have given it a favorable response.

The book contains broad and in-depth coverage of the Intermediate Accounting II topics. It covers theory and practice and is helpful as a study aid for the CPA examination. The latest pronouncements of the FASB have been woven into the text.

Each chapter thoroughly discusses the topic at hand and then concludes with a summary of the chapter. This is followed by a series of rapid-review questions that require fill-in type answers.

At this point the student should have a good, overall understanding of the material presented. What then follows is a series of solved problems that thoroughly challenge the student's grasp of the material. The student is encouraged to solve these without looking at the answers. The problems are presented in the same order as the chapter material and are keyed to the chapter sections.

Finally, the chapter concludes with approximately ten supplemental problems *without answers* for additional practice. *These may be selected by the teacher as assignment material to be done at home or in class.*

The author wishes to thank John Aliano of McGraw-Hill for his assistance in the editing of the manuscript, Annette Bodzin of The Total Book for her skill in managing the book through the editing and production phases, and Tehila Weinbaum for her patience and skill in the typing of the manuscript.

BARUCH ENGLARD
Brooklyn, N.Y.
March, 1992

Imputing interest   page 9

Marketable Equity Securities — Common + Preferred Stock

Marketable debt securities — Gov Bonds + ~~other~~ ^corporate ^bonds ~~debt~~ ~~securities~~

If assets are not used to pay an Account, then
that Account is not a leability Account

eg   Stock ^Dividends ~~Assets~~ distributable

It is a Stockholders equity Account.

Stockholders equity consists of : Paid in Capital

ie Stock +

Paid in excess

+ Retained Earnings

<u>Both</u> Cash + Stock dividends decrease Retained Earnings

CONTENTS

Chapter 1

Long-term Liabilities

1.1 INTRODUCTION

Long-term liabilities are liabilities that will be paid after 1 year or after the operating cycle (whichever is longer), counting from the balance sheet date. Examples would be bonds payable, long-term notes payable, mortgages payable, pensions, and leases. Pensions and leases will be discussed in later chapters of this book. In this chapter, the emphasis will be on bonds payable and notes payable.

1.2 BONDS PAYABLE—DEFINITIONS

A *bond* is a written promise by a corporation to pay back the principal on a loan, plus interest. When you "buy" a bond, you are really lending money to the corporation and receiving in exchange a piece of paper (the bond) containing a promise to pay back the loan plus interest. The bond is, in effect, a professional form of what is commonly referred to as an "IOU."

A bond is based upon a contract called an *indenture,* which specifies the various characteristics of the bond. Such characteristics include the maturity date, rate of interest, and call provisions.

Several kinds of bonds are common today. *Secured* bonds are backed by collateral such as real estate or other investments, while *unsecured* bonds are not. A typical example of unsecured high-risk bonds is *junk bonds*. These pay a high rate of interest due to their high risk.

Term bonds pay the entire principal on one date—the maturity date—while *serial bonds* pay the principal in installments. *Convertible bonds* may be exchanged for stock of the issuing corporation, and they will be discussed in Chapter 4.

Commodity-backed bonds are redeemable in a commodity such as oil, coal, or precious metals, rather than cash.

Deep-discount bonds ("zero coupon bonds") do not bear interest. Instead they are sold at a steep discount. Thus there is an interest *effect* at maturity when the buyer receives the full par value.

Callable bonds give the issuer (the corporation) the right to pay up the bonds before the maturity date.

1.3 ISSUANCE OF BONDS—PAR AND DISCOUNT

The amount of principal specified to be paid back at maturity is called the *face value* or *par value*. The interest rate specified in the indenture is called the *contract rate* or *nominal rate*. If the contract rate is equal to the rate currently available in the economy—the *market rate*—the bond will be issued exactly for its par.

EXAMPLE 1

Assume a bond whose par value is $100,000 and whose contract rate is 10% payable annually is issued by the Greenfield Corporation. If the market rate is also 10%, the selling price will be the par value of $100,000. Assuming the date of issue is January 1, 19X1, interest is payable every December 31 and the life of the bond is 4 years, the journal entries will be as follows:

Jan. 1, 19X1	Cash		100,000	
	Bonds Payable			100,000
Dec. 31, 19X1	Interest Expense		10,000	
	Cash			10,000
	(This entry will be repeated every December 31 through 19X4).			
Jan. 1, 19X5	On this date, Greenfield Corporation will pay back the principal and make the following entry:			
	Bonds Payable		100,000	
	Cash			100,000

1

It often happens that after a corporation prints up a bond, the market rate changes. If the market rate goes up, nobody will be willing to buy this bond since it pays a lower rate than the market. What should the corporation do? It can simply tear up the bond and print a new one with the higher rate. However, printing takes time and costs money. A better idea would be to sell the bond at a discount—below par. At maturity time, however, the corporation must pay back the full par because it is so stated in the indenture (a helpful rule to remember is: The corporation must always pay exactly what the bond says). Thus the extra payback received by the buyer at maturity compensates him or her for the low interest rate in the bond. Indeed it may be considered additional interest.

EXAMPLE 2

Hill Company wants to issue a $10,000 bond with a 4-year life on January 1, 19X1. The contract rate specifies 10%; however, the market rate has risen to 12%. To induce a buyer to buy the bond, it offers to sell it at 96. In bond terminology this means a price of 96% of the par (102 would mean 102% of the par). The entry will be:

Jan.	1, 19X1	Cash	9,600	
		Bond Discount	400	
		Bonds Payable		10,000

The discount account is a contra-liability to the Bonds Payable account. At this point in time the company only owes $9,600 ($10,000 − $400). However, as we will soon see, the discount account will slowly start to become smaller, until it reaches zero at the maturity date. At that point, therefore, there will be no contra and the company will pay back the full par value.

Dec. 31, 19X1	Interest Expense	1,000	
	Cash		1,000

The $1,000 is based upon $10,000 × 10% = $1,000. Remember the handy rule: You always pay what the bond says. The bond says $10,000 and 10%. It does *not* say $9,600 or 12%.

Dec. 31, 19X1	Interest Expense	100	
	Bond Discount		100

As mentioned earlier, the discount is really additional interest to the buyer as compensation for the low contract rate. Rather than recognizing this interest in one large amount at the maturity date, the matching principle requires that it be recognized piecemeal over the life of the bond. This is called *amortizing* the discount. The amortization per year can be calculated under the straight-line method as follows:

$$\text{Amortization per year} = \frac{\text{discount}}{\text{bond life}} = \frac{400}{4} = 100$$

Another method, the effective interest method, will be discussed later.

The purpose of the amortization entry is to shuffle the amount in the discount account into the Interest Expense account because the discount, in essence, is extra interest. The liability owed on the bond has now gotten larger because of this extra interest and is evidenced by the now smaller contra discount account.

A look at the interest expense T-account indicates $1,100 for the year, as follows:

Interest Expense	
1,000	
100	

The $1,000 represents the physical interest payment to the buyer, while the $100 represents amortization of the discount. Thus the income statement will show $1,100 of interest expense.

The Bonds Payable account and the discount account will look like this:

Bonds Payable		Bond Discount	
	10,000	400	100

Thus the balance sheet on December 31, 19X1 will show:

Bonds Payable $10,000
Less Discount ___300
$ 9,700

These entries will be repeated yearly through December 31, 19X4. On January 1, 19X5, the company will pay the full par, as the bond states, as follows:

Bonds Payable   10,000
Cash   10,000

The discount account at this point has been totally amortized and has a zero balance.

1.4 ISSUANCE OF BONDS AT A PREMIUM

If the market rate has fallen below the contract rate, then it is the corporation that will be reluctant to issue these bonds that pay such a relatively high rate. Accordingly, to compensate itself, the corporation will issue the bond at a premium—above the par. At maturity, however, it will only have to pay back par (you always pay what the bond says!). Thus the premium may be viewed as a reduction of the interest expense.

EXAMPLE 3

It is January 1, 19X1. A corporation wishes to sell a $10,000, 4-year bond. The contract rate is 10% but the market rate is only 8%. Accordingly the price is set to 104 (104% of $10,000 = $10,400). This is a premium situation.

Cash   10,400
Bonds Payable   10,000
Bond Premium   400

The premium account is not a contra; it is an *addition* to the Bonds Payable account. However, as time goes by, the premium will be slowly amortized down to zero by the maturity date. Thus, at that time, the corporation will only have to pay back the par of $10,000.

Every Dec. 31   Interest Expense   1,000
Cash   1,000
10% of 10,000
Bond Premium   100
Interest Expense   100
400 ÷ 4 = 100

The interest expense for each year will thus be only $900 ($1,000 − $100). At the end of year 19X1 the balance sheet will show:

Bonds Payable $10,000
Plus Premium ___300 (400 − 100)
$10,300

At maturity, the entry to pay back the principal will be:

Bonds Payable   10,000
Cash   10,000

1.5 SEMIANNUAL AND QUARTERLY INTEREST PAYMENTS

Until now we have been discussing bonds that pay interest once a year, annually. Some bonds pay interest twice a year (semiannually) or four times a year (quarterly). In these cases, the entries for interest expense and amortization of the discount or premium must be made semiannually or quarterly, respectively.

EXAMPLE 4

If a bond pays 16% interest compounded semiannually, instead of paying 16% once a year, it will pay 8% twice a year. Similarly, if the interest is 16% compounded quarterly, it will pay 4% four times a year. The rate is always *expressed* on an annual basis; the word "compounded" tells you how many times per year it is paid.

EXAMPLE 5

If a $100,000, 4-year bond at 12% compounded semiannually is sold on January 1, 19X1 at 95, the entries for the interest and discount amortization will be made on June 30 and December 31, as follows:

June 30	Interest Expense	6,000	
	Cash		6,000
	$100,000 \times 12\% \times \frac{1}{2}$.		
	Interest Expense	625	
	Bond Discount		625
	$5,000 discount $\div 4 \times \frac{1}{2}$.		
Dec. 31	Same entries as on June 30.		

EXAMPLE 6

When we assume the same information as in Example 5 except that the 12% is compounded quarterly, the entries will be made four times a year (March 31, June 30, September 30, and December 31) as follows:

Interest Expense	3,000	
Cash		3,000
Interest Expense	312.50	
Bond Discount		312.50

1.6 ACCRUALS OF INTEREST

Up to this point all the situations that we have discussed dealt with an interest payment date of December 31. If the payment date is other than December 31, an adjustment entry must be made on December 31 to accrue the interest from the last payment date and also to amortize the discount or premium as well.

EXAMPLE 7

On May 1, 19X1 Berger Corporation issues a $10,000, 10%, 4-year bond at 96. The bond pays interest semiannually on November 1 and May 1. The entries are:

May 1, 19X1	Cash	9,600	
	Bond Discount	400	
	Bonds Payable		10,000
Nov. 1, 19X1	Interest Expense	500	
	Cash		500
	Interest Expense	50	
	Bond Discount		50
	400 $\div$ 4 years $\times \frac{1}{2}$ year.		
Dec. 31, 19X1	Interest Expense	166.67	
	Interest Payable		166.67
	10,000 $\times$ 10% $\times$ 2/12		
	To accrue 2 months of interest.		
	This entry will be reversed on January 1, 19X2, if the company makes reversing entries.		
Dec. 31, 19X1	Interest Expense	16.67	
	Bond Discount		16.67
	400 $\div$ 4 $\times$ 2/12.		

1.7   BONDS ISSUED BETWEEN INTEREST DATES

The bond indenture specifies all the important details of the bond, including the interest dates. Usually the bond is sold on an interest date. For example, if the interest dates are January 1 and July 1, the bond will be sold on one of these dates.

Occasionally it happens that the sale is delayed until a later date. Regardless of when the sale occurs, interest still accrues from the interest date. If the interest dates are January 1 and July 1 and the bond is sold March 1, interest must still be paid from January 1 (remember: the indenture is a legal contract and all its provisions must be followed).

To avoid having to pay interest for the time period before the issuance, the corporation will raise the price of the bond by the amount of the accrued interest. This is not a premium; it is simply a recovery of the "wasted" interest.

EXAMPLE 8

A $100,000, 5-year, 8% bond whose interest is payable December 31 and July 1 is issued at par plus accrued interest on April 1. The accrued interest for December 31 to April 1 is $2,000 ($100,000 × 8% × 3/12). The entry is:

Apr. 1	Cash	102,000	
	Bonds Payable		100,000
	Interest Expense		2,000
July 1	Interest Expense	4,000	
	Cash		4,000
Dec. 31	Interest Expense	4,000	
	Cash		4,000

Note.

The interest expense for the year will only be $6,000 ($4,000 + $4,000 − $2,000) since $2,000 was recovered as a result of raising the selling price.

If a premium or discount is involved, it should be amortized from the date of the sale, *not* the originally intended issue date.

EXAMPLE 9

Assume the same information as in Example 8 except that the bond is sold at 104. The entry at the date of issuance will be:

Cash	106,000	
Bonds Payable		100,000
Bond Premium		4,000
Interest Expense		2,000

The entries on July 1 and December 31 for the interest payments will be the same as in Example 8. However, an entry must also be made for premium amortization, as follows:

July 1	Bond Premium*	210.53	
	Interest Expense		210.53

*$4,000/57 × 3 months

Dec. 31	Bond Premium†	421.05	
	Interest Expense		421.05

†$4,000/57 × 6 months

The bond life is 5 years − 3 months = 57 months.

1.8   THE PRICE OF A BOND

We've seen that when the market rate of interest is different from the contract rate, the bond will sell at a premium or discount. But precisely how much will the premium or discount be? How does one go about calculating this premium or discount? The answer is that the price is based upon the following formula:

$$\text{Bond selling price} = \text{present value of the principal}$$
$$+ \text{ present value of the interest payments}$$

Note: If you would like a quick review of present value concepts, please see the Appendix at the end of the book.

The interest payments are an annuity; the principal is not. Accordingly, both the Present Value of $1 table and the Present Value of an Annuity of $1 table (both appearing in the Appendix) must be used.

EXAMPLE 10

The Weisz Corporation wishes to issue a $50,000, 4-year, 10% bond. The interest is payable annually. Unfortunately, the market rate has risen to 12%. Clearly, the bond must sell at a discount. But how much? We must find the present value of the $50,000 principal and of the $5,000 ($50,000 × 10%) annuity. According to the tables:

Present value of $50,000, 4 periods, 12% =   .63552
                                                    × $50,000
                                                              ──────────
                                                                $31,776

Present value of $5,000 annuity, 4 periods, 12% = 3.03735
                                                    × $5,000
                                                              ──────────
                                                                 15,187
                        The bond selling price is: $46,963

Notice that 12%, not 10%, was used in looking up the table. An important rule to remember is: *Always look up the table at the market rate.*

EXAMPLE 11

If in the previous example the rates were compounded semiannually, then the annuity would be $2,500 (5,000 × $\frac{1}{2}$) instead of $5,000, the periods would be 8 instead of 4, the market rate would be 6% instead of 12%, and the calculation would be as follows:

Present value of $50,000, 8 periods, 6% =   .62741
                                                    × $50,000
                                                              ──────────
                                                                $31,371

Present value of $2,500 annuity, 8 periods, 6% = 6.20979
                                                    × $2,500
                                                              ──────────
                                                                 15,524
                        The bond selling price is: $46,894

1.9   BOND ISSUE COSTS

There are a number of different costs incurred in the issuance of bonds, such as engraving and printing costs, legal and accounting fees, and commissions and promotion costs. According to APB Opinion No. 21, these costs should be debited to a deferred charge account (an asset) and then be amortized over the life of the bond. Generally the straight-line method of amortization may be used.

EXAMPLE 12

On January 1, 19X1, the Greco Corporation issues a $100,000, 5-year bond at par. It also pays $2,000 in printing costs. The entries are:

Jan. 1	Cash	100,000	
	Bonds Payable		100,000
	Unamortized Bond Issue		
	Costs	2,000	
	Cash		2,000

Dec. 31 Bond Issue Expense	400	
Unamortized Bond Issue Costs		400
To amortize the $2,000 cost over		
the 5-year life.		

1.10 EARLY RETIREMENT OF BONDS

The bond indenture may contain a provision stating that the corporation may pay up a bond before its maturity at a specified price. This is called an *early retirement* of the bond. If the price paid is greater than the book value of the bond, the difference is a loss. If it is less than the book value, the difference is a gain. Both a loss and a gain are considered to be extraordinary items.

The book value of a bond is equal to the balance in the bonds payable account minus any discount, plus any premium. It is important to make sure that the discount or premium account has been amortized right up to the retirement date.

The journal entry for a retirement closes the bonds payable account and the related discount or premium, credits cash, and recognizes the gain or loss.

EXAMPLE 13

On January 1, 19X1 Clark Corporation issued a $100,000 bond (5-year life) at 103. After 2 years it retired the bond at 104 (as specified in the indenture). At this point, the bond accounts appear as follows:

Bonds Payable	Bond Premium	
100,000	600	3,000
	600	
		1,800

The book value is thus $101,800 ($100,000 + $1,800). Since the retirement price is $104,000 (1.04 × $100,000), the difference of $2,200 is a loss. The journal entry is:

Bonds Payable	100,000	
Bond Premium	1,800	
Loss on Retirement	2,200	
Cash		104,000

If there is an unamortized bond issue cost relating to the bond, it should be written off at this point, thus enlarging the loss, or in a gain situation, reducing the gain.

EXAMPLE 14

A $50,000, 5-year bond was issued on January 1, 19X1, at 95. Related issue costs were $1,000. After 3 years the bond is retired at 90. The accounts appear as follows:

Bonds Payable	Bond Discount		Unamortized Bond Issue Cost	
50,000	2,500	500	1,000	200
		500		200
		500		200
	1,000		400	

The book value is $50,000 − $1,000 =	$49,000	
The retirement price is .90 × $50,000 =	45,000	
The gain is therefore	$ 4,000	

However, this gain must be reduced by the $400 write-off of the bond issue cost. The entry is:

Bonds Payable	50,000	
Bond Discount		1,000
Unamortized Bond Issue Cost		400
Gain on Retirement		3,600
Cash		45,000

1.11   THE EFFECTIVE INTEREST METHOD OF AMORTIZATION

Up to this point, we've used the straight-line method to amortize a discount or premium. A more compli-cated method of amortization is the effective interest method. Because of its greater theoretical justification, the accounting profession has *required* the use of this method unless the straight-line approach provides results that are not significantly different.

To calculate the periodic amortization, it is helpful to set up an amortization table.

EXAMPLE 15

A company issues a 4-year, $100,000 bond with a contract rate of 8% payable semiannually (4%). The market rate is 10% payable semiannually (5%). Using the formula, the selling price is determined to be $93,552. The table would appear as follows:

Interest Period	(A) Interest Paid 4% of Par	(B) Interest Expense 5% of Book Value	(C) Amortization	(D) Discount Balance	(E) Book Value
Issue Date	—	—	—	$6,448	$93,552
1	$4,000	$4,678	678	5,770	94,230
2	4,000	4,712	712	5,058	94,942
3	4,000	4,747	747	4,311	95,689
4	4,000	4,784	784	3,527	96,473
5	4,000	4,824	824	2,703	97,297
6	4,000	4,865	865	1,838	98,162
7	4,000	4,908	908	930	99,070
8	4,000	4,930*	930	0	100,000

*Adjusted for rounding error of $24.

Column A represents the physical interest paid each period—4% of $100,000. Column B represents the true interest expense—the market rate of 5% times the book value.

The main column of concern is column C, which tells us the periodic amortization. Its value is column B minus column A. Notice that the amortization changes from period to period, unlike the straight-line method, which provides a constant amount.

Column D is the balance in the discount account, and column E is the book value, which equals the par of $100,000 minus the discount balance of column D.

EXAMPLE 16

In this example we look at a table for the amortization of a premium. Assume a 4-year, $100,000 bond paying interest of 8% compounded semiannually. Since the market rate is 6%, the selling price will be $106,980.

Interest Period	(A) Interest Paid 4% of Par	(B) Interest Expense 3% of Book Value	(C) Amortization	(D) Premium Balance	(E) Book Value
Issue date	—	—	—	$6,980	$106,980
1	$4,000	$3,209	791	6,189	106,189
2	4,000	3,186	814	5,375	105,375
3	4,000	3,161	839	4,536	104,536
4	4,000	3,136	864	3,672	103,672
5	4,000	3,110	890	2,782	102,782
6	4,000	3,083	917	1,865	101,865
7	4,000	3,056	944	921	100,921
8	4,000	3,079*	921	0	100,000

*Adjusted for rounding error of $51.

Column E represents the par of $100,000 plus the premium balance.

1.12   LONG-TERM NOTES ISSUED FOR CASH

Long-term notes are payable after 1 year or the operating cycle (whichever is longer) counting from the balance sheet date. They are similar to bonds in that they both have fixed maturity dates and carry either an explicit or implicit interest rate. Usually small corporations will issue notes, while large ones will issue both notes and bonds. Notes do not trade as easily as bonds in the securities markets.

When a note is issued solely for cash and the contract rate equals the market rate, it will sell at par. Otherwise there will be a discount or premium that should be amortized over the life of the note, using the effective interest method.

EXAMPLE 17

A company issues a 5-year, *non-interest*-bearing note of $100,000 for only $49,718—a steep discount of $50,282. The entry at issuance would be:

Cash	49,718	
Discount on Note	50,282	
Notes Payable		100,000

This type of note is called a "zero-coupon" or "deep discount" note.

If straight-line amortization is used, the annual amortization would be $50,282 ÷ 5 = $10,056.40. If the effective amortization method is used, we must determine what effective rate was used to calculate the selling price of $49,718.

Let X represent the unknown present value decimal factor from the present value of $1 table.

We know that ($100,000) ($X$) yields 49.718.

Therefore X = 49.718. .49718

Searching the table for 49.718, we find the rate to be 15%. Accordingly the amortization table should use 15% as the rate for column B. Column A, of course, will contain zeros since the note is non-interest-bearing.

1.13   LONG-TERM NOTES ISSUED FOR GOODS OR SERVICES

If a note is issued in exchange for goods or services and the stated rate of interest is a fair one, then the note should be recorded at its face value. However, if the note is non-interest-bearing, contains an unrealistically low rate, or the face amount of the note differs significantly from the fair market value of the goods or services, a discount should be recognized and the goods or services should be debited for their fair market value.

EXAMPLE 18

A $100,000 *non-interest*-bearing note is issued for a machine whose fair market value is $60,000. Since it is unlikely for anyone to pay $100,000 for an item worth only $60,000, we say that the extra $40,000 is really "hidden interest." Recording the machine at $100,000 would be overstating the asset Machine and understating Interest Expense. The correct entry should be:

Machine	60,000	
Discount on Note	40,000	
Notes Payable		100,000

The discount should be amortized to interest expense over the life of the note using, preferably, the effective interest method.

If the fair market value of the asset is unknown, it should be debited for the *present value* of the note, using an interest rate that the buyer, based on his or her credit rating, would have to pay in today's economy. This is called *imputing* interest.

EXAMPLE 19

A 5-year, 4%, $100,000 note is issued in exchange for a machine. The fair market value of the machine is unknown. Since 4% is very unrealistic for today's economy, we have to assume that there really is additional hidden interest in the $100,000. To determine how much that is, we must take the present value of the $100,000 principal and the present value of the $4,000 interest annuity (4% × 100,000).

If this buyer must pay 10% in today's economy to borrow money, the present value computations are:

Present value of $100,000, 5 years, 10% =   .62092
$$\times \$100,000$$

$62,092

Present value of $4,000 annuity, 5 years, 10% = 3.79079
$$\times \$4,000$$

15,163

Total present value $77,255

The true cost of the machine is $77,255; the rest is hidden interest. The entry is:

Machine	77,255	
Discount on Note	22,745	
Notes Payable		100,000

1.14   LONG-TERM NOTES ISSUED FOR CASH AND SPECIAL PRIVILEGES

Sometimes when a note is issued, special privileges are given to the lender. For example, a company may issue *at face value* a long-term non-interest-bearing note to be repaid in 3 years and agree to sell merchandise to the lender at a discount during that period. In this case the difference between the loan proceeds and the present value of the 3-year note should be debited to a discount account and credited to a liability—Unearned Revenue. The discount should be amortized to interest expense over the 3-year period. The unearned revenue is considered to be a prepayment for sales that will occur during this period, and should therefore be gradually recognized as revenue as these sales take place.

The entries for the issuance of the note are:

Cash	XXX	
Notes Payable		XXX
Discount on Note	XXX	
Unearned Revenue		XXX

1.15   OFF-BALANCE-SHEET FINANCING

Off-balance-sheet financing is an attempt to borrow money without having to show the liability on the balance sheet. As a result, the quality of the balance sheet is enhanced and credit can be obtained more easily and at lower cost.

A typical example of such financing would be a "project financing arrangement." In this case two companies form a third company for the purpose of completing a project. The third company borrows money for this project, and agrees to pay it back from the proceeds of the project. The two original companies guarantee payment of the loan if the new company defaults.

As a result of this arrangement, the original two companies manage to avoid showing any debt on their balance sheets, since technically they are only guarantors rather than borrowers. In substance, however, they have really engaged in a borrowing.

EXAMPLE 20

Company A and Company B wish to build a plant together. They don't have enough money for this project and they don't want to borrow since that would increase the liabilities on their balance sheets.

Instead, they form a new entity—Company C. Company C borrows the money and agrees to pay it back from the goods produced by the plant. Companies A and B guarantee payment on the loan should Company C default. The liability is shown on the Company C balance sheet—not on A or B. This is "off-balance-sheet" financing.

In FASB No. 47, the accounting profession has required disclosure of any unconditional long-term obligations if all of the following conditions have been met:

1. They are noncancelable, or cancelable only with the permission of the other party.

2. They are part of a supplier's project financing arrangement for the facilities that are to provide the contracted goods or services.

3. They have a remaining term in excess of 1 year.

If these conditions are met, then the following disclosures (in the footnotes) are necessary:

1. The nature and term of the obligation.

2. The total amount of the fixed portion of the obligation as of the balance sheet date and for each of the next 5 years.

3. The nature of any variable portion of the obligation.

4. The amounts purchased under the obligation in take-or-pay* contracts for each period for which an income statement is presented.

Summary

1. *Long-term liabilities* are liabilities that will be paid after 1 year or the operating cycle (whichever is longer). One typical example would be bonds payable. A *bond* is a written promise made by the corporation to pay back the principal on a loan, plus interest.

2. The amount of principal to be paid at maturity is called the *face value* or *par value*. The interest rate specified in the bond is called the *contract rate*. If the contract rate is equal to the rate in the market, the bond will be issued at exactly par. If the contract rate is less than the market rate, the bond will sell at a discount. If the contract rate is greater than the market rate, the bond will sell at a premium.

3. The *discount account* is a contra liability to the bonds payable account, and is, in effect, considered to be additional interest on the loan. Rather than recognizing this interest in one large amount at the maturity date, the matching principle requires that it be recognized piecemeal over the life of the bond. This process is called *amortization*. The entry for the discount amortization is:

Interest Expense	xxx	
Bond Discount		xxx

4. Under the straight-line method of amortization, each year receives an equal amount of amortization, using the following formula:

$$\text{Amortization per year} = \frac{\text{discount}}{\text{bond life}}$$

5. In a premium situation, the premium account is an *addition* to the bonds payable account, and is, in effect, considered to be a reduction of the interest on the loan. Once again, this reduction is recognized on a piecemeal basis via annual amortization. The entry for the amortization is:

Bond Premium	xxx	
Interest Expense		xxx

6. If the bond pays interest annually, the entries for the cash interest and the amortization of premium or discount will be made annually. However, if the interest payments are made semiannually or quarterly, then these entries will be made two times per year and four times per year, respectively.

7. If the interest payment date is other than December 31, an adjustment entry must be made on December 31 to accrue interest from the last payment date and also to amortize the discount or premium.

---

*Take-or-pay-contracts require the "parent company" to make certain minimum payments for goods even if delivery of these goods is not taken.

8. Usually a bond is sold on an interest date. It occasionally happens that the sale is delayed until later. Regardless of when the sale occurs, interest still accrues from the interest date. To avoid having to pay interest for the time period before issuance, the corporation will raise the price of the bond by the amount of the accrued interest. This is not a premium; it is merely a recovery of the "unearned" interest. If a premium or discount is involved, it should be amortized from the actual date of the sale, not the originally intended date.

9. The price of a bond is determined by using the following formula:

   Bond selling price = present value of principal + present value of interest payments
   The interest payments are an annuity; the principal is not.

10. Bond issue costs such as engraving and printing costs, legal fees, and accounting fees should be debited to a deferred charge account and then amortized over the life of the bond. Generally, the straight-line method of amortization is used.

11. A corporation may pay up a bond before its maturity date. This is referred to as an *early retirement* of the bond. If the price paid is greater than the bond book value, the difference is a loss; if it is less, the difference is a gain. Both gains and losses are considered to be extraordinary items. The book value of a bond is equal to the balance in the bonds payable account, minus any discount, plus any premium.

12. Long-term notes are payable after 1 year or the operating cycle (whichever is longer). They are similar to bonds in that they both have fixed maturity dates and carry either an explicit or implicit interest rate. Usually small corporations issue notes while large ones issue both notes and bonds.

13. If a note is issued in exchange for goods and the stated rate of interest is a fair rate, the note would be recorded at its face value. However, if the note is non-interest-bearing, contains an unrealistically low rate, or has a face amount that differs significantly from the fair market value of the goods, then a discount should be recognized and the goods should be debited at their fair market value.

14. If the fair market value of the goods is unknown, the goods should be debited for the present value of the note, using an interest rate that the buyer, based on his or her credit rating, would have to pay in the marketplace. This is called *imputing* interest.

15. Off-balance-sheet financing is an attempt to borrow money without having to show the liability on the balance sheet. As a result, the quality of the balance sheet is enhanced and credit can be more easily obtained. A typical example of such financing is a "project financing arrangement."

16. If all of the following conditions have been met, the accounting profession requires the disclosure (in the footnotes) of any unconditional long-term obligations:

   (1) The obligations are noncancelable, or cancelable only with the permission of the other party.

   (2) The obligations are part of a supplier's project financing arrangement for the facilities that are to provide the contracted goods or services.

   (3) The obligations have a remaining term in excess of 1 year.

Rapid Review

1. Long-term liabilities will be paid after ___1 year___ counting from the ___BS___ date.

2. A bond is a promise to pay ___principle___ and ___interest___.

3. Bonds backed by collateral are called ___secured___ bonds.

4. Bonds that pay back the entire principal at one time are called _____TeRm_____ bonds.

5. Bonds that pay back the principal in installments are called _____SeRiAl_____ bonds.

6. Bonds that do not pay any interest but are issued at a steep discount are _____Deep Discount_____bonds. *Zero or Coupon bonds*

7. If the issuer has the right to pay up the bond before maturity, this bond is a _____Callable_____ bond.

8. Another name for par value is _____face._____.

9. The rate stated in the contract is called the _____Contract_____ or the _____Nominal_____ rate.

10. The market rate is also known as the _____effective_____ rate.

11. If the contract rate equals the market rate, the bond will be sold at _____PAR_____.

12. If the contract rate is greater than the market rate, the bond will be sold at a _____Discount_____ *Prem*, while if it is less, the bond will be sold at a _____premium_____. *8781.*

13. The process of transferring a premium or discount to interest expense is called _____Amortization_____

14. A premium _____Credits_____ interest expense while a discount _____Debits_____ interest expense.

15. The two methods of amortization are the _____Straight line_____method and the _____effective Interest_____method.

16. The discount account is a _____Contra_____ to the bonds payable account while the premium is a(n) _____addition_____.

17. If Dec. 31 is not an interest payment date, an _____Adjustment_____ must be made to accrue _____Interest_____.

18. The price of a bond is equal to the present value of the _____Principle_____ plus the present value of the _____Interest payment_____

19. The rate to use when looking up the tables to determine the selling price is the _____Market_____ rate.

20. Bond issue costs are considered to be a _____deferred_____ charge Account (asset)

21. If the price paid at retirement is greater than the book value, there is a _____loss_____; if it is less, there is a _____gain_____.

22. The book value of a bond equals the par plus any _____premium_____, minus any _____Discount_____

23. Gains or losses on early retirements are considered to be _____extraordinary item_____

24. If a note is non-interest-bearing and the market value of the asset to be acquired is known, the asset should be debited at _____market value_____

25. An attempt to borrow money without having to show the liability on the balance sheet is called _____off Bal sheet financing._____

26. A typical example of such an arrangement is a _____project. financing arrangement_____

Answers: 1. 1 year or the operating cycle; balance sheet 2. principal; interest 3. secured 4. term 5. serial 6. zero coupon 7. callable 8. face value 9. contract; nominal 10. effective 11. par 12. premium; discount 13. amortization 14. decreases; increases 15. straight-line; effective interest 16. contra; addition 17. adjusting entry; interest 18. principal; interest 19. market 20. deferred charge (asset) 21. loss; gain 22. premium; discount 23. extraordinary 24. its market value 25. off-balance-sheet financing 26. project financing arrangement

Solved Problems

Bonds Issued at Par, Discount, or Premium

1.1 If the contract rate is 10%, determine whether the bond will sell at par, at a discount, or at a premium under the following market rate conditions:
(*a*)　12%
(*b*)　　8%
(*c*)　10%

SOLUTION

(*a*)　discount　(*b*)　premium　(*c*)　par　　　　　　　　　　　　　　　　　[Section 1.3]

1.2 Assume a 3-year, 10% bond for $200,000 is issued on January 1, 19X1, at par. Prepare the entries for the issuance, the first interest payment, and the repayment of the principal at maturity.

SOLUTION

Jan.　1, 19X1	Cash		200,000	
	Bonds Payable			200,000
Dec. 31, 19X1	Interest Expense		20,000	
	Cash			20,000
Dec. 31, 19X3	Bonds Payable		200,000	
	Cash			200,000　　[Section 1.3]

1.3 Assume the same information as in Problem 1.2 except that the interest payments are made
(*a*)　semiannually
(*b*)　quarterly
Show how the entries for the interest expense would differ.

SOLUTION

For case (*a*) there would be (2) entries per year, each entry for one-half of 20,000, as follows:

Interest Expense	10,000	
Cash		10,000

For case (*b*) there would be four entries per year, each for $5,000.　　　　[Sections 1.3, 1.5]

1.4 A $200,000, 4-year bond paying interest of 10% compounded semiannually is issued on January 1, 19X1, at 98. Prepare the entries for the issuance, the interest and amortization for the first year, and the repayment at maturity.

SOLUTION

Jan.　1, 19X1	Cash		196,000	
	Bond Discount		4,000	
	Bonds Payable			200,000
June 30, 19X1				
Dec. 31, 19X1	Interest Expense		10,000	
	Cash			10,000
	$10\% \times \$200,000 \times \frac{1}{2}$.			
	Interest Expense		500	
Straight-line	Bond Discount			500
amortization:	$4000 \div 4$ years $\times \frac{1}{2}$.			

Dec. 31, 19X4	Bonds Payable	200,000		
	Cash		200,000	[Section 1.3]

1.5   In the previous problem, how much interest expense would appear on the income statement for each year? How would the bonds be presented on the balance sheet at December 31, 19X1?

SOLUTION

The income statement would show $21,000 of interest expense ($10,000 + $10,000 + $500 + $500).
The balance sheet would show:

Bonds Payable	$200,000
Less Discount	3,000*
Net Payable	$197,000

*$4,000 − $500 − $500

1.6   A $200,000, 4-year bond paying interest of 10% payable semiannually is issued on January 1, 19X1, at 104. Prepare the entries for the issuance, the interest and amortization for the first year, and the repayment at maturity.

SOLUTION

Jan. 1, 19X1	Cash	208,000		
	Bonds Payable		200,000	
	Bond Premium		8,000	
June 30, 19X1	Interest Expense	10,000		
Dec. 31, 19X1	Cash		10,000	
	$200,000 \times 10\% \times \frac{1}{2}$.			
	Bond Premium	1,000		
	Interest Expense		1,000	
	$8,000 \div 4 \text{ years} \times \frac{1}{2}$.			
Dec. 31, 19X4	Bonds Payable	200,000		
	Cash		200,000	[Sections 1.4, 1.5]

1.7   In the previous problem, determine the interest expense for 19X1 and show how the bond would appear on the December 31 balance sheet.

SOLUTION

Interest expense would be $18,000 ($10,000 + $10,000 − $1,000 − $1,000).
The balance sheet would appear as follows:

Bonds Payable	$200,000
Plus Bond Premium ($8,000 − $1,000 − $1,000)	6,000
Net Payable	$206,000

1.8   In the previous problem, if the interest was payable quarterly, how would the entries for the interest payments and the amortization differ?

SOLUTION

The entries for the interest payments and the amortization would be made four times per year rather than two times. Each interest payment would be $5,000 ($200,000 $\times$ 10% $\times \frac{1}{4}$) and each amortization entry would be $500 ($8,000 $\div$ 4 years $\times \frac{1}{4}$).   [Section 1.5]

Accruals of Interest

1.9   A $100,000, 10-year, 10% bond whose interest is payable annually on May 1 is sold at 96 on May 1, 19X1. Prepare all of the entries for 19X1.

SOLUTION

May 1, 19X1	Cash		96,000	
	Bond Discount		4,000	
	Bonds Payable			100,000
Dec. 31, 19X1	Interest Expense		6,667	
	Interest Payable			6,667
	$100,000 $\times$ 10% $\times$ 8/12			
Dec. 31, 19X1	Interest Expense		267	
	Bond Discount			267
	$4,000 $\div$ 10 yrs. $\times$ 8/12			

[Section 1.6]

1.10   Given:

Par = $300,000

Rate = 10%, payable 5% semiannually every Dec. 31 and June 30

Life = 4 years; Bond date = January 1

Issue date = April 1, 19X1

Selling Price = par

Prepare all of the entries for 19X1.

SOLUTION

Apr. 1, 19X1	Cash		307,500	
	Bonds Payable			300,000
	Interest Expense			7,500
	To accrue the interest from Dec. 31 to Apr. 1:			
	$300,000 $\times$ 5% $\times$ 3/6			
June 30;	Interest Expense		15,000	
Dec. 31	Cash			15,000

The interest expense for 19X1 would be $22,500 ($15,000 + $15,000 − $7,500).   [Section 1.7]

1.11   Assume the same information as in the previous example except that the bond is sold at 98. Prepare all of the 19X1 entries, including the discount amortization.

SOLUTION

Cash		301,500*	
Bond Discount		6,000	
Bonds Payable			300,000
Interest Expense			7,500

*$300,000 $\times$ 98 + $7,500 interest

June 30	Interest Expense	15,000	
Dec. 31	Cash		15,000
June 30	Interest Expense	400	
	Bond Discount		400

The discount period runs from the *date of issuance* (April 1, 19X1) until the maturity date. Thus this period is 45 months long (4 years − 3 months).

$$\$6,000 \div 45 \text{ months} = \$133.33 \text{ per month}$$
$$\underline{\times \qquad 3 \text{ months (April-June)}}$$
$$\$400.00$$

Dec. 31	Interest Expense	800	
	Bond Discount		800*

---

*$133.33 × 6   [Section 1.7]

Bond Selling Prices

1.12   A company wishes to issue a $30,000, 4-year bond that pays 8% interest compounded semiannually (4% every 6 months). Determine the selling price. Assume a market rate of 10% compounded semiannually (5%).

SOLUTION

Since the bond specifies 4%, there will be an annuity of $1,200 (4% × $30,000) every 6 months. The tables, however, must be used at the market rate of 5%. Thus:

Present value of a $1,200 annuity, 5%, 8 periods* =		6.46321
		× $1,200
		$7,756
Present value, $30,000, 5%, 8 periods =	.67684	
	× $30,000	
		+ 20,305
Selling price:		$28,061

---

*4 years, 2 interest periods per year   [Section 1.8]

1.13   If the market rate is 12% compounded quarterly (3%), how much will a 3-year, $50,000 bond paying 16% quarterly (4%) sell for?

SOLUTION

The quarterly interest payment annuity is $2,000.

Present value, annuity of $2,000, 12 periods, 3% =		9.954
		× $2,000
		$19,908
Present value, $50,000, 12 periods, 3% =	.70138	
	× $50,000	
		+ 35,069
Selling price		$54,977

[Section 1.8]

1.14   To issue a 5-year bond, a corporation incurs $10,000 of printing costs. Prepare the necessary journal entries for the incurrence of these costs and for their amortization.

SOLUTION

Unamortized Bond Issue Costs	10,000	
Cash		10,000
To amortize over 5 years:		
Bond Issue Expense	2,000	
Unamortized Bond Issue Costs		2,000

[Section 1.9]

Early Retirement of a Bond

1.15   On January 1, 19X1, the Spira Corporation issued a 10-year, $40,000 bond at 103. Five years later it retired the bond at 102. Prepare the journal entry.

SOLUTION

The Bonds Payable account and the related Premium account appear as follows:

Bonds Payable		Premium	
	40,000	120	1,200
		120	
		120	
		120	
		120	
			600 balance

Book value =	$40,600	
Retirement price =	40,800	(40,000 × 1.02)
Loss	$ 200	

The entry is:

Bonds Payable	40,000	
Premium	600	
Extraordinary Loss on Retirement	200	
Cash		40,800

[Section 1.10]

1.16   A bond is retired at 97. Its related accounts appear as follows:

Bonds Payable		Bond Discount		Unamortized Bond Issue Cost	
	70,000	2,000	200	900	90
			200		90
			200		90
		1,400		630	

Prepare the entry for this retirement.

SOLUTION

Bonds Payable	70,000	
Bond Discount		1,400
Unamortized Bond Issue Cost		630
Cash		67,900*
Gain on Retirement		70

---

*.97 × $70,000

[Section 1.10]

The Effective Interest Method of Amortization

1.17 A $40,000 bond that pays interest of 6% semiannually (3%) is sold to yield the market rate of 8% (4%). The life of the bond is 3 years. Prepare an amortization table.

SOLUTION

The selling price, according to the formula discussed in Section 1.8, is $37,903.

Interest Period	Interest Paid 3% of Par	Interest Expense 4% of Book Value	Amortization	Discount Balance	Book Value
Issue Date	—	—	—	$2,097	$37,903
1	$1,200	1,516	316	1,781	38,219
2	1,200	1,529	329	1,452	38,548
3	1,200	1,542	342	1,110	38,890
4	1,200	1,556	356	754	39,246
5	1,200	1,570	370	384	39,616
6	1,200	1,585	384*	—	40,000

*Rounded   [Section 1.11]

1.18 A 5-year, $90,000 bond with a stated annual rate of 10% is sold to yield a market rate of 8%. Prepare an amortization table.

SOLUTION

The selling price is $97,186.

Interest Period	Interest Paid 10% of Par	Interest Expense 8% of Book Value	Amortization	Premium Balance	Book Value
Issue date	—	—	—	7,186	$97,186
1	9,000	7,775	1,225	5,961	95,961
2	9,000	7,677	1,323	4,638	94,638
3	9,000	7,571	1,429	3,209	93,209
4	9,000	7,457	1,543	1,666	91,666
5	9,000	7,333	1,666	—	90,000

[Section 1.11]

Long-term Notes

1.19 A company issues a $200,000, 10-year note for $75,000. What type of note is this? How should the issuance be recorded?

SOLUTION

This is a "zero-coupon" or "deep discount" note. The entry is:

Cash	75,000	
Discount on Note	125,000	
Note Payable		200,000

If the straight-line method of amortization is used, the discount should be amortized for $12,500 each year.

[Section 1.12]

1.20 A machine is purchased by issuing a $70,000, 5-year, 3% note payable. This buyer would have to pay 10% interest to borrow money from banks and other financial institutions. Prepare the journal entry for this purchase assuming that:
(a) The fair market value of the machine is $60,000.
(b) The fair market value of the machine is unknown.

SOLUTION

(a)

Machine	60,000	
Discount on Note	10,000	
Notes Payable		70,000

(b) We must calculate the present value of the principal and of the interest payments using the 10% rate:

Present value, $1.00, 5 periods, 10% =   .62092

× $70,000

$43,464

Present value, $1.00 annuity, 5 periods, 10% = 3.79079

× $2,100*

7,961

$51,425

_____

*3% × 70,000

Machine	51,425		
Discount on Note	18,575		
Notes Payable		70,000	[Section 1.13]

Supplementary Problems

1.21 On January 1, 19A, Corporation A issues a $60,000 bond at 104. The bond pays interest annually of 12% and has a 10-year life.
(a) How much is this bond selling for?
(b) Prepare journal entries for the first year. Use straight-line amortization.
(c) Show a partial balance sheet for the end of 19A.
(d) How much interest expense will the income statement report for 19A?

1.22 Use the same information as in Problem 1 but assume that the bond is sold at 96. Answer requirements (a), (b), (c), and (d).

1.23 Assume the same information as in Problem 1 and assume the bond sold at 96. However, let's change the interest rate to 12% *semiannually.*
(a) Prepare journal entries for 19A.
(b) Show a partial balance sheet on June 30, 19A.

1.24 If the contract rate in a bond is 12% but the market rate is 10%, will the bond sell at a premium or discount? Why?

1.25 A bond that has a par of $40,000, an interest rate of 10% (annually), and a date of April 1, 19A is sold on this date at 98. The life of the bond is 10 years.
(a) How much are the proceeds from this sale?
(b) Prepare all entries for 19A, including any adjusting entries, if needed.
(c) Show a partial balance sheet at December 31, 19A.
(d) How much interest expense will appear on the income statement for 19A?

1.26 A bond with a par of $40,000, an annual rate of 10%, and a date of *January 1, 19A,* is sold on April 1, 19A, at 98. The life of this bond is 10 years.
(a) How much are the proceeds from this sale?
(b) Prepare all entries for 19A.

1.27   A bond with a par of $70,000 and a life of 10 years pays 12% interest (semiannually). The market rate of interest, however, is 10%. Determine the selling price of the bond.

1.28   Assume the same information as in the previous question except that the market rate is 14%. Determine the selling price of the bond.

1.29   Company B uses the effective interest method of bond amortization. It issues a bond with a par of $30,000 and a contract rate of 10%. The market rate is 12% and the life of the bond is 3 years. All rates are compounded semiannually.
   (a)   Determine the price of the bond.
   (b)   Prepare an amortization table.
   (c)   How much would interest expense be for the first year? Assume the bond was issued on January 1.

1.30   Company C incurs engraving and printing costs of $1,000 in issuing a $50,000 bond with a life of 10 years.
   (a)   Prepare an entry for these costs.
   (b)   Prepare the annual entry to amortize these costs.

1.31   Company D issued a $70,000 bond at 104 on January 1, 19A. The bond has a life of 8 years. On January 1, 19E, it decided to retire this bond at 103. Prepare an entry to record the retirement.

1.32   Use the same information as in the previous problem but assume the retirement price is 99. Prepare the retirement entry.

1.33   Company E issued a $60,000 bond with a life of 10 years at 97 on January 1, 19A. On January 1, 19E, it retires the bond at 99.
   (a)   Prepare the retirement entry.
   (b)   What is the nature of any gain or loss incurred upon retirement of a bond?

Chapter 2

Stock Ownership

2.1 INTRODUCTION

In a partnership or sole proprietorship the owners' interest is called *capital*. In a corporation it is called *stockholders' equity*. This ownership is simply the excess of the assets of the corporation over its liabilities—in other words, $A - L$ in the accounting equation. Thus the equation now states: Assets − Liabilities = Stockholders' Equity. Another name for this ownership is *net assets*.

Stockholders' equity is created from two sources: contributions of assets by the stockholders (*contributed capital*) and earnings by the corporation (*retained earnings*). This chapter will discuss the former while the next chapter will discuss the latter.

Ownership (stockholders' equity) in a corporation is divided into a large number of individual units called *shares*. Within each class of stock, all shares are the same and equal to each other. In a corporation with 100 shares, a person owning 50 shares has a 50% ownership; a person owning 10 shares has a 10% ownership; and a person owning 1 share has a 1% ownership.

Generally, each share carries the following rights:

1. To share proportionately in profits and losses.

2. To vote for the board of directors.

3. To share proportionately in assets upon liquidation.

4. To share proportionately in any new issues of stock of the same class (the preemptive right).

If a corporation has just one class of stock, it is called *common stock*. Sometimes, in order to appeal to all types of investors, a corporation may also issue another class of stock called *preferred stock* that has certain special privileges. For example, preferred stock, unlike common stock, may be guaranteed a dividend at a fixed rate before any dividends can be distributed to the common stock. Usually, preferred stockholders do not have the right to vote.

Each share of stock has a number printed on the stock certificate called *par*. Par value is *not* the same thing as market value, and very often the market value will be higher than the par value. The significance of par is that it sets the maximum amount of responsibility for liability to be borne by the stockholder. If, for example, both the par and the selling price are $100, the stockholder cannot lose more than this amount. If the corporation cannot pay its liabilities, its creditors cannot demand payment from the personal assets of the stockholders. This is called *limited liability*. The stockholder simply loses the $100 investment and is free.

The number of shares that a corporation may issue according to its charter is called the *authorized shares*. The shares actually sold are called *issued shares* while the shares physically in the hands of the public are *outstanding shares*. The number of outstanding shares is not necessarily equal to the number of issued shares.

EXAMPLE 1

A corporation is *authorized* to issue 100,000 shares. It *issues* 25,000 and then buys back 5,000 (these are called *treasury shares*). The authorized shares are 100,000; the issued shares are 25,000; the outstanding shares are only 20,000.

2.2 STOCK ISSUANCES

When a person buys shares of stock directly from the corporation, he or she is contributing assets (usually cash) to the corporation and in exchange is receiving an ownership interest. The evidence of this ownership is the stock certificate. In terms of the accounting equation ($A - L = C$) the assets of the corporation have gone up, liabilities have stayed the same, and capital has also gone up. In this respect, investing assets in a corporation by buying its stock is no different than investing assets in a partnership or sole proprietorship.

If the stock is issued at exactly par, a capital account called Common Stock or Preferred Stock is credited. If the stock is issued above par (a premium situation) or below par (a discount situation), an account called Paid-in Capital in Excess of Par will be, respectively, credited or debited for the difference.

EXAMPLE 2

If 100 shares of $100 par common stock are sold at par, the journal entry would be:

Cash	10,000	
Common Stock		10,000

If these shares are sold at $110 per share, this is a premium situation, and the entry is:

Cash	11,000	
Common Stock		10,000
Paid-in Capital in Excess of Par		1,000

The rule is that the common stock or preferred stock account is always recorded at par.

In this case, assets have gone up by $11,000, and so has capital. The increase in capital is split over two capital accounts: the Common Stock account and the Paid-in Capital account.

EXAMPLE 3

If in the previous situation the shares were issued at $80 per share, the journal entry would be:

Cash	8,000	
Paid-in Capital in Excess of Par (Discount)	2,000	
Common Stock		10,000

Here assets have gone up by $8,000 and so has capital. The Paid-in Capital account acts as a contra to the Common Stock account in this case.

When stock is issued at a discount, the stockholders are contingently liable for the amount of the discount. Should the corporation be unable to pay its debts, its creditors may go to the personal assets of the stockholders and collect the discount. Thus in the previous example, the stockholders may end up losing $11,000 even though the cost of the stock was only $8,000.

The previous entries would be the same for preferred stock except that Preferred Stock would be credited instead of Common Stock.

Many states permit stock to be issued without a par value. One of the reasons for this is to avoid the contingent liability associated with discounts. In these states, the Common Stock or Preferred Stock account is simply credited for the full amount received. If the board of directors orally assigned a par to the stock (referred to as *stated value*), the Common Stock account would be credited for this value. If the cash received was above or below this value, the difference would go to Paid-in-Capital in Excess of Stated Value or Paid-in Capital below Stated Value, respectively.

EXAMPLE 4

If 100 shares of $50 stated value preferred stock are issued at $70, the entry is:

Cash	7,000	
Preferred Stock		5,000
Paid-in Capital in Excess of Stated Value		2,000

2.3   STOCK SUBSCRIPTIONS

Stock may be sold on a subscription basis. In this case, the selling price is payable in installments rather than in total at the time of the sale, and the stock certificates are not handed over until the final installment is paid. A temporary account called Common Stock Subscribed (or Preferred Stock Subscribed) is credited at sale time and is later replaced by the regular Common Stock account when the stock is issued.

EXAMPLE 5

Assume that 100 shares of $100 par common stock are sold at $110 on subscription, payable in two installments of $55 each in 3 months and 6 months, respectively. The entry at sale time is:

Stock Subscriptions Receivable	11,000	
Common Stock Subscribed		10,000
Paid-in Capital in Excess of Par		1,000

The Stock Subscriptions Receivable account is an asset account similar to Accounts Receivable and should therefore be shown in the assets section of the balance sheet. (It should be noted, however, that the SEC disagrees with this treatment and requires companies to show it as a contra-capital account in the stockholders' equity section.)

The Common Stock Subscribed account is a temporary common stock capital account and will later be replaced by the account Common Stock. It is, therefore, credited at par.

At the time each installment is collected, the entry would be:

Cash	5,500	
Stock Subscriptions Receivable		5,500

Finally, when all the installments have been received and the stock certificates are handed over, the Common Stock Subscribed account is replaced by Common Stock as follows:

Common Stock Subscribed	10,000	
Common Stock		10,000

2.4 LUMP-SUM SALES OF STOCK

If a corporation issues both common stock and preferred stock for a lump sum of cash (or any other asset), it must determine how much of this lump sum should be allocated to the common, and how much to the preferred. If the market values of both the common and the preferred are known, these are used as a guide in the allocation process. This is called the *proportional method*.

EXAMPLE 6

The Brown Corporation issues 1,000 shares of $10 par common stock and 2,000 shares of $20 par preferred stock for a lump sum of $100,000. The market values per share are $20 and $30, respectively. Thus the total market values are $20,000 for the common and $60,000 for the preferred. The allocation of the $100,000 would be done as follows:

Common	$20,000	20/80 × $100,000 = $25,000
Preferred	60,000	60/80 × $100,000 = $75,000
Total	$80,000	

If the market value of only one class of stock is known, then that class would be allocated exactly its fair market value, and the remainder would go to the other class. This is the *incremental method*.

EXAMPLE 7

If in the previous example the total market value of the common stock was $20,000 as mentioned, and the preferred stock's market value was unknown, then $20,000 of the $100,000 lump sum would go to the common, while the remaining $80,000 would go to the preferred.

2.5 STOCK ISSUANCES IN NONCASH TRANSACTIONS

If stock is issued for assets other than cash, the question arises as to what value to assign to these assets. The answer is: The assets should be valued at their own market value or at the market value of the stock, whichever is clearer. If both values are clear, then they will probably be the same since this is an arm's-length transaction. If neither one is clear, then the value should be set by the board of directors based upon independent appraisals.

EXAMPLE 8

Hitech Corporation issues 1,000 shares of $10 par common stock in exchange for a building. The market value of the building is $35,000; the market value of the shares is unknown. The journal entry is:

Building	35,000	
Common Stock		10,000*
Paid-in Capital in Excess of Par		25,000

---

*This follows the usual rule of crediting Common Stock at par.

EXAMPLE 9

If in the previous example the market value of the building was unknown while the market value of the stock was $40,000, the entry would be:

Building	40,000	
Common Stock		10,000
Paid-in Capital in Excess of Par		30,000

2.6 STOCK ISSUANCE COSTS

There are many costs associated with the issuance of stock. Examples are attorneys' fees, CPA fees, underwriters' fees, and printing expenses. How should these be accounted for?

One method treats these costs as a reduction of the amount paid in for the stock by debiting the paid-in capital account. The second method debits them to an intangible asset account which is slowly written off to expense over a maximum period of 40 years. Both methods are acceptable, although the first method is more popular.

EXAMPLE 10

A corporation incurs stock issuance costs of $1,000 for the issuance of 1,000 shares of $100 par common stock at $150 per share. Under both methods the entry for the stock issuance would be:

Cash	150,000	
Common Stock		100,000
Paid-in Capital in Excess of Par		50,000

Under the first method, the entry for the issuance costs would be:

Paid-in Capital in Excess of Par	1,000	
Cash		1,000

Under the second method, the entry is:

Stock Issue Costs	1,000	
Cash		1,000

2.7 TREASURY STOCK—COST METHOD

A corporation is allowed to buy back its own shares from the public. These shares are called *treasury shares*. Some reasons for doing so are to meet employee stock compensation contracts, to increase earnings per share, or to thwart hostile takeover attempts. These shares may be retired or issued again.

Treasury stock is *not* an asset (a corporation cannot own part of itself!). It is simply a reduction of its capital. When the shares were originally issued, assets and capital went up. When they are bought back, the opposite takes place—assets and capital go down.

There are two methods for handling treasury stock transactions, the cost method and the par method. Under both methods, the total stockholders' equity is the same, although the individual components are different.

Under the cost method, the account Treasury Stock is *debited* for the *cost* of the purchase. The price received for these shares when they were originally issued is ignored, and so is the par value. If the treasury shares are later reissued, the account Treasury Stock is *credited* for the *cost*. Any excess of the selling price above cost is credited to an account called Paid-in Capital from Treasury Stock. If the selling price is below cost, the excess is debited to this account if it contains a sufficient credit balance to absorb this debit. If not, the difference is debited to Retained Earnings.

EXAMPLE 11

A corporation originally issues 1,000 shares of $10 par common stock for $15. The original entry is:

Cash	15,000	
Common Stock		10,000
Paid-in Capital in Excess of Par		5,000

It then buys back 600 shares at $20. The entry is:

Treasury Stock	12,000	
Cash		12,000

Notice that the par of $10 and the original selling price of $15 are ignored in this entry.

The corporation then resells 300 shares at $25. The entry is:

Cash	7,500	
Treasury Stock		6,000
Paid-in Capital from Treasury Stock		1,500

The $6,000 credit to Treasury Stock is based upon the *cost* of $20 multiplied by 300 shares.

Finally it resells another 200 shares at $12. The entry is:

Cash	2,400	
Paid-in Capital from Treasury Stock	1,500	
Retained Earnings	100	
Treasury Stock		4,000 (200 × $20)

Since the difference between the selling price and the cost is $1,600 ($4,000 − $2,400) and the Paid-in Capital from Treasury Stock account only contains $1,500, the remaining $100 is debited to Retained Earnings.

The account Treasury Stock is a negative (contra) capital account and appears on the balance sheet as a subtraction from the contributed capital in the stockholders' equity section. Paid-in Capital from Treasury Stock also appears in the same section as a normal capital account. It is not considered to be a revenue item and therefore it will *not* appear on the income statement.

Sometimes stockholders donate shares of the corporation's own stock back to the corporation. Since there is no cost involved, Treasury Stock would be debited at the fair market value of these shares with a credit going to Donated Capital for the same amount.

EXAMPLE 12

If 100 shares of $5 par stock are donated to the corporation, and their market value is $7, the entry is:

Treasury Stock	700	
Donated Capital		700

If the donated shares are later resold, the accounting treatment is the same as per the earlier discussion for purchased shares.

Treasury shares may be retired. This means that a decision is made not to reissue these shares again. Accordingly, when this happens, all the accounts relating to these shares are canceled. Thus accounts with a debit balance (Treasury Stock) are credited, and accounts with a credit balance (Common Stock and Paid-in Capital in Excess of Par) are debited. If a debit is needed to balance this entry, it goes to Retained Earnings; if a credit, it goes to an account called Paid-in Capital from Retirement of Treasury Stock.

EXAMPLE 13

The Benevolent Corporation issues 1,000 shares of $10 par common stock for $15 and then buys back 100 treasury shares at $17. The T-accounts appear as follows:

Common Stock	Paid-in Capital in Excess of Par	Treasury Stock
10,000	5,000	1,700

It then decides to retire the treasury shares. Since these shares constitute 10% of all the shares, 10% of the Common Stock account and premium account must be canceled (debited). The entry is:

Common Stock	1,000	
Paid-in Capital in Excess of Par	500	
Retained Earnings	200	
Treasury Stock		1,700

EXAMPLE 14

Assume the same information as in the previous example except that the treasury shares were acquired at $13. The retirement entry would be:

Common Stock	1,000	
Paid-in Capital in Excess of Par	500	
Treasury Stock		1,300
Paid-in Capital from Retirement of Treasury Stock		200

2.8　TREASURY STOCK—PAR VALUE METHOD

Under this method, the account Treasury Stock is debited for the *par value* of these shares. In addition, the original Paid-in Capital in Excess of Par account relating to these shares is also canceled by a debit. If the entry now needs a credit for balancing, it goes to Paid-in Capital from Treasury Stock. If it needs a debit, it goes to Paid-in Capital from Treasury Stock if there exists a sufficient credit balance in Paid-in Capital from Treasury Stock to absorb this debit. It not, the debit goes to Retained Earnings.

When the treasury stock is resold, Cash is debited and Treasury Stock is credited for the par value. If the selling price is greater than the par value (thus requiring a credit in the entry), then Paid-in Capital in Excess of Par would be credited (as if this were an issuance of new stock). If the selling price is less than par value (thus requiring a debit in the entry), then Paid-in Capital from Treasury Stock would be debited provided it already contains a sufficient credit balance. Otherwise, Retained Earnings would be debited.

EXAMPLE 15

A company originally issues 1,000 shares of common stock, $100 par, at $120. Thus the premium is $20 per share. The original entry is:

Cash	120,000	
Common Stock		100,000
Paid-in Capital in Excess of Par		20,000

It then buys back 600 shares at $110. The entry is:

Treasury Stock (Par)	60,000	
Paid-in Capital in Excess of Par	12,000	
Cash		66,000
Paid-in Capital from Treasury Stock		6,000

Later it decides to buy back another batch of 200 shares at $160. The entry is:

Treasury Stock (Par)	20,000	
Paid-in Capital in Excess of Par	4,000	
Paid-in Capital from Treasury Stock	6,000	
Retained Earnings	2,000	
Cash		32,000

Since a debit of $8,000 is needed to balance the entry and Paid-in Capital from Treasury Stock can absorb only $6,000, the remaining $2,000 goes to Retained Earnings.

It then resells 200 shares at $130. The entry is:

Cash	26,000	
Treasury Stock (Par)		20,000
Paid-in Capital in Excess of Par		6,000

Finally, it resells another 400 at $90. The entry is:

Cash	36,000	
Retained Earnings*	4,000	
Treasury Stock		40,000 (par)

*Since Paid-in Capital from Treasury Stock at this point
has a zero balance, we must debit Retained Earnings.

If stockholders donate treasury shares, Treasury Stock is, once again, debited at par and any related premium account is canceled with a debit. The account Donated Capital is then credited for the sum of the debits.

EXAMPLE 16

Fifty shares of $100 par value stock originally issued at $120 are donated to the corporation. The entry is:

Treasury Stock (Par)	5,000	
Paid-in Capital in Excess of Par	1,000	
Donated Capital		6,000

If treasury shares are retired, Common Stock is debited and Treasury Stock credited, each at par value.

EXAMPLE 17

A corporation has the following T-accounts relating to its common stock and treasury stock:

Common Stock	Treasury Stock
75,000 (par)	50,000 (par)

The corporation now decides to retire the treasury shares. The entry is:

Common Stock	50,000	
Treasury Stock		50,000

EXAMPLE 18

A company issues 100 shares of $100 par common stock at $110. Thus the premium is $10 per share. Fifty shares are then donated back to the company and are later retired. The entries are:

Cash	11,000	
Common Stock		10,000
Paid-in Capital in Excess of Par		1,000
(For the Issuance)		
Treasury Stock	5,000*	
Paid-in Capital in Excess of Par	500†	
Donated Capital		5,500
(For the donation)		

*$50 \times 100 = \$5,000$
†$50 \times 10 = \$500$

Common Stock	5,000	(par)
Treasury Stock		5,000 (par)
(For the retirement)		

2.9   ASSESSMENTS ON STOCK

In some states corporations may assess the stockholders an additional amount above their original contribution. If the stock was originally issued at a discount, the discount account should now be credited since the new contribution reduces the discount. Conversely, if the original issuance was at a premium, the premium account should be credited since the premium is now enlarged as a result of the assessment.

EXAMPLE 19

Common stock was originally issued at a discount of $500. An assessment of $75 is now placed on the stockholders. The entry is:

Cash	75	
Paid-in Capital in Excess of Par (Discount)		75

If the stock was originally issued at par, then an account called Paid-in Capital from Stock Assessments should be credited for the receipt of the stock assessment.

2.10 FEATURES OF PREFERRED STOCK

Preferred stock is entitled to receive an annual fixed dividend. This dividend is usually expressed as a percentage of par. For example, $100 par, 5%, preferred stock would receive $5 in dividends every year. Sometimes the dividend is expressed as a dollar value rather than in percentage form. Thus, $100 par, $6 preferred stock means that the dividend is $6.

A corporation does not have to pay dividends unless so declared by the board of directors. What happens if the board does not declare ("pass") a dividend in a given year? Is the preferred stock entitled to a double share next year in order to make up for the lost year? It depends. If the preferred stock is cumulative, the answer is yes. If not, the answer is no. Unless the stock specifically states that it is noncumulative, the courts have ruled that it is cumulative.

Preferred dividends not declared in previous years are called *dividends in arrears*.

EXAMPLE 20

Assume a corporation has 1,000 shares of $100 par, 5% preferred stock outstanding, and 1,000 shares of $200 par common stock outstanding. The dividend declared is $13,000 and there are no dividends in arrears.

The preferred stockholders would get 5% × $100 × 1,000 = $5,000. The remainder of $8,000 ($13,000 − $5,000) would go to the common stockholders.

EXAMPLE 21

Assume the same information as in the previous example except that last year's dividend is in arrears. If the preferred stock is cumulative, it would get $10,000 ($5,000 for this year and $5,000 for last year). The remainder of $3,000 would go to the common.

If the preferred is noncumulative, it would only get this year's $5,000 and $8,000 would go to the common.

Preferred stock may sometimes get an additional share of the dividends over and above its fixed amount. This is called *participating preferred stock*. It may be fully participating or partially participating. Fully participating preferred follows these steps:

1. First give the preferred its fixed percentage.

2. Then give the common the same matching percentage.

3. Divide any remainder according to the ratio of par.

EXAMPLE 22

A corporation has 1,000 shares of $100 par, 5% preferred stock and 1,000 shares of $200 par common stock. The dividend declared is $24,000. The allocation would be as follows, assuming the preferred is fully participating:

	Preferred	Common	Total
1.	$5,000	—	$ 5,000
2.	—	$10,000	10,000
3.	3,000	6,000	9,000
	$8,000	$16,000	$24,000

First the preferred received 5% × $100 × 1,000 = $5,000. Then the common received the same 5% on their par of $200: 5% × $200 × 1,000 = $10,000. The remaining $9,000 is divided according to the par ratio, as follows:

	Par	
Preferred	$100,000 = 1/3 × $9,000 = $3000
Common	200,000 = 2/3 × $9,000 = $6000
Total	$300,000

If the preferred is partially participating, it will only participate to a certain percentage above its par. For example, if 5% preferred stock participates to 7%, it will receive an extra 2% of par.

The allocation procedure for partially participating preferred follows these steps:

1. First give the preferred its fixed percentage.
2. Then give the common the same matching percentage.
3. Then give the preferred its additional participation.
4. Finally, give any remainder to the common.

EXAMPLE 23

Assume the same information as in the previous example except that the preferred is partially participating up to 7%. The allocation is:

	Preferred	**Common**	**Total**
1.	$5,000	—	$ 5,000
2.	—	$10,000	10,000
3.	2,000*	—	2,000
4.	—	7,000	7,000 (remainder)
	$7,000	$17,000	$24,000

*2% × $100 × 1,000

Summary

1. In a corporation, owners' equity or capital is referred to as *stockholders' equity*. It represents the excess of the corporation's assets over its liabilities.

2. Ownership (stockholders' equity) in a corporation is divided into a large number of individual units called *shares* of stock. Within each class of stock, all the shares are the same and equal to each other.

3. Generally, each *common* share has the right to share in profits and losses, vote for the board of directors, share in assets upon liquidation, and share in any new issues of stock of the same class.

4. A second class of stock is *preferred* stock. It is usually guaranteed a dividend at a fixed rate before any dividends can be distributed to the common stock. Preferred stockholders usually do not have the right to vote.

5. The number of shares that a corporation is permitted to issue under its charter is called the *authorized shares*. The shares sold are the *issued shares* while the shares physically in the hands of the public are the *outstanding shares*.

6. When stock is issued, the account Common Stock (or Preferred Stock) is credited at par. *Par* is the number printed on the stock certificate. If the stock is issued at a price above par (a *premium*) or at a price below par (a *discount*), an account Paid-in Capital in Excess of Par will be, respectively, credited or debited for the difference.

7. If the stock has no par, then common stock (or preferred stock) is credited for the full amount of the issue price. If the board of directors *orally* assigned a par to the stock (*stated value*), this is now considered as par and would be credited to Common Stock. Any amount above or below this value would go to Paid-in Capital in Excess of Stated Value or Paid-in Capital below Stated Value, respectively.

8. If stock is sold on a subscription basis, the selling price is payable in installments rather than in total at the time of the sale, and the stock certificates would not be issued until the final installment is paid. A temporary account called Common Stock Subscribed would be credited for the par at the time of sale. This account is later replaced by the Common Stock account after the stock is issued.

9. If a corporation issues both common and preferred stock for a lump sum, it must determine how much of this sum should be allocated to the common, and how much to the preferred. If the market values are known, these should be used as a guide. This is called the *proportional method*.

10. If the market value of only one class of stock is known, that class would be allocated its market value, and the remainder would go to the other class. This is the *incremental method*.

11. If stock is issued for assets other than cash, the assets should be valued at their own market value or at the market value of the stock, whichever is clearer. If neither one is clear, the value should be set by the board of directors based upon independent appraisals.

12. Stock issuance costs are various costs associated with the sale of shares. Examples include attorney fees and CPA fees. One method treats these costs as a reduction of the amount paid in for the stock and thus debits the paid-in capital account. Another method debits these costs to an intangible asset account which is written off to expense over a maximum 40-year period. Both methods are acceptable.

13. A corporation may buy back its own shares from the public. These are called *treasury shares*. These shares are not an asset of the corporation; they simply represent a reduction of the corporation capital.

14. There are two methods for handling treasury stock transactions, the *cost method* and the *par method*. Under both methods, total stockholders' equity is the same, although the individual components are different.

15. Under the cost method, the account Treasury Stock is debited for the *cost* of the purchase. The par value of the shares is ignored. If these shares are later resold, this account is credited at *cost*. Any excess of the selling price above cost is credited to Paid-in Capital from Treasury Stock. If the selling price is below cost, the excess is debited to this account if it contains a sufficient credit balance to absorb this debit. If not, the difference is debited to Retained Earnings.

16. If stockholders donate their shares to the corporation, Treasury Stock would be debited for the fair market value of these shares and Donated Capital would also be credited for this amount.

17. Treasury shares may be *retired*. This means a decision has been made not to reissue these shares. In this case, all the accounts relating to these shares are closed. Thus accounts with a *debit* balance (such as Treasury Stock) are credited, while accounts with a *credit* balance (such as Common Stock and Paid-in Capital in Excess of Par) are debited. If a debit is needed to balance this entry, it goes to Retained Earnings. If a credit is needed, it goes to Paid-in Capital from Retirement of Treasury Stock.

18. Under the par value method, Treasury Stock is debited for the *par* value of the shares acquired. In addition, the original Paid-in Capital in Excess of Par relating to these shares is canceled via a debit. If the entry now needs a credit for balancing, it goes to Paid-in Capital from Treasury Stock. If it needs a debit, it also goes to this account provided it contains a sufficient credit balance to absorb this debit. If it does not, the debit goes to Retained Earnings.

19. If the treasury stock is resold, Cash is debited and Treasury Stock is credited for the *par* value. If the selling price is greater than par value (thus requiring a credit in the entry), then Paid-in Capital in Excess

of Par is credited. If the selling price is less than par value, then Paid-in Capital from Treasury Stock is debited provided this account contains a credit balance. If not, Retained Earnings would be debited.

20. If stockholders donate treasury shares, Treasury Stock is debited at *par* and any related premium account is closed with a debit. The account Donated Capital is then credited for the sum of these debits. If treasury shares are retired, Common Stock is debited and Treasury Stock credited, each at par.

21. A corporation does not have to pay dividends unless so declared by the board of directors. If preferred stock is cumulative and the directors omitted a dividend in one year, these shares are entitled to a "make up" in the following year. Such dividends are called *dividends in arrears*.

22. Fully participating preferred stock is entitled to receive an additional dividend over and above its fixed share, using the following steps:
1. First give the preferred its fixed percentage.
2. Then give the common the same matching percentage.
3. Divide any remainder according to the ratio of par.

23. Partially participating preferred is also entitled to additional dividends, as follows:
1. First give the preferred its fixed percentage.
2. Then give the common the same matching percentage.
3. Then give the preferred its additional percentage of participation.
4. Finally, give any remainder to the common.

Rapid Review

1. The general name for capital in a corporation is ___Stockholder equity___

2. Ownership in a corporation is divided into units called ___shares___.

3. Stock that has special privileges is called ___preferred___.

4. The number printed on the stock certificate is called ___par___.

5. The number of shares a corporation is allowed to issue is called ___authorized___ shares.

6. The shares sold are the ___issued___ shares, while the shares physically in the hands of the public are the ___O/S___ shares.

7. If stock is sold above par, it is a ___premium___ situation; if below par it is a ___discount___ situation.

8. The Common Stock and Preferred Stock accounts are always credited at ___par___.

9. When the board of directors orally assigns a par to no-par stock, this is called ___stated___ value.

10. When shares are sold on the installment basis, the arrangement is referred to as a ___subscription___

11. The two methods used for lump-sum sales of stock are the ___proportional___ method and the ___incremental___ method.

12. Stock issuance costs may be debited to an ___intangible asset___ account which should be written off over a maximum period of ___40 years___

13. When a corporation buys back its own shares, they are called ___treasury___ shares.

14. The two methods of accounting for such shares are the _____Cost_____ method and the _____par_____ method.

15. For shares donated back to the corporation, the account Donated Capital is credited at _____market_____ value. (cost method)

16. If a company decides not to reissue treasury stock, it _____retires_____ them.

17. If dividends have not been declared in any given year, they are called _____in arrears_____

18. If preferred stock is entitled to receive prior years' dividends that were skipped, it is _____cumulative_____ preferred stock.

19. The two types of preferred stock that receive dividends over and above their fixed percentage are _____fully participating_____ and _____partially participating_____

Answers: 1. Stockholders' equity 2. Shares 3. Preferred stock 4. Par 5. Authorized 6. Issued; outstanding 7. Premium; discount 8. Par 9. Stated 10. Stock subscription 11. Proportional; incremental 12. Asset; 40 years 13. Treasury 14. Cost; par 15. Market (cost method) 16. Retires 17. Dividends in arrears 18. Cumulative 19. Fully participating; partially participating

Solved Problems

Stock Issuances

2.1   The Micro Corporation is authorized to issue 100,000 shares of common stock. It issues 30,000 shares and then buys back 5,000 shares for the treasury. As a result of these transactions, determine:
   (*a*)   The authorized shares
   (*b*)   The issued shares
   (*c*)   The outstanding shares

   SOLUTION
   (*a*)   100,000
   (*b*)   30,000
   (*c*)   25,000   [Section 2.1]

2.2   The Stern Corporation is authorized to issue 100 shares of $100 preferred stock. Prepare the journal entries for the issuance if the price per share is:
   (*a*) $100
   (*b*) $110
   (*c*) $80

   SOLUTION

(*a*)	Cash		10,000	
	Preferred Stock			10,000
(*b*)	Cash		11,000	
	Preferred Stock			10,000
	Paid-in Capital in Excess of Par			1,000

(c)	Cash		8,000		
	Paid-in Capital in Excess of Par				
	(Discount)		2,000		
	Preferred Stock			10,000	[Section 2.2]

2.3 In the previous problem determine the effect of each case on the accounting equation (Assets − Liabilities = Stockholders' Equity).

SOLUTION

(a) Assets: +$10,000; Liabilities: No change; Stockholders' Equity: +$10,000
(b) Assets: +$11,000; Liabilities: No change; Stockholders' Equity: +$11,000
(c) Assets: +$8,000; Liabilities: No change; Stockholders' Equity: +$8,000   [Section 2.2]

2.4 How would the entries for Problem 2.2 differ if common stock was issued instead of preferred?

SOLUTION

They would be the same except that the account Common Stock would be credited instead of Preferred Stock.
[Section 2.2]

2.5 A corporation issued 50 shares of no-par common stock for $100 per share. Prepare the entries if:
(a) There is no stated value.
(b) There is a stated value of $80.

SOLUTION

(a)	Cash		5,000		
	Common Stock			5,000	
(b)	Cash		5,000		
	Common Stock			4,000	
	Paid-in Capital in Excess of Stated Value			1,000	[Section 2.2]

Stock Subscriptions

2.6 What type of account is:
(a) Stock Subscriptions Receivable?
(b) Common Stock Subscribed?

SOLUTION

(a) Asset—accounts receivable.
(b) Capital—temporary in nature.   [Section 2.3]

2.7 The Czinner Corporation issues 200 shares of $100 par preferred stock for $115 on subscription. One-half of the selling price is payable upon subscription while the other half is payable in two equal installments. Prepare all necessary journal entries.

SOLUTION

Cash	11,500	
Stock Subscriptions Receivable	11,500	
Preferred Stock Subscribed		20,000*
Paid-in Capital in Excess		3,000
of Par		

Cash		5,750	
Stock Subscriptions Receivable			5,750
Cash		5,750	
Stock Subscriptions Receivable			5,750
Preferred Stock Subscribed		20,000	
Preferred Stock			20,000*

*At par   [Section 2.3]

Lump-Sum Sales

2.8 The House of Fashion issues 50 shares of common stock and 100 shares of preferred stock for a lump sum of $10,000. The par value of each class of stock is $30 and the market values are $200 and $400, respectively. Determine the amount to allocate to each class and prepare the journal entries.

SOLUTION

Market Value

Common:	$10,000 = 10/50 × $10,000 = $2,000	
Preferred:	40,000 = 40/50 × $10,000 = $8,000	
Total	$50,000	

Cash	2,000	
Common Stock		1,500
Paid-in Capital in Excess of Par—Common		500
Cash	8,000	
Preferred Stock		3,000
Paid-in Capital in Excess of Par—Preferred		5,000

[Section 2.4]

2.9 In the previous problem assume that the market value of the common was $50 and the preferred's market value was unknown. Determine the allocation to each class.

SOLUTION

Under the incremental method the common would be allocated $2,500 (50 × $50) and the remaining $7,500 ($10,000 − $2,500) would go to preferred.   [Section 2.4]

Noncash Transactions

2.10 S & W Metals Corporation issues 1,000 shares of $100 par common stock for equipment. Prepare the journal entry for this transaction if:
(a) The market value of the equipment is $90,000 and the market value of the stock is unknown.
(b) The market value of the stock is $115,000 and the market value of the equipment is unknown.
(c) Both market values are unknown.

SOLUTION

(a)	Equipment	90,000	
	Paid-in Capital in Excess of Par (Discount)	10,000	
	Common Stock		100,000
(b)	Equipment	115,000	
	Common Stock		100,000
	Paid-in Capital in Excess of Par		15,000

(c) The value would have to be determined by the board of directors.   [Section 2.5]

2.11 Distra Corporation issues 100 shares of $100 par preferred stock for $120 and incurs stock issue costs of $500. Prepare the entry for these costs using the more popular method.

SOLUTION

Paid-in Capital in Excess of Par	500		
Cash		500	[Section 2.6]

2.12 Prepare the entry for the previous problem using a different method.

SOLUTION

Stock Issue Costs	500	
Cash		500

Under this method, the Stock Issue Costs account would be amortized yearly to expense by the following entry:

Stock Issue Costs Expense	XXX	
Stock Issue Costs		XXX

The amortization period cannot be longer than 40 years.   [Section 2.6]

Treasury Stock

2.13 A corporation issues 1,000 shares of $100 par common stock at $120. Prepare the journal entries for the following transactions using the *cost method:*
(a) It buys back 600 shares at $130.
(b) It then resells 300 at $140.
(c) It later resells another 200 at $105.
(d) It retires the remaining 100 shares.

SOLUTION

The original entry at issuance is:

Cash	120,000	
Common Stock		100,000
Paid-in Capital in Excess of Par		20,000

The T-accounts appear as follows:

Common Stock	Paid-in Capital in Excess of Par
100,000	20,000

(a)	Treasury Stock	78,000	
	Cash		78,000
(b)	Cash	42,000	
	Treasury Stock		39,000*
	Paid-in Capital Treasury Stock		3,000

*300 × $130

(c)	Cash	21,000	
	Paid-in Capital Treasury Stock	3,000	
	Retained Earnings	2,000	
	Treasury Stock		26,000*

*200 × $130

Since the Paid-in Capital Treasury Stock account only has a credit of $3,000, the maximum it can be debited for is $3,000. Accordingly, the remaining $2,000 is debited to Retained Earnings.

(d)

Common Stock	10,000 (100 × $100)	
Paid-in Capital in Excess of Par	2,000*	
Retained Earnings	1,000	
Treasury Stock		13,000

*The premium per share is $20 ($120 − $100)
and $20 × 100 shares = $2,000.

If in the above a credit was needed to balance the entry, it would have gone to Paid-in Capital from Retirement of Treasury Stock.   [Section 2.7]

2.14   One hundred shares having a par value of $100 and a market value of $80 are donated back to the corporation. Prepare the journal entry under the cost method.

SOLUTION

Treasury Stock	8,000	
Donated Capital		8,000

[Section 2.7]

2.15   The Gold Corporation has just retired treasury stock which has the following related T-accounts:

Common Stock	Paid-in Capital in Excess of Par	Treasury Stock
1,000	100	900

Prepare the entry for the retirement under the *cost* method.

SOLUTION

Common Stock	1,000	
Paid-in Capital in Excess of Par	100	
Treasury Stock		900
Paid-in Capital from Retirement of		200
Treasury Stock		[Section 2.7]

2.16   The Zinner Corporation engages in the following transactions involving its common stock:
(a)   Issues 500 shares, $100 par, for $125.
(b)   Purchases 250 shares for the treasury for $115.
(c)   Purchases 150 shares for the treasury for $140.
(d)   Resells 100 shares at $130.
(e)   Resells another 100 shares at $90.
Prepare the journal entries for these transactions. Use the par value method.

SOLUTION

(a)

Cash	62,500	
Common Stock		50,000
Paid-in Capital in Excess of Par		12,500

The premium is $25 per share.

(b)   Treasury Stock (Par)   25,000
             Paid-in Capital in Excess of Par   6,250*
                 Cash   28,750
                 Paid-in Capital Treasury Stock   2,500

             _____

             *250 × $25

(c)   Treasury Stock (Par)   15,000
             Paid-in Capital in Excess of Par   3,750
             Paid-in Capital Treasury Stock   2,250
                 Cash   21,000

At this point the balance in Paid-in Capital Treasury Stock is $2,500 − $2,250 = $250.

(d)   Cash   13,000
                 Treasury Stock   10,000
                 Paid-in Capital in Excess of Par   3,000

(e)   Cash   9,000
             Paid-in Capital Treasury Stock   250
             Retained Earnings   750
                 Treasury Stock   10,000

Since Paid-in Capital Treasury Stock only has a $250 credit balance, the most it can absorb is a $250 debt. The remaining $750 goes to Retained Earnings.

2.17   The Feldbrand Corporation issued 300 shares of $200 par common stock at $220. Some time later the stockholders donated 100 shares which were retired. Prepare the journal entries under the par value method.

SOLUTION

          Cash   66,000
              Common Stock   60,000
              Paid-in Capital in Excess of Par   6,000
          Treasury Stock (Par)   20,000
          Paid-in Capital in Excess of Par   2,000*
              Donated Capital   22,000

          _____

          *100 × $20 premium

          Common Stock   20,000
              Treasury Stock   20,000   [Section 2.8]

Preferred Dividends

2.18   A corporation has 100 shares, 7%, $100 par preferred stock outstanding.
   (a)   How much is the dividend per share?
   (b)   How much in dividends must the preferred get before the common can get anything?
   (c)   If the dividends are 2 years in arrears, how much must preferred get before common?

SOLUTION

   (a) $7 (7% × $100)
   (b) $700 ($7 × 100 shares)

(*c*) If the preferred is noncumulative, the answer is still $700. However if it is cumulative, it is entitled to $700 for this year plus $700 for each of the two past years. Thus the answer is $2,100.   [Section 2.10]

2.19 A corporation has 100 shares of $100 par common stock outstanding and 100 shares of $50 par preferred stock, 8%. The total dividend declared is $30,000 and the preferred stock is *fully* participating. Show how the dividend would be allocated.

SOLUTION

Common	Preferred	Total
—	$ 400	$ 400 (8% × $50 × 100)
$ 800	—	800 (8% × $100 × 100)
19,200*	9,600*	28,800 (remainder)
$20,000	$10,000	$30,000

	Par	
*Common	$10,000 = 10/15 × $28,800 = $19,200	
*Preferred	5,000 = 5/15 × $28,800 = $9,600	
Total	$15,000	[Section 2.10]

2.20 Assume the same information as in the previous problem except that the preferred is *partially* participating up to 10%. Show the dividend allocation.

SOLUTION

Common	Preferred	Total
—	$400	$ 400
$ 800	—	800
—	100	100 (2% × $50 × 100)
28,700	—	28,700 (remainder)
$29,500	$500	$30,000 [Section 2.10]

Comprehensive Problem

2.21 Determine the effect each of the following transactions has on assets, liabilities, capital (stock accounts and other paid-in capital accounts), and retained earnings. For increases place a " + " sign in the column; for decreases a " − " sign and if no effect place "NE."
   (1) Issued common stock for cash.
   (2) Entered into a subscription agreement.
   (3) Issued common stock at a discount.
   (4) Issued common stock for equipment.
   (5) Received authorization from the state to issue stock.
   (6) Issued subscribed stock *after* full payment had already been received.
   (7) Bought treasury stock (cost method).
   (8) Sold treasury stock above cost (cost method).
   (9) Sold treasury stock below cost; no balance exists in the Paid-in Capital Treasury Stock account (cost method).
   (10) Received donated treasury shares (cost method).
   (11) Retired treasury stock; debit needed to balance the entry (cost method).

SOLUTION

	Assets	Liabilities	Capital	Retained Earnings
(1)	+	NE	+	NE
(2)	+	NE	+	NE
(3)	+	NE	+	NE
(4)	+	NE	+	NE
(5)	NE	NE	NE	NE
(6)	NE	NE	+, −*	NE
(7)	−	NE	−	NE
(8)	+	NE	+	NE
(9)	+	NE	+	−
(10)	NE	NE	+, −	NE
(11)	NE	NE	+, −	−

---

*The entry for this is:

Common Stock Subscribed   xx

Common Stock   xx

Thus one capital account goes up and another goes down.

Supplementary Problems

2.22 Corporation A is authorized to issue 50,000 shares of common stock. It issues 20,000 shares but buys back 7,000 shares as treasury stock. Determine the number of authorized shares, issued shares, and outstanding shares.

2.23 Corporation B is authorized to issue 50,000 shares of $70 par common stock. It issues 10,000 shares. Prepare the journal entry if:
(a)   these shares are issued at $80 per share.
(b)   these shares are issued at $50 per share.

2.24 Corporation C issues 10,000 shares no-par common stock at $90 per share. Prepare an entry if:
(a)   the shares have no stated value.
(b)   the shares have a stated value of $60.

2.25 Corporation D issues 1,000 shares of $120 par common stock on subscription at $150 per share. The subscription price is payable in two installments of $75 each. Prepare entries for the subscription, the receipt of each installment, and the final issuance of the stock.

2.26 Corporation E issues 1,000 shares of $75 par common stock and 2,000 shares of $100 par preferred stock for a lump-sum price of $400,000. The market value of the common is $125 per share; the market value of the preferred is unknown. Prepare the necessary journal entry.

2.27 Corporation F issues 500 shares of $100 par preferred stock for a piece of equipment. Prepare an entry if:
(a)   the market price of the equipment is $75,000 and the market price of the stock is unclear.
(b)   the market price of the stock is $125 per share and the market price of the equipment is unclear.

2.28 Company G issues 100 shares of $180 par common stock at $190. It also incurs $900 in attorney fees relating to the issuance.
(*a*) Prepare an entry for the issuance.
(*b*) Prepare an entry for the attorney fees. (Use both methods discussed in the chapter.)

2.29 Corporation H issues 1,000 shares of $90 par common stock at $100 per share. Prepare the journal entry for the issuance and for the following additional transactions, under the *cost* method:
(*a*) It buys back 600 shares at $110.
(*b*) It then resells 300 shares at $120.
(*c*) It then resells another 200 at $95.
(*d*) It retires the remaining 100 shares.

2.30 Prepare the entries for the previous problem using the *par* method.

2.31 Corporation I issues 400 shares of $100 par common stock at $120. Some time later the shareholders donate 200 shares back to the corporation. At this time the fair market value of the shares is $150 per share. Prepare the entries for the original issuance, the donation and the retirement, under the cost method.

2.32 For the previous problem, prepare journal entries under the par method.

Remember Treasury Stock is not an Asset — it is a contra Capital Account

Chapter 3

Stockholders' Equity: Retained Earnings

3.1 DEFINITION

The previous chapter dealt with the portion of stockholders' equity contributed by the stockholders—contributed capital. This chapter will deal with the other major portion of stockholders' equity—retained earnings.

Retained earnings are created for the most part by the earnings of the corporation. These earnings (referred to as *net income*) are closed into the retained earnings T-account.

EXAMPLE 1

Suppose a corporation earned $100,000 of net income. The closing journal entry would be:

Income summary	100,000	
Retained Earnings		100,000

In previous years many companies used the name "earned surplus" instead of "retained earnings." This practice has been discouraged by the profession because the term "surplus" is misleading since it connotes a pool of cash. Accordingly, "retained earnings" will be used throughout this book.

Not only does the retained earnings account contain the net income; it also contains many other items, as the following T-account shows.

Retained Earnings	
1. Net losses	1. Net income
2. Prior-period adjustments	2. Prior-period adjustments
3. Cash or scrip dividends	3. Adjustments due to quasi-reorganizations
4. Stock dividends	
5. Property dividends	

The remainder of this chapter will discuss these items.

3.2 CASH DIVIDENDS

In a sole proprietorship, when the owner decides to withdraw cash for his or her own personal use, that is called a *drawing*. In a corporation, this decision must be made by the board of directors and is called a *dividend*. Usually dividends are paid from the earnings that have accumulated in the retained earnings account, but occasionally, as will be discussed later, they may be paid out of other accounts.

There are three dates associated with dividends: the date of declaration, the date of record, and the date of payment. On the date of declaration the board of directors holds a meeting and decides how much to pay out as a dividend. This is called *declaring a dividend*.

But who is entitled to receive the dividend? As we know, ownership of the shares changes from day to day since shares are bought and sold daily on the stock market. To resolve this problem, the board of directors must decide on a cutoff date called the *date of record*.

EXAMPLE 2

On June 1, the board of directors declares a dividend of $100 per share to all stockholders owning the shares on July 1. The date of declaration is June 1. The date of record is July 1. Anyone not owning shares on July 1 is not entitled to a dividend. Therefore, if someone owned shares on June 29 but sold them before July 1, he or she will not get a dividend. Conversely, if someone bought shares the last minute of June 30, he or she thus owns them on July 1 and *will* be entitled to a dividend.

If in the above example the dividends will actually be paid on August 1, that is the date of payment.

Journal entries need to be made on the date of declaration and date of payment. But no entry is made on the date of record.

EXAMPLE 3

Suppose that, as in the above example, on June 1 the board of directors declared a dividend of $100 per share payable on August 1 to all common stockholders of record on July 1. Also assume that on the date of record there are 1,000 shares of common stock outstanding, plus 200 shares of treasury stock. The journal entries would be:

June 1	(date of declaration)	Retained Earnings	100,000	
		Cash Dividends Payable		100,000
		(1,000 shares @ 100 = 100,000)		
July 1	(date of record)	No entry		
Aug. 1	(date of payment)	Cash Dividends Payable	100,000	
		Cash		100,000

Notice that no dividends are declared or paid on shares in the treasury.

The Cash Dividends Payable account is a liability account, and since it is usually paid within a few months, it is a current liability.

In the previous example the dividend was expressed as a fixed dollar amount per share. Sometimes (as in the case of preferred stock) it is expressed as a percentage of par. If the preferred stock is, say, $100 par and the dividend is 6% of par, then each share will receive $6.00.

3.3 PROPERTY DIVIDENDS

Sometimes a corporation may not wish to issue a dividend in cash because it needs the cash in the business. Instead it may issue a dividend in the form of property (usually shares of stock it owns in other corporations).

According to APB Opinion No. 29, a journal entry must first be made to raise or lower the property on the books to its fair market value. Fair market value can be determined by reference to quoted market prices or by independent appraisals.

EXAMPLE 4

On June 1, X Company declares a property dividend to be paid from its portfolio of 5,000 shares of General Motors stock. On its books, these shares were recorded at their cost of $10,000. However, today their fair market value is $11,000. The journal entries are:

Date of declaration	Investments—Securities	1,000	
	Gain on Appreciation of Securities		1,000
	Retained Earnings	11,000	
	Property Divid. Payable		11,000
Date of payment	Property Divid. Payable	11,000	
	Investments—Securities		11,000

If the fair market value had been less than the book value, a loss, rather than a gain, would have been recognized.

3.4 SCRIP DIVIDENDS

If a corporation wishes to pay a cash dividend but has no cash at the moment, it may issue a special type of note payable to the stockholders promising to pay later. This is called *scrip*. If the scrip pays interest, the interest portion of the payment should be debited to Interest Expense and not be treated as part of the dividend. The interest period runs from the *date of record* to the date of payment.

EXAMPLE 5

On January 1, a corporation declares a scrip dividend of $300,000 payable on June 1 to stockholders of record on April 1. The scrip pays interest at 10%.

The journal entries are:

Date of declaration	Retained Earnings	300,000	
	Notes Payable to Stockholders		300,000
Date of payment	Interest Expense	5,000	
	Notes Payable to Stockholders	300,000	
	Cash		305,000

The interest computation is: $300,000 \times .10 \times 2/12 = 5,000$.

The interest period is from the date of record to the date of payment—2 months.

3.5 LIQUIDATING DIVIDENDS

As stated earlier, most dividends are paid out of retained earnings and are simply distributions to the stockholders of the corporate earnings. Sometimes, however, a dividend may be paid out of contributed capital instead. These dividends are called *liquidating dividends* and represent a reduction of the corporate paid-in capital. This information must be disclosed in the footnotes to the financial statements.

EXAMPLE 6

If a corporation declares a dividend of $100,000, of which $70,000 is to be considered a liquidating dividend, the journal entry is:

Retained Earnings	30,000	
Additional Paid-in Capital	70,000	
Cash Dividends Payable		100,000

3.6 STOCK DIVIDENDS

If a company decides to pay a dividend in the form of its *own* shares, this is called a *stock dividend*. If this dividend is less than 20 to 25% of the company's outstanding common stock (at the date of declaration) then retained earnings should be debited for the fair market value of the stock dividend. This is called a *small (ordinary) stock dividend*. Otherwise it is a *large stock dividend* and retained earnings is debited at par.

EXAMPLE 7

Suppose a corporation has 100,000 shares of common stock, $10 par outstanding, with a market value of $15 per share. It declares a stock dividend of 10%. It will therefore pay out to the stockholders a total of 10,000 shares (100,000 × 10%) as a dividend. Since this is less than 20 to 25%, fair market value must be used as the basis for debiting Retained Earnings. The journal entries would be:

Date of declaration:

Retained Earnings	150,000*	
Stock Dividend Distributable		100,000 (par)
Paid-in Capital in Excess of Par		50,000

Date of payment (when the shares were issued):

Stock Dividend Distributable	100,000	
Common Stock		100,000

*(10,000 × $15)

The Stock Dividend Distributable account is *not* a liability account. It is a temporary capital account which is replaced by the Common Stock account at the date of payment.

EXAMPLE 8

If in the previous example a 30% dividend was declared, then 30,000 shares (100,000 × 30%) would be issued and par value, rather than market value, would be used. The journal entries would be:

Retained Earnings	300,000	
Stock Dividend Distributable		300,000
Stock Dividend Distributable	300,000	
Common Stock		300,000

*(30,000 × $10 par)

3.7 STOCK SPLITS

If a corporation's stock is selling at a very high price on the market, many people will not be able to afford it. To make the stock less expensive and thus more attractive to the buying public, the corporation may effect what is called a *stock split*. This involves two steps:

1. Increasing the number of shares outstanding.

2. Reducing the par of each share proportionately.

EXAMPLE 9

Suppose a corporation has 100,000 shares outstanding, $12 par. It then splits the stock 2:1 by distributing another 100,000 shares to the stockholders and halving the par of *all* the shares from $12 to $6.

The total shares outstanding will now be 200,000.

The par value of every share will now be $6.

A stockholder who held 100 shares of $12 par will now hold 200 shares of $6 par.

No journal entry is made for a stock split. However, a memorandum note is made to indicate that there are now more shares outstanding.

Notice that in the above example the *total* par has not changed. Originally, it was $1,200,000 (100,000 × $12), and now it is also $1,200,000 (200,000 × $6).

EXAMPLE 10

If in the previous example the stock is split 3:1 then:

The total shares outstanding will now be 300,000.

The par value of each share will now be $4.

A stockholder who held 100 shares of $12 par will now be holding 300 shares of $4 par.

3.8 APPROPRIATIONS OF RETAINED EARNINGS

As discussed, dividends are paid out of retained earnings. For various reasons, companies may wish to restrict the amount of retained earnings available for dividends. These restrictions are called *appropriations*.

In some states restrictions must be placed on retained earnings prohibiting dividends in an amount equal to the cost of any treasury stock acquired.

It should be emphasized that appropriations do not involve the actual setting aside of cash for these purposes. They are, rather, merely journal entries indicating that a "lock" has been placed on retained earnings prohibiting a certain amount of dividends from being distributed.

EXAMPLE 11

A company decides to appropriate $10,000 each year for the next 5 years for the purpose of plant expansion. Each year the journal entry would be:

Retained Earnings	10,000	
Retained Earnings Appropriated for Plant Expansion		10,000

This entry removes $10,000 from retained earnings (by debiting it) and places it in a restricted "area."

Of course, the total retained earnings has not changed at all—it has merely been split into two parts: the restricted ("appropriated") part, and the unrestricted part.

EXAMPLE 12

In the previous example the appropriated retained earnings account will eventually contain a balance of $50,000. At that point, if we assume that the plant expansion has been completed, there will no longer be a need for the restriction. Accordingly, the following entry reverses the previous entries and returns the $50,000 back to the unrestricted "area":

Retained Earnings Appropriated for Plant Expansion	50,000	
Retained Earnings		50,000

3.9 QUASI-REORGANIZATIONS

We have seen that when a corporation earns net income, it is credited to retained earnings. Conversely, net losses are debited to retained earnings.

If a corporation consistently incurs net losses over a period of years, the debits may exceed the credits, thereby resulting in a debit balance in the account. This is called a *deficit*.

In many states, a corporation may not legally declare a dividend as long as a deficit exists. Accordingly, several years may go by without dividends as the corporation struggles to earn enough income to offset this deficit. Such nonpayment of dividends may damage the company name and even cause the price of the stock to fall. Naturally, no corporation wants this to happen.

A procedure provided for under the laws of many states yields a quick solution to this problem. Referred to as a *quasi-reorganization,* it permits the company to "start from scratch" (be reorganized) and instantly "wipe out" the deficit. In order to do this, the following steps are taken:

1. Revalue the assets to their fair market value.

2. Offset the deficit against other paid-in capital accounts.

If there aren't any, then they must be created either by having the par value of the stock reduced or by having the stockholders donate some of their stock to the corporation.

EXAMPLE 13

Assume the capital accounts of XYZ company appear as follows, at June 1, 1988:

Common Stock	Retained Earnings
100,000	40,000
(10,000	(deficit)
shares of	
$10 par stock)	

The plant, which is carried on the books at $60,000, has a fair market value of 55,000. The entry to revalue the plant is:

Retained Earnings	5,000	
Plant		5,000

The retained earnings account now has a deficit of $45,000 ($40,000 and $5,000). As there are no other capital accounts in existence to offset the deficit, they must be created.

If the corporation decides to reduce the par of the stock from $10 to $5, more than enough capital will be created for this purpose. The entry is:

Common Stock	50,000	
Paid-in Capital from Reorganization		50,000

Now, to offset the deficit:

Paid-in Capital from Reorganization	45,000	
Retained Earnings		45,000

The retained earnings account now has a zero balance.

For approximately 10 years after the reorganization, the retained earnings on the balance sheet must indicate that a reorganization took place, and also the date of the reorganization.

3.10   PRIOR PERIOD ADJUSTMENTS

If a company discovers that it made an error in a previous period, it should correct it via the retained earnings account. This is called a *prior period adjustment.* According to APB Opinion No. 9, settlements of lawsuits relating to prior periods were also accorded this treatment. However, FASB No. 16 in 1977 amended the APB and restricted it to error corrections only.

EXAMPLE 14

Assume that in 19X5 a company discovers that as a result of a computational error, it understated the depreciation for 19X3 by $10,000. The correction is:

Retained Earnings	10,000	
Accumulated Depreciation		10,000

The account Depreciation Expense is *not* debited because this account may only show depreciation relating to the current year.

Summary

1. Retained earnings are created in most part by a corporation's net income, which is closed into this account. The title "earned surplus" has been discouraged by the accounting profession because it connotes a pool of cash instead of a capital account.

2. Credits to the retained earnings account include the net income, prior period adjustments and adjustments due to quasi-reorganizations. Debits include net losses, prior period adjustments, cash dividends, scrip dividends, stock dividends, and property dividends.

3. There are three dates associated with dividends: the date of declaration, the date of record, and the date of payment. For cash dividends, an entry is made on the date of declaration debiting retained earnings and crediting Cash Dividends Payable. No entry is made on the date of record. On the date of payment, the payable is debited and Cash is credited.

4. Dividends on preferred stock are usually expressed as a percentage of par. For example, if the par is $200 and the dividend is 7%, each share will receive $14.

5. If a property dividend is declared, an entry must first be made to bring its book value into line with the market value. This will usually result in the recognition of a gain or loss.

6. *Scrip* dividends are a special kind of note payable promising to pay the stockholders a dividend at a later date. This note bears interest from the date of record.

7. Most dividends are paid out of retained earnings and represent distributions of the net income. *Liquidating dividends,* however, are different. They represent a return of contributed capital and must be debited to a paid-in capital account instead of to retained earnings.

8. A *stock dividend* is paid out of a corporation's *own* shares. If the dividend is less than 20 to 25% of the outstanding shares, then retained earnings should be debited for the fair market value of the stock dividend. Otherwise, it should be debited at par.

9. In order to reduce the market price of a stock, a corporation may effect a *stock split*. This involves two steps:
   (1) Increasing the outstanding shares.
   (2) Reducing the par of each share proportionately.
   No journal entry is made for a stock split.

10. A restriction on retained earnings preventing the declaration of dividends is called an *appropriation*. The entry is:

Retained Earnings	xxx	
Retained Earnings Appropriated for ...		xxx

    If the board of directors later decides this appropriation is no longer needed, the above entry would be nullified by a reversal entry.

11. A debit balance in the retained earnings account resulting from consistent net losses is called a *deficit*. In most states, no dividends may be declared if a deficit exists. Many states provide a means of wiping out this deficit and enabling the corporation to start from scratch. This procedure is called a *quasi-reorganization* and involves the following steps:
    (1) Revaluing the assets to their fair market value.
    (2) Offsetting the deficit against other paid-in capital accounts. If no such accounts exist, they are created by reducing the par value of the stock.

12. Prior period adjustments are corrections of errors made in previous periods. If these errors originally *reduced* the net income, they are now corrected by *crediting* the retained earnings account; otherwise, they are *debited* to retained earnings. The settlements of lawsuits pertaining to a prior period are *not* considered to be prior period adjustments.

Rapid Review

1. The net income of a corporation is closed into the account called ___R. E___.

2. Distributions made by the corporation to its stockholders are called ___Dividends___

3. The three dates associated with dividends are date of ___Dec.___, date of ___Rec___, and date of ___payment___.

4. When a corporation issues a note promising to pay a dividend in the future, that is called a ___Scrip___ dividend.

5. Dividends paid out of contributed capital rather than out of retained earnings are ___Liquidatip___ dividends.

6. If a stock dividend is less than ___20 – 25___%, it is debited to retained earnings at fair market value.

7. When a corporation reduces the par of its stock to make it more affordable to the public, that is called ___Stock Split___

8. A restriction on retained earnings is called a (an) ___Appropriation___

9. A debit balance in retained earnings is referred to as a ___defict___.

10. To eliminate a deficit, a corporation will engage in a ___quasi-reorganzal___

11. Corrections of errors in previous periods are called ___prior perin___ and must flow through the ___R.E___ account. ___Adjustments___

12. Dividends may be paid in the form of ___Cash___, ___Stock___, or ___property___.

Answers: 1. Retained Earnings; 2. dividends; 3. declaration, record, payment; 4. scrip; 5. liquidating; 6. 20–25%; 7. stock split; 8. appropriation; 9. deficit; 10. quasi-reorganization; 11. prior period adjustments; Retained Earnings; 12. cash, stock, property.

Solved Problems

3.1 XYZ Corp. has 8,500 shares of $30 par value common stock outstanding and retained earnings of $320,000. The company declares a cash dividend of $3.00 per share and a 5% stock dividend. The market price of the stock at the date of declaration is $40 per share.
(*a*) Give the journal entries for the declaration and payment of the cash dividends.
(*b*) Give the journal entries for the declaration and payment of the stock dividend.
(*c*) Assume the stock dividend is 40% rather than 5%.
Prepare the journal entries.

SOLUTION

(*a*)

Retained Earnings		25,500*	
Cash Dividends Payable			25,500
Cash Dividends Payable		25,500	
Cash			25,500

*(8,500 × 3)

(b)   Retained Earnings   17,000

                  Stock Dividend Distributable   12,750
                  Paid-in Capital in Excess of Par   4,250

            _____

            *(.05 × 8,500 × $40 market value = 17,000)

            Stock Dividend Distributable   12,750
                  Common Stock (Par)   12,750

            _____

            Note: The Common Stock account is
            always credited at par.

(c)   Since the percentage is more than 25%, par value must be used.

            Retained Earnings   102,000
                  Stock Dividend Distributable   102,000
            Stock Dividend Distributable   102,000
                  Common Stock   102,000

                                                                [Sections 3.2, 3.6]

3.2   Assume in the above example that the stock is split 2:1. Prepare the journal entries.

SOLUTION

No journal entries are required for a stock split. A memorandum entry must be made stating that the shares outstanding are now 17,000 instead of 8,500, and that the par value is now $15 instead of $30.   [Section 3.7]

3.3   The stockholders' equity section of Quincy Co. has the following balances on April 1, 1987:

            Common Stock, $1 par, 30,000 shares outstanding $ 30,000
            Paid-in Capital in Excess of Par   160,000
            Retained Earnings   650,000

The market value is $3 per share.
Prepare the journal entries for:
(a)   The declaration of a 6% dividend.
(b)   The declaration of a 100% dividend.
(c)   A 1.5:1 stock split.

SOLUTION

(a)   Retained Earnings   5,400

                  Stock Dividend Distributable   1,800 (at par)
                  Paid-in Capital in
                     Excess of Par   3,600

      The $5,400 debit to retained earnings is computed as follows:
                        30,000 shares × 6% × $3 = $5,400

(b)   Here retained earnings is debited at par since the dividend is larger than 20–25%.

            Retained Earnings   30,000
                  Stock Dividend Distributable   30,000

(c)   No journal entry is made for the stock split. The shares outstanding increase from 30,000 to 45,000, and the par is cut from $1.00 to 67 cents.   [Sections 3.6, 3.7]

3.4   The following data were taken from the balance sheet of High-Tech Company on December 31, 19X9:

Investments	500,000
Common Stock ($10 par)	440,000
Paid-in Capital in Excess of Par	100,000
Retained Earnings	750,000

Prepare entries for the following:
(*a*)   A scrip dividend of $75,000 is declared. The date of record is March 1; the date of payment is May 1, and the note pays interest at 12%.
(*b*)   The stock is split 5:1.
(*c*)   A dividend is declared from bonds held as an investment. The bonds have a book value of $60,000 and a fair market value of $90,000.

SOLUTION

(*a*)

Retained Earnings	75,000	
Notes Payable to Stockholders		75,000
Interest Expense	1,500	
Notes Payable to Stockholders	75,000	
Cash		76,500

The interest period is 2 months (March 1–May 1) and the interest calculation is: $75,000 × 12% × 2/12.
(*b*)   No entry
(*c*)   First, the bonds must be increased to their fair market value:

Investments	30,000	
Gain on Appreciation of Investments		30,000

The entry for the dividend declaration is:

Retained Earnings	90,000		
Property Dividend Payable		90,000	[Sections 3.3, 3.4]

3.5   GX Corp. has common stock ($50 par), 12,000 shares outstanding, and a retained earnings account with a deficit of $200,000. There are no other paid-in capital accounts.
    A quasi-reorganization was approved that reduced the par to $25, wrote down plant assets by $65,000, and eliminated the deficit. Prepare the appropriate journal entries.

SOLUTION

To write down the plant:

Retained Earnings	65,000	
Plant		65,000

The deficit is now $265,000 ($200,000 + $65,000). To reduce the par:

Common Stock	300,000	
Paid-in Capital from Reorganization		300,000

To eliminate the deficit:

Paid-in Capital from Reorganization	265,000		
Retained Earnings		265,000	[Section 3.9]

3.6   On January 1, 19X7, the stockholders' section of the Wizard Corp. appeared as follows:

Common Stock, $50 par, issued 12,000 shares	600,000
Retained Earnings (deficit)	(200,000)
Total	400,000

The officers of the corporation voted for a quasi-reorganization (on July 1) which accomplished the following:

(1)   The par value of the stock was reduced to $20 per share to create additional paid-in capital.

(2)   Inventories were revalued downward by $30,000.

(3)   The deficit was written off.

(4)   A liquidating cash dividend of 5,000 was declared.

(a)   Prepare journal entries for the above.

(b)   Assuming the company earned $50,000 for the year 19X7, show the stockholders' equity section of the balance sheet, on December 31, 19X7.

SOLUTION

(a)

	(1)	Common Stock	360,000	
		Paid-in Capital from Reorganization		360,000
		To reduce the par.		
	(2)	Retained Earnings	30,000	
		Inventories		30,000
		To revalue inventory.		

The deficit is now 230,000 (200,000 + 30,000).

	(3)	Paid-in Capital from Reorganization	230,000	
		Retained Earnings		230,000
		To eliminate the deficit.		
	(4)	Paid-in Capital from Reorganization	5,000	
		Cash Dividends Payable		5,000
		For the liquidating dividend.		

(b)

STOCKHOLDERS' EQUITY

Common stock, $20 par, 12,000 shares outstanding	240,000	
Paid-in Capital from Reorganization	125,000	
Retained Earnings (after quasi-reorganization of July 1, 19X7)	50,000	
Total Stockholders' Equity	415,000	[Section 3.9]

3.7   In both 19X5 and 19X6, the Lucky Corp. appropriated $60,000 of retained earnings for a future machine acquisition. In 19X7, the company bought the machine for $130,000 cash.

Prepare entries for:

(a)   The appropriations.

(b)   The acquisition of the machine.

(c)   The disposition of the appropriations.

SOLUTION

(a)   In both 19X5 and 19X6, the following entry is to be made:

Retained Earnings	60,000	
Retained Earnings Appropriated for Machine		60,000

(b)   Machine   130,000
                                Cash   130,000

(c) To "unlock" the appropriation:

            Retained Earnings Appropriated for Machine   120,000
                    Retained Earnings   120,000

                                                                    [Section 3.8]

3.8   Use the following data to prepare a retained earnings statement for Widget Corp. for the year 19X7:

Total retained earnings originally reported on Dec. 31, 19X6 (including $100,000 appropriated for treasury stock)	$275,000
Cash dividends declared in 19X7	40,000
Net income for 19X7	125,000
Additional appropriation for plant expansion	20,000
Understatement of 19X6 ending inventory, discovered in 19X7	8,000

SOLUTION

Widget Corp.
Retained Earnings Statement 19X7
For the Year Ending Dec. 31, 19X7

Appropriated:			
Balance Jan. 1, 19X7 (for treasury stock)	100,000		
Additional appropriation during 19X7 (for plant)	20,000		
Total appropriated		120,000	
Unappropriated:			
Balance Jan. 1 19X7	175,000		
Add: Correction of prior period inventory error	8,000		
Adjusted balance, Jan. 1, 19X7	183,000		
Add: Net Income	125,000		
	308,000		
Less: Dividend Declared	(40,000)		
Appropriation for Plant (above)	(20,000)	248,000	
Total Retained Earnings, Dec. 31, 19X7		368,000	[Section 3.10]

3.9   The stockholders' equity section of the Gimmick Corp. balance sheet at January 1, 19X7, contained the following:

Common Stock, $10 par, 50,000 shares authorized, 20,000 shares outstanding	$200,000
Paid-in Capital in Excess of Par	60,000
Unappropriated Retained Earnings	200,000

During 19X7, the following took place:

Feb.   1   The board of directors appropriated 90,000 of retained earnings for bond redemption.
Mar. 10   Declared a cash dividend of $1.00 per share and a 5% stock dividend. (Market value per
          share was $30).
Dec. 31   Closed the net income of 150,000.
(a)   Prepare journal entries for the above.
(b)   Prepare a retained earnings statement for 19X7.
(c)   The appropriation was eliminated on July 1, 19X8.

SOLUTION

(a)

Retained Earnings	90,000	
Retained Earnings Appropriated for Bond Redemption		90,000
Retained Earnings	20,000*	
Cash Dividend Payable		20,000

    *(20,000 × 1.00)

Notice that the shares outstanding, rather than the shares authorized, are used for the dividend.

Retained Earnings	30,000	
Stock Dividend Distributable (Par)		10,000
Paid-in Capital in Excess of Par		20,000
Income Summary	150,000	
Retained Earnings		150,000

    (20,000 × 5% × $30)

(b)

Gimmick Corp.
Retained Earnings Statement
For the Year Ended Dec. 31, 19X7

Appropriated:			
Balance Jan. 1, 19X7		–0–	
Appropriated during 19X7 for bonds		90,000	
Total appropriated			90,000
Unappropriated			
Balance Jan. 1, 19X7		200,000	
Add: Net Income		150,000	
		350,000	
Less: Cash dividend declared	20,000		
Stock dividend declared	30,000		
Appropriation for bonds	90,000	(140,000)	210,000
Total retained earnings			
Dec. 31, 19X7			300,000

(c)

Retained Earnings Appropriated for Bond Redemption	90,000	
Retained Earnings		90,000

[Section 3.8]

3.10   Indicate whether the following increase, decrease, or have no effect on retained earnings:
(a)   Declared cash dividend.
(b)   Declared stock dividend.
(c)   Recorded prior period adjustment (gain).
(d)   Revalued plant assets downward.

(e) Eliminated a deficit via a quasi-reorganization.
(f) Declared a scrip dividend.
(g) Split the stock 2:1.
(h) Recorded a net loss.
(i) Appropriated retained earnings for plant expansion).
(j) Eliminated an appropriation.

SOLUTION

Debits to Retained Earnings decrease retained earnings, while credits increase retained earnings.
(a) Decrease
(b) Decrease
(c) Increase
(d) Decrease
(e) Increase (from a minus to zero).
(f) Decrease
(g) No effect
(h) Decrease
(i) No effect (retained earnings are simply "shuffled" from an "unlocked" area to a "locked" area).
(j) No effect

Supplementary Problems

3.11 Corporation A had net income during 19X1 in the amount of $100,000 and had 10,000 shares of common stock outstanding. On June 30, it declared a cash dividend of $1 per share payable on October 1 to stockholders of record on August 1.
(a) Prepare an entry for the net income.
(b) What is the name given to each of the three dates (June 30, August 1, October 1)?
(c) Prepare the necessary entry for each date.

3.12 On April 1, 19A, Corporation B declares a dividend to be paid out of its merchandise inventory. On this date, the book value of the inventory is $5,000 while its market value is $4,000.
(a) What type of dividend is this?
(b) Prepare entries for the declaration and the payment.

3.13 On January 1, 19A, Corporation C declares a scrip dividend of $100,000 payable on May 1 to stockholders of record on April 1. The scrip pays interest at a 10% annual rate. Prepare entries for these three dates.

3.14 Corporation D declares a dividend of $80,000, of which $20,000 is considered to be a liquidating dividend. Prepare the necessary journal entry.

3.15 Corporation E has 10,000 shares of $60 par common stock outstanding. On February 1, 19A, when the market value of the stock is $80 per share, it declares a 10% stock dividend. Prepare the entries for both the declaration and the payment.

3.16 For the previous problem, prepare the journal entries if the dividend was 30% rather than just 10%.

3.17 Corporation F has 20,000 shares of $120 par value common stock, with a market value of $180 per share.
(a) If the stock is split 2:1, what will be the *new* par value per share, *new* market value per share, and total number of shares outstanding?
(b) What will your answers be to these questions if the stock is split 3:1?

3.18 On February 1, Corporation G decides to appropriate $50,000 of its $120,000 retained earnings for the retirement of bonds payable. On June 1, the corporation decides it no longer needs the appropriation. Prepare the entries for the original appropriation and its elimination.

3.19 During 19B, Corporation H discovers it understated depreciation for 19A in the amount of $40,000.
  (a) What type of correction entry is needed?
  (b) Prepare the correction entry. (Ignore income taxes.)

3.20 Corporation I has the following capital accounts on January 1, 19A:

Common Stock	Retained Earnings
200,000	30,000

The common stock consists of 20,000 shares of $10 par each. Corporation I now decides to effect a quasi-reorganization by reducing the par of the stock to $5 per share. It also revalues its equipment (which is carried on the books at $20,000) to its market value of $18,000. Prepare the required journal entries.

Examination I

Chapters 1, 2, 3

A. True-False Questions. Place the letter T or F next to the question.

1. _____ To determine the price of a bond, you must look up the tables at the *stated* rate.

2. _____ The gain or loss on retirement of a bond is *not* considered to be extraordinary.

3. _____ A corporation must pay the face value of a bond at maturity, even if it was sold at a premium or discount.

4. _____ If a bond is sold after an interest date, the interest starts to accrue from the date of the sale.

5. _____ Initially, bond issue costs are debited to an expense account.

6. _____ The bond contract is called a *debenture.*

7. _____ The preferred method of premium/discount amortization is the effective interest method.

8. _____ Deep discount bonds bear a low rate of interest.

9. _____ Retained earnings should be debited at par value for a stock dividend of 15%.

10. _____ Errors in prior periods should be reported in the current income statement.

11. _____ Appropriations involve the setting aside of cash.

12. _____ For property dividends an adjusting entry must first be made to adjust the book value to market value.

13. _____ In a stock split, the par value is *doubled.*

14. _____ The account Stock Subscriptions Receivable is a capital account.

15. _____ Issued shares are equal to outstanding shares.

16. _____ Both the cost and par value methods of treasury stock result in the same total stockholders' equity.

17. _____ The account Stock Issue Costs is a deferred charge.

18. _____ If stock is issued for a noncash asset, the asset should be debited at par.

19. _____ Treasury stock is an asset.

20. _____ When a company issues stock, assets and liabilities go up.

B. Completion Questions. Fill in the blanks.

21. In a corporation, the Income Summary account is closed into _____ .

22. The cutoff date that determines whether or not one is entitled to a dividend is the _____ .

23. A note payable that promises to pay a dividend is called _____ .

24. Dividends that are paid out of contributed capital are _____ dividends.

25. For a stock dividend to be debited at fair market value, it must be no larger than _____ %.

26. Restrictions of retained earnings are _____ .

27. Unsecured high risk bonds are called _____ bonds.

28. The face value of a bond is also referred to as _____ .

29. When the market rate of interest is greater than the contract rate, the bond will sell at a _____ .

30. Amortization of bond premium _____ interest expense while amortization of bond discount _____ interest expense.

31. If a bond is sold between interest dates, its selling price will be raised by the amount of _____ interest.

32. An attempt to borrow money without having to show the liability on the balance sheet is called _____ financing.

33. A temporary capital account that is credited for the par value of a stock subscription is called _____ .

34. Stock that is repurchased from the public is _____ stock.

35. The two methods of accounting for stock repurchased from the public are the _____ method and the _____ method.

36. A par value orally assigned to stock by the board of directors is called _____ value.

37. When stock is issued, assets go _____ , liabilities _____ , and capital _____ .

38. In some states, stockholders are personally liable for any _____ on the purchase price of the stock.

39. When an asset or treasury stock is donated to a corporation, the account to be credited is _____ .

40. When stock is issued for a noncash asset, the asset should be debited at its own _____ or at the _____ , whichever is more clear.

C. Problems

41. On January 1, 19X1, the board of directors declares a cash dividend of $1.00 per share and a stock dividend of 10% to all common stockholders of record as of February 1, payable on March 1. The number of shares presently outstanding is 10,000, and the par and market values are $10 and $12, respectively.

   Required:
      Prepare journal entries for *all* dates for:
      (*a*) The cash dividend.
      (*b*) The stock dividend.
      (*c*) The stock dividend if it was 30% instead of 10%.

42. The Clark Corporation declared a property dividend payable from its investment in General Motors stock. The stock is carried on the books at $5,000 but has a market value of $7,000. It also declares a liquidating dividend of $12,000.

   Required:
      Prepare the entries at the *declaration date* for both of these dividends.

43. A $200,000, 2-year, 8% bond paying interest semiannually (4%) is sold to yield a market rate of 6% (3%). Compute the bond selling price and prepare the journal entry for the sale.

44. In the above problem determine the amortization:
    (*a*)   under the straight-line method.
    (*b*)   under the effective interest method and prepare an amortization table.

45. The following transactions relate to the stock of the Rich Corporation:
    (*a*)   Issued 300 shares, $10 par common stock at $13
    (*b*)   Purchased 100 shares treasury stock at $11
    (*c*)   Resold 50 shares at $8
    (*d*)   Retired the remaining 50 shares
    Prepare journal entries for these transactions under both the cost and par methods.

46. Fifty shares of preferred stock, $20 par, are donated back to a corporation. These shares were originally issued at $25, and their present market value is $35. Prepare the journal entry under both the cost and par methods.

Answers to Examination I

True-False Questions
1. F   2. F   3. T   4. F   5. F   6. F   7. T   8. F   9. F   10. F   11. F   12. T

13. F   14. F   15. F   16. T   17. T   18. F   19. F   20. F

Completion Questions
21. retained earnings   22. date of record   23. scrip   24. liquidating   25. 20–25   26. appropriations

27. junk   28. par   29. discount   30. decreases; increases   31. accrued   32. off-balance-sheet

33. stock subscribed   34. treasury   35. par; cost   36. stated   37. up; stays same; up   38. discount

39. donated capital   40. fair value; stock's fair value

Problems
41. (*a*)   Date of declaration:

Retained Earnings	10,000	
Cash Dividends Payable		10,000

Date of record:

No entry

Date of payment:

Cash Dividend Payable	10,000	
Cash		10,000

(*b*)

Retained Earnings	12,000	
Stock Dividend Distributable		10,000
Paid-in Capital in Excess of Par		2,000

Date of record:

No entry

Date of payment:

Stock Dividend Distributable	10,000	
Common Stock		10,000

(c) Date of declaration:

Retained Earnings	30,000*	
Stock Dividend Distributable		30,000

_____

*10,000 × 30% × $10

Date of record:

No entry

Date of payment:

Stock Dividend Distributable	30,000	
Common Stock		30,000

42.

Investments—Securities	2,000	
Gain on Appreciation of Securities		2,000
Retained Earnings	7,000	
Property Dividend Distributable		7,000
Additional Paid-in Capital	12,000	
Cash Dividend Payable		12,000

43.

Present value, 3%, 4 periods = .88849 × $200,000 = $177,698

Present value, annuity, 3%, 4 periods = 3.7171 × 8000 = 29,737

$207,435

Cash	207,435	
Bonds Payable		200,000
Bond Premium		7,435

44. (a) Straight-line: 7,435/4 periods = $1,859 per period.

(b) Effective interest method:

Period	Physical Interest—4%	Interest Expense—3%	Amortization	Book Value
Now	—	—	—	$207,435
1	$8,000	$6,223	$1,777	205,658
2	8,000	6,170	1,830	203,828
3	8,000	6,115	1,885	201,943
4	8,000	6,058	1,942	200,001

45. *Cost Method:*

(a)

Cash	3,900	
Common Stock		3,000
Paid-in Capital in Excess of Par		900

(b)

Treasury Stock	1,100	
Cash		1,100

(c)	Cash	400	
	Retained Earnings	150	
	Treasury Stock		550

(d)	Common Stock	500	
	Paid-in Capital in Excess of Par	150*	
	Treasury Stock		550
	Paid-in Capital from Retirement of Treasury Stock		100

---

*3 × 50

Par Method:
(a)   Same as under cost method

(b)	Treasury Stock	1,000	
	Paid-in Capital in Excess of Par	300	
	Cash		1,100
	Paid-in Capital from Treasury Stock		200

(c)	Cash	400	
	Paid-in Capital from Treasury Stock	100	
	Treasury Stock		500

(d)	Common Stock	500	
	Treasury Stock		500

46. *Cost Method:*

Treasury Stock	1,750	
Donated Capital		1,750

Par Method:

Treasury Stock	1,000	
Paid-in Capital in Excess of Par	250*	
Donated Capital		1,250

---

*$50 × 5

Chapter 4

Dilutive Securities and Earnings per Share

4.1 INTRODUCTION

During the past 30 years, a wide variety of new financial instruments have been introduced into the market-place. In addition to the traditional basic securities of common stock, preferred stock, and bonds, one can now also own convertible bonds, convertible preferred stock, bonds with detachable stock warrants, stock rights, and employee stock options. The first half of this chapter will discuss each one of these instruments; the second half will discuss earnings per share and demonstrate the role that these instruments play in the determination of earnings per share.

4.2 CONVERTIBLE BONDS

Many corporations issue *convertible bonds*. These bonds may be traded in by the investor before maturity for common stock. Thus the investor has the option of either holding the bonds until maturity and collecting principal and interest or trading them in at an earlier date for stock. Because of this attractive feature, convertible bonds will usually pay a lower rate of interest than nonconvertibles.

The accounting for these bonds at the date of issuance is no different from nonconvertibles.

EXAMPLE 1

The Large Corporation issues $100,000 par, 5-year, 8% bonds at 103. The bonds are convertible into 5,000 shares of $15 par common stock after 3 years. The entry at issuance is:

Cash	103,000	
Bonds Payable		100,000
Bond Premium		3,000

Notice that no indication is made in the entry regarding the conversion feature.

If a conversion eventually takes place, the entry is made based upon *book values*. Market values are ignored. Therefore, no gain or loss is recognized upon the conversion.

EXAMPLE 2

Assume the bonds in the previous example are converted after 3 years, and the straight-line method of premium amortization has been used. The T-accounts would appear as follows:

Bonds Payable		Bond Premium	
	100,000	600	3,000
		600	
		600	
			1,200

Thus the book value at this time is $101,200. Assuming the market value of these bonds at this point is 104, the entry would be:

Bonds Payable	100,000	
Bond Premium	1,200	
Common Stock (Par)		75,000
Paid-in Capital in Excess of Par		26,200

The Bonds Payable and Premium accounts are closed and replaced by the Common Stock and Paid-in Capital in Excess of Par accounts. Notice that the market value of 104 is totally ignored.

Sometimes a corporation may try to induce the bondholder to trade in the bond by giving a cash payment. This is called a "sweetener" and is debited to an expense account.

EXAMPLE 3

If in the previous example the bondholder refused to convert the bonds unless paid a sweetener of $5,000, an additional entry would be made as follows:

Debt Conversion Expense	5,000	
Cash		5,000

4.3 CONVERTIBLE PREFERRED STOCK

Once again, as was the case for convertible bonds, the book value method is used and market values are ignored. The Preferred Stock account and any related premium accounts are canceled (debited) and Common Stock is credited at par. If a credit is needed to balance the entry, it goes to Paid-in Capital in Excess of Par; if a debit is needed, it goes to retained earnings.

EXAMPLE 4

Preferred stock of $1,000 par with a related premium of $100 is converted into 100 shares of $9 par common stock. The entry is:

Preferred Stock	1,000	
Paid-in Capital in Excess of Par — Preferred	100	
Common Stock		900
Paid-in Capital in Excess of Par — Common		200

EXAMPLE 5

Assume the same information as in the previous example except that the par of the common is $13. The entry is:

Preferred Stock	1,000	
Paid-in Capital in Excess of Par — Preferred	100	
Retained Earnings	200	
Common Stock		1,300

4.4 BONDS WITH DETACHABLE STOCK WARRANTS

A stock warrant is a certificate that enables its holder to purchase shares of stock at a certain fixed price for a given time period. Many times corporations will attach these warrants to a bond in order to make the bond more attractive. A key difference between these bonds and convertible bonds is that in the latter case, the investor *trades* in the bond for stock, while in the former case, he or she *keeps* the bond and hands in the warrant plus cash.

Since these warrants are detachable and can be traded separately from the bonds, the profession has ruled that the sale of this entire package be considered an issuance of both debt and equity securities. Accordingly, the entry involves a credit to the Bonds Payable account and to a stockholders' equity account as well. The allocation between the two is based upon their respective market values. This is called the *proportional method*.

EXAMPLE 6

Bell Labs issued 100 bonds, $100 par, each with a detachable stock warrant. Each warrant may be exercised to purchase 1 share of $100 par common stock at $110. The total selling price is the par of $10,000 ($100 × 100). At the time of the sale, the market value of the bonds (without the warrants) is 102, while the market value of the warrants is $30. The allocation of the $10,000 selling price is as follows:

		Market Value
Bonds: 100 × 102	=	$10,200
Warrants: 100 × $30	=	3,000
Total market value	=	$13,200

Bond allocation: 10,200/13,200 × $10,000 = $7,727 (rounded)

Warrant allocation: 3,000/13,200 × $10,000 = $2,273

Thus the bonds have been issued at a discount of \$2,273 (\$10,000 par − \$7,727). The entries are:

Cash	7,727	
Bond Discount	2,273	
Bonds Payable		10,000
Cash	2,273	
Paid-in Capital — Stock Warrants*		2,273

---

*A stockholders' equity account

EXAMPLE 7

If in the previous example the warrants are exercised by the investors to purchase 100 shares at \$110, the entry would be:

Cash (100 × \$110)	11,000	
Paid-in Capital — Stock Warrants	2,273	
Common Stock		10,000*
Paid-in Capital in Excess of Par		3,273

---

*At par: 100 × \$100

If the warrants were instead allowed by the investors to expire, the following entry would be made:

Paid-in Capital — Stock Warrants	2,273	
Paid-in Capital — Expired Stock Warrants		2,273

In the above situation, the market values of *both* the warrants and the bonds were known. If, however, only one market value is known, then that security would be allocated market value for its share of the total selling price, while the remainder would go to the other security. This is referred to as the *incremental method*.

EXAMPLE 8

If in Example 6 only the market value of the warrants was known (\$3,000), the original entries would be:

Cash	7,000	
Bond Discount	3,000	
Bonds Payable		10,000
Cash	3,000	
Paid-in Capital — Stock Warrants		3,000

Of the \$10,000 selling price, the warrants received their market value of \$3,000 and the remaining \$7,000 was allocated to the bonds.

The previous discussion centered around bonds with *detachable* warrants. If the warrants are nondetachable, no recognition would be made in the entries for the warrants. Thus the entire selling price would go to the bonds.

EXAMPLE 9

A corporation issues 100 bonds, \$100 par per bond, with *nondetachable* stock warrants for \$10,000. The market values of the bonds and the warrants are 102 and \$30, respectively. The entry is:

Cash	10,000	
Bonds Payable		10,000

Notice that the warrants are ignored in the entry.

4.5 STOCK WARRANTS ISSUED ALONE

In the previous section we discussed a situation where the stock warrants were attached to a bond. Sometimes corporations issue stock warrants unattached to any bond. These warrants, as before, give the holder the right to buy shares of stock at a certain fixed price for a given time. They are usually given to common stockholders to enable them to be first on line when new shares are issued.

No journal entry is required for the issuance of these stock warrants. The corporation merely makes a memorandum entry indicating how many warrants are outstanding.

4.6 EMPLOYEE STOCK OPTIONS

Corporations often establish stock option plans where employees may purchase shares of stock, for a limited time, at a discount. The purpose of these plans is to help recruit high-quality employees and as additional compensation for superior performance.

Such plans may be divided into two categories:

1. Noncompensatory, and

2. Compensatory

The latter involves an expense to the company and must be recorded as such; the former does not.

In order for a plan to be considered noncompensatory, it must meet *all* four of the following conditions:

1. Substantially all the full-time employees must be eligible.

2. It must be offered to all the employees *on an equal basis.*

3. The length of the option period must be reasonable.

4. The discount from the market price should not be greater than 15%.

If any one of these conditions is not met, the plan is considered to be compensatory.

EXAMPLE 10

Corporation A issues stock options, on an equal basis, to all of its employees to purchase 20 shares of stock at $20 per share for the next 6 months. At this time, the market price per share is $30.

This plan is compensatory because while the first three conditions have been met, the fourth has not, since the discount is greater than 15% ($30 - 20 = 10 \div 30 = 33\,1/3\%$).

For noncompensatory plans no special entry is required for the issuance of the options. Later, when the stock is issued upon exercise of the options, the regular entry for stock issuances is made, i.e., debit Cash, credit Common Stock, debit or credit Paid-in Capital in Excess of Par.

For compensatory plans, an entry must be made at the "measurement date" to recognize a cost called "compensation cost." The *measurement date* is the point in time when *both* the number of shares that the employees are entitled to receive *and* the option price are known. Usually this is the date of the grant.

The *compensation cost* is the difference between the option price and the market price on the market date, and this cost should be spread evenly over the service period, beginning from the date of the grant and ending on the date when the employee has no further service obligations and may exercise the options.

EXAMPLE 11

If options are granted to purchase 1,000 shares at $20 and the market price on the grant date is $50, total compensation cost would be ($50 - $20) × 1,000 = $30,000. If the service period is 5 years, then $6,000 of this cost ($30,000 ÷ 5) would be recognized each year.

If the option price is greater than the market price on the measurement date, no compensation cost is recognized, and no entry would be made.

When an entry has to be made (because the market price is greater), the entry would be:

Deferred Compensation Cost	XXX	
Paid-in Capital — Employee Stock Options		XXX

The deferred compensation cost can be thought of as a prepaid asset (similar to prepaid insurance) since the employee is being paid this compensation in advance. However, the custom is to show it in the stockholders' equity section as a contra-capital item to the Paid-in Capital — Employee Stock Option account.

When the stock is later issued, the Paid-in Capital account and Cash would be debited, and Common Stock would be credited.

EXAMPLE 12

On January 1, 19A, Distra Corporation grants options to one of its five employees to purchase 1,000 shares of $40 par common stock at $50 per share, beginning on January 1, 19D, and ending on January 1, 19E. The service period is from the grant date (1/1/19A) until the earliest exercise date (1/1/19D) — a total of 3 years.

On the grant date the market price per share was $56. Since on this date we know both the total number of shares and the market price, it is considered to be the measurement date. Since only one employee out of five has been given these options, condition 1 has not been fulfilled and this plan is thus a compensatory one. The entries are:

Jan. 1, 19A	Deferred Compensation Cost	6,000*	
	Paid-in Capital — Employee Stock Options		6,000

*(56 − 50) × 1,000

Dec. 31, 19A			
Dec. 31, 19B	Compensation Expense	2,000†	
Dec. 31, 19C	Deferred Compensation Cost		2,000

†6,000 ÷ 3 years

The income statement for 19A would show compensation expense of $2,000 and the December 31, 19A, balance sheet would contain the following in its stockholders' equity section:

Paid-in Capital — Employee Stock Options	$6,000
Less Deferred Compensation Cost ($6,000 − $2,000)	(4,000)
	$2,000

EXAMPLE 13

If in the previous example the employee exercises the options during 19D to purchase 1,000 shares at $50, the entry is:

Cash	50,000	
Paid-in Capital — Employee Stock Options	6,000	
Common Stock (Par)		40,000
Paid-in Capital in Excess of Par		16,000

If the employees do not exercise the options and allow them to lapse, an entry would be made debiting Paid-in Capital — Employee Stock Options, and crediting Paid-in Capital — Lapsed Stock Options.

4.7 STOCK APPRECIATION RIGHTS (SARs)

This is a plan that involves the issuance of certain rights (SARs) to employees, which upon exercise require the company to pay *cash* for the difference between the grant price and the market price of the company stock on the exercise date. For example, if the grant price is $10 per share and the market price is $15, the company will give the employee a bonus of $5 per share.

The total compensation cost must be allocated, as discussed previously, to the service period involved. Since neither the market price nor the exercise date is known in advance, estimates must be made each year to record annual compensation expense.

The entry each year, based upon an estimate using that year's ending market price, is:

Compensation Expense	XXX	
Stock Appreciation Plan Liability		XXX

At the date of exercise, the liability would be debited and cash would be credited.

EXAMPLE 14

On January 1, 19B, General Motors grants one employee 4,000 SARs. For each SAR the employee is entitled to receive the difference between the grant price of $10 and the market price of the company's stock on the measurement date. The measurement date is 4 years later on December 31, 19E. The employee may not exercise these rights before that date. The service period is thus 4 years.

The year-end market prices were as follows:

19B:	$12	19D:	$13
19C:	$13	19E:	$15

For each year (19B–19E) an entry must be made to recognize compensation cost. Since the market price on the measurement date is presently unknown, we use each year's ending market price as a best estimate.

For December 31, 19B:

Compensation Expense	2,000	
Stock Appreciation Plan Liability		2,000

The $2,000 is based upon $(12 - 10)\$4,000 = \$8,000 \div 4$ years $= \$2,000$.

For December 31, 19C:

Compensation Expense	3,333*	
Stock Appreciation Plan Liability		3,333

*($13 − $10)4,000 = $12,000
Less 19B amount = (2,000)
$10,000 ÷ 3 remaining years = $3,333

For December 31, 19D:

Same entry as last year since the market price did not change.

For December 31, 19E:

Compensation Expense	11,334*	
Stock Appreciation Plan Liability		11,334

*($15 − $10)4,000 = $20,000
Less 19B amount =   (2,000)
Less 19C amount =   (3,333)
Less 19D amount =   (3,333)
$11,334

When the rights are exercised, the entry is:

Stock Appreciation Plan Liability	20,000	
Cash		20,000

4.8 EARNINGS PER SHARE—BASIC

A very popular ratio used by financial analysts to evaluate a company's performance is *earnings per share (EPS)*. Broadly speaking, this ratio determines how much of the net income "pie" has been "earned" for each share of *common stock*.

There are three types of EPS: basic, primary, and fully diluted. Basic EPS is used for a "simple capital structure"—a corporation that has no convertible securities (convertible bonds, convertible preferred stock, or stock warrants) outstanding. Primary and fully diluted EPS are used for complex capital structures.

The formula for basic EPS is:

$$\text{EPS} = \frac{(\text{net income} - \text{preferred dividend})}{\text{weighted average of common shares outstanding during year}}$$

If the preferred stock is cumulative, then the preferred dividend must be subtracted *regardless* of whether or not it was declared. However, if it is noncumulative, it is subtracted only if declared.

The calculation of a weighted average will be discussed later on toward the end of this chapter.

EXAMPLE 15

Corporation C had net income of $110,000 in 19X5 and 20,000 shares of common stock were outstanding during the year. There were also 1,000 shares of $100 par, 10%, preferred stock outstanding as well. Thus the preferred dividend is $10\% \times \$100 \times 1,000 = \$10,000$. Basic EPS is:

$$\frac{\$110,000 - \$10,000}{20,000} = \$5.00$$

4.9 PRIMARY AND FULLY DILUTED EPS—CONVERTIBLE PREFERRED STOCK

In a complex capital structure containing either convertible preferred stock, convertible bonds, or stock warrants, the accounting profession requires the presentation of primary and fully diluted EPS, rather than basic EPS. Certain adjustments must be made to the numerator and the denominator of the basic EPS formula. Let's discuss convertible preferred stock first.

If there is preferred stock outstanding that can be converted into common stock, we "make-believe" *as if* the conversion has actually taken place. Accordingly, in the numerator we will *not* subtract the preferred dividend—because the preferred stock has "magically" been converted into common—and thus there is no preferred dividend. In the denominator we will add the additional common shares created by this "conversion."

For primary EPS, two conditions must be met for us to assume that a conversion has occurred. They are:

1. At the time of issuance the dividend rate on the preferred stock must have been less than two-thirds of the Aa bond rate, and
2. The conversion privilege must be exercisable within 5 years of the balance sheet date.

If these conditions are met, the preferred stock is considered to be a "common stock equivalent."

The logic behind the first condition is that since the rate is so far below the Aa bond rate, the investors will be unhappy and thus will probably exercise the conversion privilege.

Both of the above conditions must be met for primary EPS. If either condition (or both conditions) is not met, the conversion is not assumed to have taken place. For fully diluted EPS, however, none of the above conditions need to be met, provided the conversion privilege is exercisable within 10 years.

EXAMPLE 16

A company had net income of $110,000 in 19X5 with 20,000 shares of common stock outstanding. There were also 1,000 shares of $100 par, 7% convertible preferred stock outstanding as well. These shares can be converted into 2,000 shares of common stock *after* 6 years. The Aa bond rate is 12%.

For primary EPS, condition 1 has been fulfilled since 7% is less than 2/3 of 12%. However condition 2 (5 years) has not been met. Thus no conversion is assumed, and EPS would be:

$$\frac{(\$110,000 - \$7,000)}{20,000} = \$5.15$$

Fully diluted EPS *would* assume conversion since it is exercisable *within* 10 years. Thus EPS would be:

$$\frac{\$110,000}{(20,000 + 2000)} = \$5.00$$

Notice that because we assume conversion into common stock has taken place, we do *not* subtract the preferred dividend in the numerator, and in the denominator we add the new 2,000 common shares.

If the convertible preferred stock has been outstanding for only part of the year, then the denominator should be increased by a prorated amount representing that fraction.

EXAMPLE 17

If in the previous example the preferred stock was issued April 1 and thus was outstanding for only three-fourths of the year, the denominator would only be increased by 3/4 × 2,000 = 1,500 shares. Thus EPS would be $5.12.

4.10 PRIMARY AND FULLY DILUTED EPS—CONVERTIBLE BONDS

If a corporation has *bonds* outstanding that are convertible into common stock and they fulfill the two conditions listed above, then for primary EPS we consider them "as if" converted. For fully diluted EPS the two conditions need not be met, provided the conversion privilege is exercisable within 10 years.

When conversion is assumed, the denominator must be increased by the number of common shares the bonds are convertible into.

The numerator containing the net income must also be increased. This is because net income = revenue − expense. Bonds generate interest expense. Since we are "assuming" the bonds have been converted into stock, there is no interest expense and therefore this interest must be added back into the net income.

EXAMPLE 18

A company had 10,000 shares of common stock outstanding, net income of $90,000 and a $100,000 par, 10% bond convertible into 20,000 shares of common stock within 3 years. The Aa bond rate is 20%, and to simplify, there are no taxes. This bond meets both of the conditions for primary EPS. Thus the denominator would be increased by 20,000 and the numerator by $10,000 ($100,000 × .10). Primary EPS thus is:

$$\frac{(\$90,000 + \$10,000)}{30,000} = \$3.33$$

In the above example we assumed no taxes. Since in the real world there *are* taxes, the interest saving is made smaller by the tax. To get the net saving, we must multiply the interest by 1 − the tax rate.

EXAMPLE 19

If in the above example the tax rate was 30%, the interest saving would be $10,000(1 − .30) = $7,000.

If the bonds have been outstanding for less than a full period, the interest saving in the numerator and the increase of shares in the denominator would have to be reduced accordingly.

EXAMPLE 20

If a $100,000 par, 10% bond convertible into 20,000 shares was outstanding for only one half year, and the tax rate is 30%, the denominator would only be increased by 10,000 (20,000 × $\frac{1}{2}$). The numerator would be increased by the interest of 10,000 × (1 − .30) × $\frac{1}{2}$ year = $3,500.

If the bond was sold at a premium or discount, the interest adjustment in the numerator must take this into account. Discounts increase interest expense while premiums reduce interest expense.

EXAMPLE 21

Assume a 10-year, $1,000 par, 10% convertible bond was sold at 102. The use of the straight-line method of premium amortization results in a reduction of the interest by the amount of $2 ($20 ÷ 10 years). Thus the interest savings would be $98 (10% × $1,000 − $2).

EXAMPLE 22

If the bond in the previous example was sold at 95, the discount amortization per year would be $50 ÷ 10 = $5, which increases the annual interest expense. Therefore the interest saving would be $105 ($100 + $5).

It is very common for conversion agreements to specify a changing conversion ratio over time. For primary EPS, the earliest conversion ratio should be used. For fully diluted EPS, the most advantageous ratio (from the bondholder's viewpoint) should be used.

EXAMPLE 23

A bond agreement states that the conversion ratio should be 10 shares of stock per bond for the first 3 years and 15 shares of stock for the second 3 years. For primary EPS use 10 shares; for fully diluted EPS use 15 shares.

4.11 PRIMARY AND FULLY DILUTED EPS — STOCK WARRANTS

If there are stock warrants (options) outstanding enabling the holder to purchase stock, we once again "make-believe" these warrants were exercised. For primary EPS they must be exercisable within 5 years; for fully diluted EPS within 10 years.

The proceeds received by the corporation upon the exercise of these warrants are assumed to be used to purchase treasury shares in the marketplace. For primary EPS the purchase price of the treasury shares is the average market price for the period. For fully diluted EPS the purchase price is the ending market price, provided this price is higher than the average price.

EXAMPLE 24

A corporation has 10,000 stock warrants outstanding enabling the holders to purchase 1 common share per warrant at a price of $100, within 4 years.

At first glance it would seem that since we assume conversion, we must add 10,000 shares to the denominator. However, the corporation has now received $1 million (10,000 × $100). What does it do with this money? We assume it uses this money to go into the marketplace and buy back its own shares for the treasury.

Let's assume the average market price for common stock is $110 while the ending price is $120. For primary EPS, $1 million can buy back 9,091 shares ($1,000,000 ÷ $110 = 9,091 rounded). Thus, while on the one hand it has issued 10,000 shares, on the other hand it has bought back 9,091 shares! The net increase is, therefore, only 909 shares, which would be added into the denominator.

CHAP. 4] DILUTIVE SECURITIES AND EARNINGS PER SHARE 69

For fully diluted EPS, it can buy back $1,000,000 ÷ $120 = 8,333 shares, thus creating a net change of 10,000 − 8,333 = 1,667 shares.

EXAMPLE 25

If in the previous example the ending market price was $108, it would *not* be used for fully diluted EPS since it is *less* than the average price of $110. Rather, the $110 price would be used, just as for primary EPS.

If the stock warrants were only outstanding for a partial period, then the effect of the conversion should be prorated, as discussed previously for convertible bonds and preferred stock.

There is a limitation on the number of shares that we assume can be repurchased for the treasury. The maximum is 20% of the presently outstanding common shares. If there are any funds still left over, we assume they are used to retire short-term and long-term debt, and then to buy U.S. government securities. Any interest savings or earnings on these items should be added to the numerator.

EXAMPLE 26

Assume a corporation has 70,000 shares of common stock outstanding and 20,000 stock warrants that can be used to purchase 20,000 shares at $50 per share, thus bringing in $1,000,000 (20,000 × $50). If the market value of the stock is $55, then 18,182 shares can then be repurchased for the treasury ($1,000,000 ÷ $55). However, the maximum is limited to 14,000 shares (20% of 70,000 shares outstanding). Accordingly the denominator can only be increased by 14,000.

Thus 14,000 × $55 = $770,000 will be spent on treasury stock. The remainder of the $1,000,000 ($330,000) can be used to retire short- and long-term debt. If there is no debt and U.S. government securities yielding 10% interest are purchased instead, the interest of $33,000 minus taxes are added into the numerator.

4.12 THE ANTIDILUTIVE AND 3% TESTS

In general, primary EPS will be less than or equal to basic EPS, and fully diluted EPS will be less than or equal to primary EPS. The order, from highest to lowest, thus is:

1. Basic
2. Primary
3. Fully diluted

The reason for this hierarchy is that primary and fully diluted, having added more shares to the denominator, create a smaller fraction.

Occasionally, a convertible item may add so much more to the numerator than to the denominator that the result is a primary EPS figure higher than basic EPS (or a fully diluted EPS higher than primary). Such items are called *antidilutive* and should be ignored in all EPS calculations.

EXAMPLE 27

A company's basic EPS is $100,000/20,000 shares = $5.00. For primary EPS there are convertible bonds, 15%, $100,000 par, convertible into 2,000 shares of stock. The tax rate is 10%.

Thus the numerator will now be increased by the interest saving: $100,000 × .15 × (1 − .10) = $13,500, and the denominator by 2,000. The result will be: ($100,000 + $13,500)/22,000 = $5.16.

Since $5.16 is greater than basic EPS of $5.00, these convertible bonds must be ignored, and primary EPS will be the same as basic EPS.

If the difference between basic EPS and fully diluted EPS is less than 3%, no presentation of primary and fully diluted EPS is made since the difference is trivial. Only basic EPS would be presented.

EXAMPLE 28

Basic EPS is $5.00. If fully diluted EPS is $4.85 or less, it would be shown. Otherwise, only the basic EPS of $5.00 is shown.

4.13 WEIGHTED AVERAGE SHARES

If the number of common shares changes during the period, we must use a weighted average. This is done by multiplying the shares by the number of months they were outstanding, and then dividing the total by 12.

EXAMPLE 29

The Nice Corporation engaged in the following stock transactions during 19X1:

Jan.   1   Issued 10,000 shares.
July   1   Issued another 5,000 shares.
Sept. 1   Bought back 2,000 treasury shares.
Oct.   1   Issued 7,000 shares.

The weighted average calculation is as follows:

Jan. 1–July 1	=	6 months × 10,000 shares	=	60,000
July 1–Sept. 1	=	2 months × 15,000* shares	=	30,000
Sept. 1–Oct. 1	=	1 month × 13,000† shares	=	13,000
Oct. 1–Dec. 31	=	3 months × 20,000 shares	=	60,000
		Total	=	163,000
			÷	12
		(rounded)		13,583 shares

*10,000 + 5,000
†10,000 + 5,000 − 2,000

If a stock dividend or stock split occurred *during* the year, we treat it as if it took place at the *beginning* of the year. Accordingly, a retroactive adjustment must be made.

EXAMPLE 30

The following stock transactions took place for Corporation X during 19X1:

Jan.   1   Issued 9,000 shares.
Apr.   1   Issued another 1,000 shares.
June   1   Issued a 100% stock dividend (10,000 shares).
Sept. 1   Issued 4,000 shares.

We treat the stock dividend of June 1 as if it were issued on January 1. Thus the stock transactions of January 1 and April 1 must be retroactively adjusted by multiplying them by a factor of 2. The computations are:

Jan. 1–Apr. 1	=	3 months × 9,000 shares × 2	=	54,000
Apr. 1–June 1	=	2 months × 10,000 shares × 2	=	40,000
June 1–Sept. 1	=	3 months × 20,000* shares	=	60,000
Sept. 1–Dec. 31	=	4 months × 24,000 shares	=	96,000
		Total		250,000
			÷	12
		(rounded)		20,833

*(9,000 + 1,000) × 2

Summary

1. *Convertible* bonds contain an option enabling the holder to exchange these bonds for common stock. At the date of issuance these bonds are accounted for in the same manner as nonconvertibles. If conversion eventually takes place, the common stock is recorded at the *book value* of the bonds. The market value is ignored and, thus, no gain or loss is recognized on the conversion.

2. Sometimes the corporation may try to provide an incentive for the bondholder to convert the bond by giving him or her a cash payment. This is called a "sweetener" and is debited to an expense account.

3. Stock warrants (rights) are certificates that enable the holder to purchase shares of stock at a fixed price for a given time period. Corporations will often attach these warrants to a bond in order to make the bond more attractive.

4. If the warrants are *detachable* and can thus be traded separately from the bond, the sale of the entire package should be considered an issuance of *both* debt and equity securities. Accordingly, the entry requires a debit to Cash and a credit to Bonds Payable and to a stockholders' account. The allocation between the two is based upon their respective market values.

5. If the warrants are *nondetachable,* the sale of the package is considered to be an issuance of *debt securities* only, and no recognition would be made for the warrants. Thus the entire selling price would be allocated to the bond.

6. *Employee stock option plans* may be divided into two categories: *noncompensatory* and *compensatory.* The latter is considered an expense; the former is not. In order for a plan to be considered noncompensatory, it must meet *all* four of the following conditions:
   (*a*) Substantially all the full-time employees must be eligible.
   (*b*) It must be offered to all the employees on an equal basis.
   (*c*) The option period must be reasonable.
   (*d*) The discount from the market price should not be greater than 15%.

7. Noncompensatory plans require no special entry when the options are issued. Compensatory plans require an entry at the measurement date to recognize compensation cost. This is the difference between the option price and the market price on the measurement date, and must be spread evenly over the service period beginning from the date of the grant and ending on the date when the employee has no further service obligations and may exercise the options. If the option price is greater than the market price, no compensation cost would be recognized and thus no entry would be made.

8. When an entry is made, the entry is:

Deferred Compensation Cost	xxx	
Capital-in Capital — Employee Stock Options		xxx

   The Deferred Compensation Cost account is shown as a contra item to the paid-in capital account in the stockholders' equity section of the balance sheet and is amortized evenly over the service period via the following entry:

Compensation Expense	xx	
Deferred Compensation Cost		xx

9. *Stock appreciation rights (SARs)* are rights that require the company to pay cash for the difference between the grant price and the market price of the company's stock on the date the rights are exercised. Since neither the market price nor the exercise date is known in advance, estimates must be made each year to record the annual compensation expense.

10. Broadly speaking, *earnings per share (EPS)* calculates how much of the net income has been earned by each share of *common stock*. There are three types of EPS: basic, primary, and fully diluted. Basic EPS is used for a simple capital structure — a situation in which there are no convertible securities outstanding.

11. Basic EPS takes the net income, subtracts the preferred dividend, and then divides the result by the weighted average of common shares outstanding during the year. If the preferred stock is cumulative, the preferred dividend must be subtracted *regardless* of whether or not it was declared. However, if it is noncumulative, it is subtracted only if declared.

12. In a complex capital structure there are convertible bonds, convertible preferred stock, or stock options outstanding. Primary EPS "makes believe" the bonds or preferred stock have been converted if the following two conditions have been met:

    (1) The rate of return on these securities is less than two-thirds the Aa rate, and

    (2) The conversion option is exercisable within 5 years of the balance sheet date.

    If these conditions have been met we assume conversion has taken place. Thus, for preferred stock, we will not subtract the preferred dividend in the numerator, and for bonds we will add back the interest savings (net of tax) in the numerator. In both cases, the denominator will be increased by the new, converted shares.

13. For fully diluted EPS these conditions need *not* be met provided the option is exercisable within 10 years.

14. If the convertible bonds or preferred stock have been outstanding for only part of the year, the changes to the numerator and denominator must be prorated, accordingly.

15. Stock options are also considered to have been converted if the options are exercisable within 5 years for primary EPS, and within 10 years for fully diluted EPS.

16. The proceeds received by the corporation upon the assumed conversion of stock options are assumed to be used to purchase treasury stock on the open market. Accordingly, the number of shares resulting from the exercise of the options is reduced by these treasury shares. For primary EPS, the purchase price of the treasury shares is the average market price for the year; for fully diluted EPS it is the closing market price.

17. There is a limitation on the number of shares we can assume are repurchased for the treasury. The maximum is 20% of the presently outstanding shares. Any excess funds available are assumed to be used to retire short-term and long-term debt, and to buy U.S. government securities. Any interest savings or earnings resulting from these transactions are added to the numerator.

18. Occasionally, a convertible security may add so much more to the numerator than to the denominator that the result is a primary EPS figure which is higher than basic EPS (or a fully diluted EPS higher than primary). Such securities are considered *antidilutive* and should be ignored in all EPS calculations.

19. If the difference between basic EPS and fully diluted EPS is less than 3%, no presentation of primary or fully diluted EPS would be made since the difference is insignificant. Only basic EPS would be shown.

20. If the number of common shares outstanding during the year changes, we must use a weighted average in our denominator. If a stock dividend or stock split occurred *during* the year, we treat it as if it took place at the *beginning* of the year.

Rapid Review

1. Bonds that can be exchanged for common stock are called ___Convertible___ bonds.

2. When these bonds are exchanged for stock the stock is recorded at ___PAR Book___ value instead of ___Market___ value.

3. A certificate that enables its holder to buy stock at a fixed price per share is called a stock ___Warrant___.

4. The two methods of allocating the proceeds from the sale of bonds with detachable stock warrants are the ___proportional___ method and the ___incremental___ method.

5. The two classes of employee stock options are ___compensatory___ and ___noncompensatory___.

6. For the type of stock option not considered to be an expense, the discount from market price should not be greater than ___15%___.

7. The Deferred Compensation Cost account is a ___contra capital___ in the stockholders' equity section.

8. Cash bonuses given to employees for the difference between the grant price and the market price are called ___SARs___. Stock appreciation rights

9. The three types of EPS are ___Basic___, ___Primary___, ___Fully dilutive___

10. Basic EPS is used for a ___Simple___ capital structure, while the others are used for a ___complex___ capital structure.

11. If preferred stock is noncumulative, then its dividend is subtracted in the numerator only if ___declared___.

12. For convertible bonds and preferred stock, the yield rate must be ___less than $\frac{2}{3}$___ of the Aa bond rate, under ___primary___ EPS.

13. For primary EPS the conversion privilege must be exercisable within ___5___ years, while for fully diluted EPS the period is ___10___ years.

14. For convertible bonds, the numerator is increased by the ___interest___ savings less the ___premium___. TAX

15. If the conversion ratio varies over time, then the ___earliest___ ratio must be used for primary EPS, while the most ___advantageous___ ratio must be used for fully diluted EPS.

16. The proceeds received by the corporation upon the exercise of stock warrants are assumed to be used to purchase ___Treasury___. stock

17. For primary EPS the purchase price in the above question is the ___Average___ market price, while for fully diluted EPS it is the ___closing___ market price.

18. The maximum number of treasury shares that can be purchased is limited to ___20%___.

19. If a security causes primary EPS to be higher than basic EPS, it is ___antidilutive___ and should be ___ignored___.

20. The difference between basic EPS and fully diluted EPS should be at least ___3%___.

21. For weighted average purposes, stock dividends and splits are assumed to have taken place at ___the Beginning of the period___.

Answers: 1. convertible 2. book; market 3. warrant (option) 4. proportional; incremental 5. compensatory; noncompensatory 6. 15% 7. contra-capital 8. stock appreciation rights 9. basic; primary; fully diluted 10. simple; complex 11. declared 12. less than 2/3; primary 13. 5; 10 14. interest; tax 15. earliest; advantageous 16. treasury stock 17. average; closing 18. 20% of common shares presently outstanding 19. antidilutive; ignored 20. 3% 21. year beginning

Solved Problems

Convertible Bonds

4.1 A corporation issues a $200,000 par, 4-year bond at 95. The bond is convertible into 1,000 shares of $120 par common stock. Two years later the bond is converted when the market value of the stock is $150. Prepare the entries at the date of issuance and at the date of conversion.

SOLUTION

At issuance:

Cash	190,000	
Bond Discount	10,000	
Bonds Payable		200,000

No indication is made in the entry for the conversion feature.

At conversion date, the discount account has a balance of $5,000 under the straight-line method. The entry is:

Bonds Payable	200,000	
Bond Discount		5,000
Common Stock (Par)		120,000
Paid-in Capital in Excess of Par		75,000

The market value of the stock is ignored.   [Section 4.2]

4.2 In the above problem assume that a "sweetener" of $10,000 cash is paid to the bondholder to induce the conversion. Prepare any necessary additional entries.

SOLUTION

There would be one additional entry, as follows:

Debt Conversion Expense	10,000	
Cash		10,000

[Section 4.2]

Convertible Preferred Stock

4.3 Convertible preferred stock, par $48,000, with a related premium of $1,000 is converted into 1,000 shares of $50 par common stock whose market price is $48. Prepare the conversion entry.

SOLUTION

Preferred Stock (Par)	48,000	
Paid-in Capital in Excess of Par — Preferred	1,000	
Retained Earnings	1,000	
Common Stock (Par)		50,000

Once again, the market value is ignored.   [Section 4.3]

Bonds with Attached Stock Warrants

4.4 A corporation issues 100 bonds, $50 par, each with a detachable stock warrant enabling the holder to purchase 1 share of common stock at $100. The selling price of the package is 102. At the time of sale, the market value of the bonds without the warrants is $48 and the market value of the warrants is $20 each. Prepare the journal entries for this issuance.

SOLUTION

Using the proportional method, we allocate the selling price of $5,100 (100 × $50 × 102) as follows:

		Market Value
Bonds:	100 × $48 =	$4,800
Warrants:	100 × $20 =	2,000
Total		$6,800

Bonds: (4,800 ÷ 6,800) × $5,100 = $3,600

Warrants: (2,000 ÷ 6,800) × $5,100 = $1,500

The entries are:

Cash	3,600	
Bond Discount	1,400	
Bonds Payable		5,000
Cash	1,500	
Paid-in Capital — Stock Warrants		1,500 [Section 4.4]

4.5   For the previous problem determine the allocation if the market value of the bonds is $40 and the market value of the warrants is unknown.

SOLUTION

Using the incremental method we allocate the market value to the bonds and the remainder to the warrants, as follows:

Total selling price =	$5,100	
To bonds: 100 × $40 =	− 4,000	
Remainder to warrants	$1,100	[Section 4.4]

4.6   A $10,000 par bond with a *nondetachable* stock warrant is sold at par. The market value of the bond by itself is $10,300 and the market value of the warrant is $80. Prepare the entry.

SOLUTION

Since the warrant is *nondetachable* the entire proceeds are attributed to the bond. Thus the entry would make no mention of the warrant, and the market values would be ignored. The entry would be:

Cash	10,000	
Bonds Payable		10,000 [Section 4.4]

4.7   A corporation has the following T-account relating to outstanding stock warrants:

Paid-in Capital—Stock Warrants

	10,000

These warrants enable the holder to purchase 100 shares of $90 par common stock at $110. Prepare the necessary entry if:

(a)   The holder exercises this option.

(b)   The holder allows the option to expire.

SOLUTION

(a)

Cash	11,000	
Paid-in Capital — Stock Warrants	10,000	
Common Stock (Par)		9,000
Paid-in Capital in Excess of Par		12,000

(b)   Paid-in Capital — Stock Warrants   10,000
                           Paid-in Capital — Expired Stock Warrants   10,000   [Section 4.4]

4.8   A company's stock option plan grants all of its employees, on an equal basis, the option of buying stock at a 10% discount for the next 50 years. Is this plan noncompensatory? Why?

SOLUTION

It is not because the length of the option period is unreasonably long and, thus, condition 3 has not been met.
[Section 4.6]

4.9   S & W Metals Corporation developed a stock option plan where all its employees, on an equal basis, have the option of buying its stock at a 20% discount for the next 6 months. Is this plan noncompensatory? Why?

SOLUTION

It is not, because the discount exceeds the maximum of 15%.   [Section 4.6]

4.10   If options are granted to purchase 2,000 shares at $10, the market price on the grant date is $30, and the service period is 4 years, determine:
(a)   Total compensation cost
(b)   Annual compensation cost

SOLUTION

(a)   ($30 − $10)2,000 = $40,000.
(b) $40,000 ÷ 4 years = $10,000.   [Section 4.6]

4.11   If the option price is $50 and the market price is $40, what entry should be made to recognize compensation cost?

SOLUTION

None. There is no compensation cost since the option price is too high.   [Section 4.6]

4.12   On January 1, 19A, Corporation B grants options to its single employee to purchase 3,000 shares of its $50 par common stock at $60 per share, beginning January 1, 19D, and ending on January 1, 19G. On the grant date the market price is $80 per share.
(1)   Is this plan compensatory or not?
(2)   What is the measurement date?
(3)   How long is the service period?
(4)   What is the total compensation cost, if any?
(5)   What is the annual compensation cost, if any?
(6)   Prepare all necessary journal entries.

SOLUTION

(1)   It is compensatory since the discount is greater than 15%, as follows:
$$\frac{80 - 60}{80} = 25\%$$
(2)   The measurement date is the grant date since both the total number of shares and the option price are known at this point.
(3)   Three years — January 1, 19A, through January 1, 19D.
(4)   (80 − 60)3,000 shares = $60,000.
(5) $60,000 ÷ 3 years = $20,000.

Remember

(6)　January 1, 19A:

Deferred Compensation Cost	60,000	
Paid-in Capital — Employee Stock Options		60,000

December 31, 19A, December 31, 19B, December 31, 19C:

Compensation Expense	20,000	
Deferred Compensation Cost		20,000

[Section 4.6]

4.13　In the previous problem, prepare the necessary entries if
(a)　The employee exercises the options on January 1, 19F.
(b)　The employee allows the options to lapse.

SOLUTION

(a)

Cash	180,000*	
Paid-in Capital Stock Options	60,000	
Common Stock (Par)		150,000
Paid-in Capital in Excess of Par		90,000

*3,000 × $60

(b)

Paid-in Capital — Employee Stock Options	60,000	
Paid-in Capital — Lapsed Stock Options		60,000

[Section 4.6]

Basic Earnings per Share

4.14　Corporation C has net income of $10,000 and 1,000 shares of common stock outstanding. It also has 500 shares of *noncumulative,* $100 par, 5% preferred stock. Determine basic EPS if:
(a)　The preferred dividend was declared.
(b)　The preferred dividend was *not* declared.
(c)　The preferred stock was cumulative.

SOLUTION

(a)　$\dfrac{\$10,000 - \$5(500)}{1,000} = \$7.50$

(b)　$\dfrac{\$10,000}{1,000} = \$10.00$

(c)　Since the preferred is cumulative, the dividend must be subtracted regardless of whether or not declared. Therefore the answer is $7.50, as in part (a).　　　　　[Section 4.8]

Primary and Fully Diluted Earnings per Share

4.15　Corporation X has $80,000 of net income, 20,000 shares of common stock outstanding, and 1,000 shares of 7%, $100 par preferred stock, convertible into 4,000 shares of common stock within 3 years. The Aa bond rate is 10%. Compute:
(a)　Basic EPS
(b)　Primary EPS
(c)　Fully diluted EPS

SOLUTION

(a)　$\dfrac{\$80,000 - \$7,000}{20,000} = \$3.65$

(b) Since the 7% rate is greater than two-thirds of the Aa rate, we do not assume conversion. Accordingly, the answer is the same as for basic EPS ($3.65).

(c) $\dfrac{\$80,000}{20,000 + 4,000} = \$3.33$ [Section 4.9]

4.16 In the preceding problem if the preferred stock was convertible into just 1,000 shares of common, find fully diluted EPS.

SOLUTION

$$\frac{\$80,000}{20,000 + 1,000} = \$3.81$$

Since $3.81 is greater than basic EPS of $3.65, it is considered antidilutive and should be ignored. Thus, fully diluted EPS will also be $3.65.   [Section 4.9]

4.17 A company has 1,000 shares of 6%, $100 par preferred stock convertible into 5,000 shares of common after 12 years. The Aa rate is 19%. For primary and fully diluted EPS, how will the numerator and denominator be affected?

SOLUTION

There will be *no* effect since the conversion privilege cannot be exercised within 10 years.   [Section 4.9]

4.18 A company has 100 shares of 5%, $100 par preferred stock convertible into 200 shares of common stock after 7 years. The preferred stock has been outstanding only since October 1. How will the denominator be affected for both primary and fully diluted EPS?

SOLUTION

For primary EPS the denominator will *not* be affected since conversion cannot take place within 5 years. For fully diluted EPS, since the stock has only been outstanding for one-fourth of a year, we will add $\frac{1}{4} \times$ 200 shares $= 50$ shares.   [Section 4.9]

4.19 The Gradowsky Corporation had net income of $150,000 during 19X5, with 10,000 shares of common stock outstanding. It also had 1,000 shares of *nonconvertible* 5%, $100 par preferred stock, and $25,000 par, 6% bonds *convertible* into 1,000 shares of common stock after 3 years. The Aa bond rate is 8% and the tax rate is 30%. Compute basic, primary, and fully diluted EPS.

SOLUTION

Basic: $\dfrac{\$150,000 - 5,000^*}{10,000} = \$14.50$

$\overline{}$
*1,000 × 5% × $100

Primary: Since the bond rate of 6% is greater than 2/3 the Aa rate, the bonds do not qualify for conversion. Thus the answer is also $14.50.

Fully diluted: $\dfrac{\$150,000 - 5,000 + .70(1,500)^\dagger}{10,000 + 1,000} = \$13.28$

$\overline{}$
$^\dagger(1 - .30) \times (.06 \times \$25,000)$ [Section 4.10]

4.20 If in the preceding example the bonds were only outstanding for half the year, how would fully diluted EPS change?

SOLUTION

The numerator would only be increased by $\frac{1}{2}(.70 \times .06 \times 25,000)$ and the denominator by $\frac{1}{2}(1,000$ shares) yielding a new EPS of $13.86.   [Section 4.10]

4.21   A $100,000 par, 6% convertible bond has an annual discount amortization of $600. If the tax rate is 30%, how much in interest savings should be added to the numerator for primary EPS? Assume the two conditions for conversion have been met.

SOLUTION

The annual interest is $6,000 + $600 = $6,600. Thus the numerator would be increased by $(1 - .30) \times$ $6,600 = $4,620.   [Section 4.10]

4.22   If the bond agreement states that the bonds are convertible into 1,000 shares of common stock for the first 2 years, 2,000 shares for the next 2 years, and 1,500 shares for the last 2 years, how much should be added into the denominator?

SOLUTION

For primary EPS add the earliest figure of 1,000. For fully diluted EPS add the best figure of 2,000.
                                                                                         [Section 4.10]

4.23   A corporation had a net income of $100,000, with 75,000 shares of common stock outstanding and no preferred stock. There were also 10,000 stock warrants outstanding enabling the holder to purchase 10,000 shares of $100 par common stock at $90. The average market price of the stock for the year has been $100, while the closing price was $110. Determine primary and fully diluted EPS.

SOLUTION

Primary EPS:

We use the *average* market price in our calculations:

Shares assumed to be issued:	10,000
Less shares repurchased for the treasury:	
10,000 × $90 = $900,000	
÷ 100	
=	9,000
Net increase in outstanding shares	1,000

Thus EPS is: $\dfrac{\$100,000}{75,000 + 1,000} = \$1.32$

Fully diluted EPS:

We use the closing market price. Therefore 10,000 new shares $-$ ($900,000 ÷ $110) = 1,818 net increase in shares. Thus EPS is:

$$\frac{\$100,000}{75,000 + 1,818} = \$1.30$$
                                                                                         [Section 4.11]

4.24   In the previous problem, how would fully diluted EPS differ if the closing market price was $98?

SOLUTION

It would be the same as primary EPS ($1.32) since the closing price is less than the average price and therefore cannot be used.   [Section 4.11]

4.25   In the previous problem, how would EPS differ if there were only 35,000 shares of common stock presently outstanding? Assume, once again, that the closing price is $98. Also assume that any excess funds are used to purchase U.S. government securities yielding 10% and that the tax rate is 30%.

*This is
A very
good
problem*

SOLUTION

We must apply the 20% maximum rule, as follows:

Shares assumed to be issued:	10,000
Maximum shares repurchased for the treasury: 20% × 35,000 =	(7,000)
Net increase in outstanding shares	3,000

Thus the denominator will be increased by 3,000. In the numerator we must add in the interest on U.S. government securities purchased with any excess funds. The calculation is:

Proceeds from exercise of warrants: 10,000 × $90 =	$900,000
Less amount used to purchase treasury stock: 20% × 35,000 × $100 =	700,000
Excess funds	$200,000
Interest of 10% =	$ 20,000 ($200,000 × 10%)

This $20,000 (minus taxes) is added into the numerator.

Thus EPS is: $$\frac{\$100,000 + 20,000(1 - .30)}{75,000 + 3,000} = \$1.46$$

Once again, the closing market price of $98 is ignored since it is less than the average market price.

[Section 4.11]

The Antidilutive and 3% Tests

4.26 A company's basic EPS is $100,000 ÷ 10,000 = $10.00. There are convertible bonds that add $25,000 to the numerator and 1,000 shares to the denominator for both primary and fully diluted EPS. Does this create any problems?

SOLUTION

Yes. Since the new EPS is $125,000 ÷ 11,000 = $11.36, which is higher than the basic EPS of $10.00, these bonds are "antidilutive." They, therefore, should be ignored and EPS will be only $10.00.   [Section 4.12]

4.27 Corporation E has the following EPS figures:

Basic:	$20.00
Primary:	$19.80
Fully diluted:	$19.70

Does this require any special treatment?

SOLUTION

Yes. Since the difference between basic and fully diluted is less than 3%, only basic EPS would be presented.

[Section 4.12]

Weighted Average Shares

4.28 Corporation Q engaged in the following stock transactions during 19A:

Jan.   1   Issued 5,000 shares.
Mar.   1   Issued 3,000 shares.
June   1   Split the shares 2:1 (8,000 additional shares).
Oct.   1   Issued 2,000 shares.

Determine the weighted average number of shares outstanding.

SOLUTION

Jan. 1–Mar. 1	=	2 months × 5,000 shares × 2	=	20,000
Mar. 1–June 1	=	3 months × 8,000 shares × 2	=	48,000
June 1–Oct. 1	=	4 months × 16,000* shares	=	64,000
Oct. 1–Dec. 31	=	3 months × 18,000 shares	=	54,000
				186,000
				÷ 12
				15,500 shares

*(5,000 + 3,000) × 2   [Section 4.13]

Supplementary Problems

4.29 Corporation A issues a $100,000, six-year convertible bond at 104 on January 1, 19B. This bond is convertible into 1,000 shares of $100 par common stock. Three years later, when the market value of the stock is $120, the bondholder converts the bond and receives a $500 "sweetener." Prepare the entries for the original issuance and the conversion.

4.30 Corporation B issues 200 bonds, $150 par each, at par. Each bond contains a *detachable* stock warrant enabling the holder to purchase 1 share of $120 par common stock at $130. At the time of the sale, the market value of the bonds (without the warrants) is $140, while the market value of the warrants is $20. Prepare an entry for the issuance of the bonds.

4.31 For the previous problem assume that the warrants are *nondetachable* and prepare the required journal entry.

4.32 Corporation C earned net income of $250,000 during 19A. It also had 20,000 shares of common stock and 5,000 shares of $100 par, 6% preferred stock outstanding during the year. No dividends were declared this year. Determine basic EPS if:
(a) the preferred stock is cumulative.
(b) the preferred stock is noncumulative.

4.33 Corporation D earned net income of $70,000 during 19A and had an average of 10,000 shares of common stock outstanding. It also had a $50,000, 8% bond payable convertible after 3 years into 2,000 shares of common stock. The Aa rate is 11%; the tax rate is 20%. There is no preferred stock outstanding. Determine basic EPS, primary EPS, and fully diluted EPS.

4.34 Assume the same information as in the previous problem except that the bond was issued on October 1. Once again, determine basic, primary, and fully diluted EPS.

4.35 Corporation E had net income of $130,000 and 5,000 shares of common stock outstanding during 19A. It also had 1,000 shares of 6% preferred stock ($100 par) convertible into 500 shares of common stock after 6 years. The Aa rate is 12%; the tax rate is 20%. Determine basic, primary, and fully diluted EPS.

4.36 Corporation F earned income of $40,000 during 19A and had 10,000 shares of common stock outstanding. It did not have any preferred stock, but it did have 1,000 stock options outstanding. These options are convertible after 3 years into 500 shares common stock at $70 per share. The *average* market price of common stock for the year was $80; the closing price was $85. Determine basic, primary, and fully diluted EPS.

4.37 Corporation G had the following transactions involving its own common stock during 19A:

Jan. 1 Issued 1,000 shares.
Mar. 1 Issued 3,000 shares.
May 1 Bought back 500 shares.
Oct. 1 Issued 2,000 shares.
Dec. 1 Issued 1,000 shares.

Determine the weighted average number of shares outstanding during the year.

4.38 Use the same information as in the previous example but assume Corporation G split its stock 2:1 on April 1. Determine the weighted average number of shares outstanding.

Chapter 5

Investments: Temporary and Long-term

5.1 INTRODUCTION

It is very common for companies to invest their idle cash in a variety of investments. These investments may be *temporary* (current) in nature, or *long-term* (noncurrent). The first part of this chapter will discuss temporary investments while the second part will discuss long-term investments. The chapter will then conclude with a discussion of stock rights, stock dividends, and the cash surrender value of life insurance.

5.2 TEMPORARY INVESTMENTS—MARKETABLE EQUITY SECURITIES

Temporary investments consist of marketable equity securities (preferred and common stock) and marketable debt securities (government and corporate bonds). In order for an investment to be classified as temporary, it must meet *both* of the following conditions:

1. Be readily marketable, and

2. be intended for conversion into cash within 1 year or the operating cycle (whichever is longer).

"Ready marketable" means that the item can easily be sold. If the stock is not publicly held, there may exist only a limited market for its purchase, thus making it difficult to sell. If this is the case, condition 1 has not been met and the stock would not be classified as a temporary marketable security.

When marketable equity securities are purchased, an asset account should be debited for the purchase price plus any broker's fee or taxes incurred in this transaction. Brokers' fees and taxes are not expenses; they are an addition to the cost of the stock. When the stock is later sold, such fees are considered to be a reduction of the selling price. If the selling price is higher than the purchase price, the difference is a gain and it is credited to a gain account; if it is lower it is a loss and it is debited to a loss account.

EXAMPLE 1

A corporation buys 100 shares of IBM stock for a total price of $1,000 and pays a broker's fee of $100. It later sells these shares for $2,000 and pays a broker's fee of $200. Assume the shares meet both of the above-mentioned conditions. The entries are:

Investment in Short-term Equity Securities	1,100	
Cash		1,100
Cash	1,800*	
Investment in Short-term Equity Securities		1,100
Gain on Sale of Securities		700

*$2,000 − 200

EXAMPLE 2

If in the previous example the selling price was $900 and the broker's fee was $90, there would be a loss of $290 [($900 − $90) − $1,100].

If dividends are received on short-term shares of stock, an entry is made debiting Cash and crediting Dividend Revenue.

At the end of the accounting period, a comparison must be made between the *aggregate* cost of the company's stock portfolio and the *aggregate* market value. If the market price has fallen below cost, an entry must be made to reduce the cost down to the market value. However, if the market price is above cost, no entry is made to raise the cost up to the market value. This is called *lower of cost or market (LCM)*.

When an entry has to be made, an *unrealized* loss account is debited for the difference and the credit goes to an account called Allowance to Reduce Cost to Market. This account acts as a contra to the investment account.

EXAMPLE 3

A company has three stock investments: X, Y, and Z, whose cost and market values on December 31, 19A, are as follows:

	Cost	Market Value
X	$ 500	$ 300
Y	900	1,000
Z	400	350
Aggregate	$1,800	$1,650

Since the market value is lower than the cost, an adjusting entry must be made to reduce the cost (book value) by $150. The entry is:

Unrealized Loss Due to Market Decline	150	
Allowance to Reduce Cost of Short-term Equity		
Securities to Market		150

The unrealized loss appears on the income statement as an expense. The allowance appears on the balance sheet as a contra account, as follows:

Investment in Short-term Equity Securities	$1,800
Less: Allowance to Reduce Cost to Market	(150)
Net Investment	$1,650

If in later years the market price rises, the previous unrealized loss may be recovered and credited to a revenue account. However, no recognition is given to a price rise that is above the original cost.

EXAMPLE 4

Assume that on December 31, 19B, the cost and market values of the stocks from the previous example are as follows:

	Cost	Market Value
A	$ 600	$ 400
B	800	1,000
Z	400	450
Aggregate	$1,800	$1,850

Not only has the $150 unrealized loss been recovered; there is a "gain" of $50 as well. The $150 recovery is recognized; the $50 "gain" is not. The entry is:

Allowance to Reduce Cost of Short-term	150	
Equity Securities to Market		
Recovery of Unrealized Loss		150

If the aggregate market price was only $1,750 instead of $1,850, the recovery would only be $100 ($1,750 − $1,650) and the above entry would be made for only this amount.

If an equity security is transferred from the short-term portfolio to the long-term portfolio, or vice versa, it must be transferred at the LCM value and a *realized* loss should be recognized if the market value has fallen below cost.

EXAMPLE 5

On March 15, 19A, a company reclassifies its investment in an equity security from short-term to long-term. The original cost was $1,000; the market value today is $800. The entry is:

Investment in Long-term Equity Securities	800	
Loss on Reclassification	200	
Investment in Short-term Equity Securities		1,000

EXAMPLE 6

If in the previous example the market price was $1,200, the reclassification entry would be made at the cost of $1,000 and no gain would be recognized.

5.3   TEMPORARY INVESTMENTS — MARKETABLE DEBT SECURITIES

Marketable debt securities are investments in bonds and other debt instruments that meet the two conditions mentioned earlier, namely:

1. They are readily marketable, and

2. the intention is to sell them within 1 year or the operating cycle (whichever is longer).

As was the case for marketable equity securities, these investments are debited for their cost plus any broker's fee or taxes incurred at the date of purchase. A question arises, however, as to whether or not they should be given the LCM treatment at year-end. FASB No. 12, which prescribed the LCM treatment for marketable *equity* securities, is silent on the treatment for marketable *debt* securities. Logic and consistency dictate that these securities should be treated no differently. Indeed, many companies over the past 10 years have used LCM for debt securities. Accordingly, we will do so as well.

If these securities are purchased above or below par, a discount or premium situation arises. The discount or premium should *not* be amortized since the intention is to hold the securities for only a short time period. Accordingly, the investment account is debited at the *net* amount paid, and no use is made of a discount or premium account.

EXAMPLE 7

A $100,000 bond is purchased as a short-term investment at 98 on January 1, 19A. The entry is:

Investment in Short-term Debt Securities	98,000	
Cash		98,000

Notice that the investment account is debited at the net price of $98,000 and no discount account is used. The $2,000 reduction from par would *not* be amortized.

Since debt securities pay interest, an entry must be made crediting Interest Revenue. If the interest has been received, then Cash is debited. If not, it must be accrued on December 31 by debiting Interest Receivable.

EXAMPLE 8

If in the previous example the bond paid interest of 10% annually and the payment date is December 31, 19A, the following entry would be made on that date:

Cash	10,000	
Interest Revenue		10,000

If the interest payment date is not until the next day (January 1, 19B) then on December 31, 19A, an adjusting entry for the accrual would be made, as follows:

Interest Receivable	10,000	
Interest Revenue		10,000

If a bond is purchased between interest dates, its price will be increased by the amount of accrued interest thus far. This increase should be debited to Interest Revenue since its effect is to reduce the amount of interest earned.

EXAMPLE 9

A short-term bond dated January 1, 19A, is purchased on April 1, 19A, at its par of $100,000. The interest rate is 10% and is payable on December 31. The accrued interest thus far is $2,500 ($100,000 $\times$ 10% $\times \frac{1}{4}$). The selling price will therefore be $102,500. At the time of purchase the entry is:

Investment in Short-term Debt Securities	100,000	
Interest Revenue	2,500	
Cash		102,500

On December 31, the entry for the interest is:

Cash	10,000	
Interest Revenue		10,000*

---

*(10% × $100,000)

Thus the net interest revenue is $7,500 ($10,000 − $2,500).

5.4   LONG-TERM INVESTMENTS—DEBT SECURITIES

Long-term investments in debt securities consist of bonds or other debt instruments whose principal is payable after 1 year or the operating cycle (whichever is longer), and there is no intention to sell them before the due date. Thus, condition 2 mentioned earlier for marketable securities has not been met.

EXAMPLE 10

A company purchases a 5-year, 10%, $100,000, long-term bond at par, on January 1, 19X1. The entry is:

Investment in Long-term Debt Securities	100,000	
Cash		100,000

Every December 31, an entry must be made either to accrue interest on the bond, or to record the actual receipt of interest, if this date is an interest payment date.

EXAMPLE 11

In the previous example, if December 31 is an interest payment date, and interest is payable annually, the entry would be:

Cash	10,000	
Interest Revenue		10,000

If interest is payable annually on June 30, the entry on December 31 would be:

Interest Receivable	5,000	
Interest Revenue		5,000*

---

*To accrue six months of interest:
$100,000 × 10% × 6/12

When the bond matures, an entry would be made debiting Cash and crediting the investment account.

If the bond is purchased at a price above or below the par value, the investment account would be debited at par, and the difference would go to a premium or discount account, which would be amortized over the life of the bond. Amortization can be calculated under either the straight-line method or the effective interest method. Because the latter method was discussed in detail in the chapter on long-term liabilities, we will use the simpler, straight-line method in this chapter.

If the bond is purchased at a premium, the amortization entry debits the Interest Revenue account, thus reducing the interest earned. Conversely, if the bond was purchased at a discount, Interest Revenue would be increased.

EXAMPLE 12

The Greenfield Company purchases a $100,000 par, 10% bond at 102 on January 1. The interest is payable annually on December 31 and the bond matures in 10 years. The premium is $2,000, and the annual amortization is $200 ($2,000 ÷ 10). The entries are:

Jan.	1	Investment in Long-term Debt Securities	100,000	
		Bond Premium	2,000	
		Cash		102,000

Dec. 31	Cash	10,000	
	Interest Revenue		10,000
Dec. 31	Interest Revenue	200	
	Premium		200

The net interest revenue is $9,800 ($10,000 − $200).

EXAMPLE 13

Assume the same information as in the previous example except that the bond was purchased at 98. The entries are:

Jan. 1	Investment in Long-term Debt Securities	100,000	
	Cash		98,000
	Bond Discount		2,000
Dec. 31	Cash	10,000	
	Interest Revenue		10,000
Dec. 31	Discount	200	
	Interest Revenue		200

The net interest revenue is $10,200 ($10,000 + $200).

The premium account acts as an addition to the investment account on the balance sheet, while the discount account acts as a minus (a contra). Thus, in the previous example, the balance sheet after the first year would appear as follows:

Investment in Long-term Debt Securities	$100,000
Less Discount ($2,000 − $200)	(1,800)
Net Investment	$ 98,200

If the bond is purchased between interest dates, its price will be increased by the amount of the accrued interest. This increase should be debited to the Interest Revenue account since, in effect, it causes a decrease in the interest earned.

EXAMPLE 14

A company purchases a $100,000, 12%, 10-year bond at par on April 1. The bond pays interest annually on December 31. Thus interest in the amount of $3,000 has accrued ($100,000 × 12% × $\frac{1}{4}$). This entry is:

Investment in Long-term Debt Securities	100,000	
Interest Revenue	3,000	
Cash		103,000

On December 31, the entry for the receipt of the interest would be:

| Cash | 12,000 | |
| Interest Revenue | | 12,000* |

---

*100,000 × 12%

The net interest revenue is thus only $9,000 ($12,000 − $3,000).

If the bond investment is sold before it reaches maturity, the investment account and its related premium or discount should be closed. If the selling price is greater than the book value of the bond, a gain should be recognized. Otherwise, a loss should be recognized. The "book value" is the investment account plus any premium, minus any discount.

EXAMPLE 15

A 4-year, $100,000 bond is purchased at 102 on January 1, 19X1. After 2 years go by, the bond is sold for $99,000. At this point, the T-accounts would appear as follows:

Investment in Long-term Debt Securities		Premium	
100,000		2,000	500
			500
		1,000	

The entry for the sale would be:

Cash	99,000	
Loss on Sale of Securities	2,000	
Investment in Long-term Debt Securities		100,000
Premium		1,000

EXAMPLE 16

Assume the same information as in the previous example except that the bond was purchased at 98 and sold for $95,000. The entry is:

Cash	95,000	
Loss on Sale of Securities	4,000	
Discount	1,000	
Investment in Long-term Debt Securities		100,000

5.5   LONG-TERM INVESTMENTS—EQUITY SECURITIES

Long-term investments in equity securities involve the purchase of stock to be held on a long-term basis. If Company A purchases more than 50% of the outstanding stock of Company B, then the statements of both companies generally should be consolidated. This is discussed in detail in Advanced Accounting. In this chapter we will discuss situations involving a purchase of 50% or less.

There are two methods of accounting for these investments. They are:

1.   The cost method

2.   The equity method

If as a result of this purchase Company A acquires "significant influence" over Company B, then the equity method should be used. Otherwise, the cost method is more appropriate. The accounting profession, in APB Opinion No. 18, has ruled that a purchase of between 20 and 50% of the stock is presumed to lead to significant influence, unless the facts clearly indicate otherwise.

Under the equity method, when Company B (the "subsidiary") earns income, it is as if Company A (the "parent") also "earns" income, and thus Company A must make a journal entry for its share of this income. Furthermore, dividends received from the subsidiary are not considered to be income but withdrawals, and therefore the investment account must be reduced.

Under the cost method, the parent does not "earn" income when the subsidiary earns income, and dividends received are treated as revenue rather than withdrawals.

EXAMPLE 17

Parent Company purchases 30% of Subsidiary Company's 100,000 outstanding shares (30,000 shares) for $100,000. During the next year, Subsidiary earns $50,000 net income and distributes a cash dividend of 25 cents per share. If we assume that Parent has no significant influence and, therefore, the cost method is appropriate, the entries for these transactions would be:

Investment in Long-term Equity Securities	100,000	
Cash		100,000

No entry for the $50,000 earnings would be made.

Cash	7,500	
Investment Revenue		7,500*

----

*.25 × 30,000

The investment account balance is $100,000.

EXAMPLE 18

If in the previous example there is significant influence, and thus the equity method must be used, the entries would be:

Investment in Long-term Equity Securities	100,000	
Cash		100,000
Investment in Long-term Equity Securities	15,000	
Investment Revenue		15,000
(30% of $50,000 earnings)		
Cash	7,500	
Investment in Long-term Equity Securities		7,500

The investment account balance would now show $107,500 ($100,000 + $15,000 − $7,500). Notice that this differs from the $100,000 balance under the cost method.

If the subsidiary incurs a loss instead of earning net income, the parent would debit an account called Investment Loss and credit the investment account.

Under the *cost method,* a comparison would be made at the end of each period of the cost price to the market price. If the market price is lower, an entry would be made to recognize the difference, as discussed in the section on marketable equity securities. However, there is one major difference. For marketable securities, the debit goes to an income statement account (an expense account). For long-term securities, the debit goes directly to a stockholders' equity account, thus bypassing the income statement. This account is a contra-capital account.

EXAMPLE 19

On December 31, 19X5, the market value of a company's investment in stock X is $500 while the cost (under the cost method) is $550. The entry to recognize the lower-of-cost-or-market value is:

Unrealized Loss Due to Market Decline	50	
Allowance to Reduce Cost of Long-term Equity Securities to Market		50

Under the equity method, the above entry would not be made.

It often happens that the price a parent pays for the stock of a subsidiary is greater than the book value. This is usually a result of an understatement of the plant assets on the subsidiary's books, and sometimes it is due to unrecorded goodwill of the subsidiary. (For a discussion of goodwill, see Part I of this book). Under the equity method, these understatements must be accounted for, and they will have an effect on the amount of the subsidiary income to be recognized by the parent.

EXAMPLE 20

Company A buys 30% of Company B's outstanding stock for $40,000. The net worth (stockholders' equity) of Company B, according to its books, is $100,000. Since 30% of $100,000 is only $30,000, Company A has overpaid for this investment by $10,000. Let us assume that $6,000 of this difference is due to an understatement in the asset building (whose remaining life is 10 years) and $4,000 is due to unrecorded goodwill, with an estimated life of 40 years. Let us also assume there is significant influence.

In addition to the above, Company B earned $50,000 net income during the first year after this purchase. The entries are:

For the purchase:

Investment in Long-term Equity Securities	40,000	
Cash		40,000

For the recognition of Company B income:

Investment in Long-term Equity Securities	15,000	
Investment Revenue		15,000*

---

*$50,000 × .30

For the recognition of the effect of depreciation and amortization:

Investment Revenue	700	
Investment in Long-term Equity Securities		700

Building depreciation:	$6,000 ÷ 10 years	=	$600
Goodwill amortization:	$4,000 ÷ 40 years	=	100
			$700

The situation where the cost of an investment is less than the book value is discussed in Advanced Accounting.

5.6 STOCK DIVIDENDS

Unlike cash dividends, dividends received in the form of additional shares of stock are not considered to be revenue and thus no formal journal entry would be made. However, they do reduce the cost per share of the stock investment and a memorandum entry should be made to record this information.

EXAMPLE 21

A company purchases 100 shares of stock at $10 per share. The entry is:

Investment in Long-term (or Short-term) Equity Securities	1,000	
Cash		1,000

It then receives a 10% stock dividend (10 shares). No entry is made for this receipt. However, the cost per share has now fallen to $9.09 ($1,000 ÷ 110).

If the company now sells 50 shares at $9.50, it would recognize a gain, as follows:

Cash	475	
Investment in Long-term Equity Securities		454.50*
Gain on Sale of Securities		20.50

*50 × $9.09

Had the company sold these shares at $9.50 before it received the stock dividend, it would have recognized a loss on the sale instead of a gain.

5.7 STOCK RIGHTS

Stock rights are certificates that permit the holder to buy shares of stock at a fixed price for a certain period of time. These certificates are called *warrants*.

These certificates are usually issued to the present stockholders to enable them to be first on line when the corporation issues new shares of stock. Generally stockholders receive 1 right for every share they own. But it often takes more than 1 right to purchase a new share.

When stockholders receive rights, it is not considered as if they received the rights for free. Rather, the original cost of the stock must now be allocated partially to the rights, based upon respective market values.

EXAMPLE 22

The Giant Corporation purchased 100 shares of General Motors stock at $100 per share. The entry for this was:

Investment in Equity Securities	10,000	
Cash		10,000

It then received 100 rights (1 right per share) to purchase 50 new shares of General Motors stock at $90. Thus, 2 rights are needed per share. These rights expire in 3 months. At the time the rights are received the market value per share and per right are $98 and $6, respectively. The following entry must be made, based upon these market values:

Investment in Stock Rights   577
    Investment in Equity Securities   577*

Stock: $ 98 = $\dfrac{98}{104}$ × \$10,000 = \$ 9,423   (rounded)

*Rights: $\dfrac{6}{\$104}$ = $\dfrac{6}{104}$ × \$10,000 = $\dfrac{577}{\$10,000}$ (rounded)

Thus, the cost assigned to the rights is \$577, which comes out to \$5.77 per right (\$577 ÷ 100).

Stockholders may take three possible actions with the stock rights. They can exercise them to purchase new shares, sell them, or allow them to expire. If new shares are purchased, their cost is the cash given plus the rights given. If the rights are sold, there may be a gain or loss which needs to be recognized. If the rights expire, a loss should be recognized.

EXAMPLE 23

Assume in the previous example that of the 100 rights received, 40 are exercised, 40 are sold for \$6.50 each, and the remaining 20 expire. The entries are:

For the exercise:

Investment in Equity Securities   2,030.80
    Cash   1,800.00*
    Investment in Stock Rights   230.80[†]

*20 × \$90 (40 rights can purchase only 20 shares)
[†]40 × \$5.77

For the sale:

Cash   260
    Investment in Stock Rights   230.80
    Gain on Sale of Rights   29.20

For the expiration:

Loss on Expiration of Stock Rights   115.40*
    Investment in Stock Rights   115.40

*20 × \$5.77

5.8 LIFE INSURANCE POLICIES ON OFFICERS

Corporations often take out life insurance policies on the lives of their key officers. The corporation pays the annual premium and frequently is the beneficiary of the proceeds when the officer dies.

Life insurance policies may be surrendered while the insured is still alive for a certain amount of money. This is called the *cash surrender value* and it increases each year. Accordingly, the yearly insurance premium should not be totally expensed; part of it is an asset—the cash surrender value.

EXAMPLE 24

If the premium for 19X2 is \$1,000 and the cash surrender value increases this year from \$300 to \$450, the entry for the premium is:

Insurance Expense   850
Cash Surrender Value   150*
    Cash   1,000

*450 − 300

The asset Cash Surrender Value is considered to be a long-term investment and would be shown in that section on the balance sheet.

When an officer dies, the corporation receives the proceeds of the insurance policy, and the cash surrender value becomes null and void. Thus the corporation would recognize a gain for the amount of the proceeds less the cash surrender value.

EXAMPLE 25

If the proceeds at death are $100,000 and the cash surrender value at that time is $18,000, the entry would be:

Cash	100,000	
Cash Surrender Value		18,000
Gain on Insurance Settlement		82,000

Summary

1. Companies may use their idle cash to purchase a variety of investments. These investments may be either temporary (marketable securities) or long-term, and consist of stocks or bonds.

2. In order for an investment to be considered temporary, it must meet *both* of the following conditions:

    (1) Be readily marketable, *and*

    (2) be intended for conversion into cash within 1 year or the operating cycle (whichever is longer).

    "Readily marketable" means it can easily be sold in an established market.

3. Brokers' fees and taxes incurred on the purchase of marketable securities are not expenses; they are an addition to the cost of the securities. When these securities are later sold, such fees are considered to be a reduction of the selling price.

4. At the end of the accounting period, a comparison must be made between the aggregate cost of the marketable securities and its aggregate market value. If the market price has fallen below cost, an entry should be made to reduce the cost to the maket value. However, if the market price has risen above cost, no entry is made to recognize this increase. This is called *lower of cost or market (LCM)* and applies to both equity and debt securities.

5. If in later years the market price rises, any such losses previously recognized may be recovered and credited to a revenue account. However, no recognition is given to a price rise above the original cost.

6. If an equity security is transferred from the short-term portfolio to the long-term portfolio, or vice versa, it should be transferred at the LCM value and a realized loss should be recognized if the market value has fallen below cost.

7. A premium or discount on the purchase of marketable debt securities (bonds) should *not* be amortized since the intention is to hold these securities for only a short period. Accordingly, the investment account is debited for the *net* amount paid, and no use is made of a premium or discount account.

8. If a marketable debt security is purchased between interest dates, its price will be increased by the accrued interest. This increase should be debited to Interest Revenue since its effect is to reduce the interest earned.

9. If a long-term bond is purchased above or below par, the investment account would be debited at par, and the difference would go to a premium or discount account. This would then be amortized over the life of the bond using either the straight-line method or the effective interest method of amortization.

10. If the bond is sold before maturity, the investment account and related premium or discount accounts must be closed. If the selling price is greater than the book value of the bond, a gain is recognized; if it is less, a loss is recognized.

11. If Company A purchases more than 50% of Company B stock as a long-term investment, the statements of both companies should generally be consolidated. If the purchase is between 20 and 50%, the equity method of accounting is used, provided that Company A has acquired a "significant influence" in Company B. If the purchase is less than 20%, or if no significant influence is acquired, the cost method is used.

12. When a purchase is between 20 and 50%, we may automatically assume there is significant influence, unless the facts clearly indicate otherwise.

13. Under the equity method, earnings of Company B (the subsidiary) increase the parent's investment account while dividends decrease this account. Under the cost method, the subsidiary earnings are not recognized (and do not affect the investment account) and dividends are recorded as dividend revenue, rather than as a decrease in the investment account.

14. Occasionally, the purchase price of the stock investment will be greater than the corresponding book value. This is usually due to either an understatement of the subsidiary's plant assets or unrecognized goodwill. For the equity method, these understatements must be accounted for by reducing the amount of subsidiary income recognized by the parent.

15. Stock dividends require no formal journal entry. However, they do reduce the cost per share of the stock investment.

16. Stock rights are certificates that permit the holder to buy shares of stock at a fixed price for a fixed period of time. Generally, 1 right is received for every share owned. The cost of the original stock investment must be allocated partially to the rights, based upon respective market values.

17. Holders of stock rights may either exercise them, sell them, or allow them to expire. If the rights are exercised to purchase new shares, the cost of these shares is the cash given plus the rights surrendered. If the rights are sold, there may be a gain or loss which needs to be recognized. If the rights expire, a loss should be recognized.

18. Life insurance policies may be surrendered while the insured is still alive for a certain amount of money. This is called the *cash surrender value,* and it is considered an asset. Thus the yearly insurance premium should not be totally expensed; part of it is an asset representing the cash surrender value.

19. When an officer dies, the corporation receives the proceeds of the insurance policy, and the cash surrender value becomes null and void. Thus the corporation would recognize a gain for the amount of the proceeds less the cash surrender value.

Rapid Review

1. If an investment can readily be sold, and the intention of management is to sell it in the short-term, it is called a ___Mar. Sec___.

2. Brokers' fees are to be debited to an ___Asset___ account rather than to an ___expense___ account.

3. The nature of the Allowance to Reduce Cost to Market account is that of a ___contra asset___

4. If a security is transferred from the short-term portfolio to the long-term portfolio, or vice versa, the transfer should be made at the ___LCM___ value.

5. If a bond investment is purchased between interest dates, its price will be increased by the amount of ___Accrued Int___

6. Amortization of a bond premium _Debits_ interest revenue, while amortization of a bond discount _Credits_ interest revenue.

7. If a bond investment is sold before maturity at a price greater than its book value there is a _gain_.

8. If a company purchases 20 to 50% of another company's stock, the _equity_ method should be used, unless it has no _significc_ influence.

9. Under the cost method, dividends are considered to be _Revenue_, while under the other method, they are considered to be _A Decrease in Investment_

10. For short-term investments, the unrealized loss account is considered to be a(n) _expense income st_ account, while for long-term investments it is a _Contra Corp._ account.

11. The receipt of a stock dividend _reduces_ the cost per share of the investment.

12. Certificates that permit one to buy stock at a fixed price are called _Stock rights_ or _St Warrants_.

13. A part of the annual life insurance premium should be debited to an asset account called _Cash Surrendered value_.

Answers: 1. marketable security 2. asset; expense 3. contra asset 4. lower-of-cost-or-market 5. accrued interest 6. decreases; increases 7. gain 8. equity; significant 9. revenue; withdrawals 10. expense; contra-capital 11. decreases 12. stock rights; warrants 13. cash surrender value

Solved Problems

Temporary Investments — Marketable Equity Securities

5.1 A corporation purchases 1,000 shares of Xerox stock as a short-term investment. The cost per share is $100 and there is a broker's fee of $2,000. It later sells these shares at $110 each and incurs a $3,000 broker's fee. Prepare entries for these transactions.

SOLUTION

Investment in Short-term Equity Securities	102,000	
Cash		102,000
Cash	107,000	
Investment in Short-term Equity Securities		102,000
Gain on Sale of Securities		5,000 [Section 5.2]

5.2 The Feldbrand Corporation purchases 1,000 shares of IBM at $100 and 1,000 shares of Bell Labs at $125. It receives dividends of $1.00 per share on all shares. On December 31, 19X1, the market values of these shares are $90 and $127, respectively. Prepare all the necessary entries for this information, and show how these investments would appear on the December 31 balance sheet. Assume these shares are short-term investments.

SOLUTION

Investment in Short-term Equity Securities	100,000	
Cash		100,000
Investment in Short-term Equity Securities	125,000	
Cash		125,000
Cash	1,000	
Dividend Revenue		1,000
Cash	1,000	
Dividend Revenue		1,000
Unrealized Loss Due to Market Decline	8,000*	
Allowance to Reduce Cost of Short-term Equity Securities to Market		8,000*

	*Cost	Market	
IBM	$100,000	$ 90,000	
Bell	125,000	127,000	
Total	$225,000	$217,000	Difference = $8,000

The balance sheet would appear as follows:

Investment in Equity Securities	$225,000	
Less Allowance to Reduce Cost to Market	(8,000)	
Net Investment	$217,000	[Section 5.2]

5.3 If in the previous example the market prices rise one year later to $95 and $128, and then to $130 and $135 one year after that, prepare the necessary journal entries.

SOLUTION

December 31, 19X2:

	Cost	Market	
IBM	$100,000	$ 95,000	
Bell	125,000	128,000	
	$225,000	$223,000	Difference = $2,000

In this case, since the market price is only $2,000 below cost, while the allowance shows $8,000, we may recover $6,000 by *debiting* the allowance account. The entry is:

Allowance to Reduce Cost of Long-term Equity Securities to Market	6,000	
Recovery of Unrealized Loss Due to Market Decline		6,000

December 31, 19X3:

	Cost	Market
IBM	$100,000	$130,000
Bell	125,000	135,000
	$225,000	$265,000

We may recover the remaining $2,000 in the allowance account, and stop. We may not go above the cost. The entry is:

Allowance to Reduce Cost of Long-term Equity Securities to Market	2,000	
Recovery of Unrealized Loss Due to Market Decline		2,000

[Section 5.2]

Temporary Investments — Marketable Debt Securities

5.4 A $1,000 bond paying 10% interest annually on December 31 is purchased at 110. Prepare all the entries for the first year if:

(1) The bond was purchased on January 1.

(2) The bond was purchased on April 1.

In addition, compute the annual premium amortization using the straight-line method. Assume the bond is a short-term investment.

SOLUTION

(1)

Investment in Short-term Debt Securities	1,100	
Cash		1,100
Cash	100	
Interest Revenue		100

(2)

Investment in Short-term Debt Securities	1,100	
Interest Revenue	25*	
Cash		1,125

*$1,000 × .10 × 3/12

There will be no premium amortization since the investment is short-term. [Section 5.3]

Investments in Long-term Debt Securities

5.5 A $1,000 bond, paying interest annually on December 31, is purchased on January 1 at 110 as a long-term investment. The life of the bond is 5 years. Prepare entries for the first year and use the straight-line method of premium amortization. Also, calculate the *net* interest revenue for the year. The interest rate is 10%.

SOLUTION

Investment in Long-term Debt Securities	1,000	
Premium	100	
Cash		1,100
Cash	100	
Interest Revenue		100
Interest Revenue	20	
Premium		20*

*$100 ÷ 5 years

Net interest revenue = $80 (100 − 20). [Section 5.4]

5.6 Assume the same information as in the previous problem except that the bond was purchased at 95. Prepare all the entries.

SOLUTION

Investment in Long-term Debt Securities	1,000	
Cash		950
Discount		50
Cash	100	
Interest Revenue		100
Discount	10	
Interest Revenue		10

Net interest revenue = $110 (100 + 10). [Section 5.4]

5.7 A company purchases a $100,000, 10-year bond on January 1, 19X1 at 107. After 5 years, it sells the bond at 102. Prepare the entry for the sale.

SOLUTION

Investment in Long-term Debt Securities			Premium	
100,000			7,000	700*
				700
				700
				700
				700
			Balance 3,500	

*7,000 ÷ 10

Cash	102,000	
Loss on Sale of Security	1,500	
Investment in Long-term Debt Securities		100,000
Premium		3,500 [Section 5.4]

5.8 A company purchases a 10-year, $100,000 bond on January 1, 19X1 at 98. Five years later, it sells this bond at 102. Prepare the entry for the sale.

SOLUTION

The $2,000 discount would be amortized at the rate of $200 yearly, thus leaving a balance of $1,000 in the discount account after 5 years ($2,000 − 5[200]).

The entry is:

Cash	102,000	
Discount	1,000	
Investment in Long-term Debt Securities		100,000
Gain on Sale of Security		3,000 [Section 5.4]

Long-term Investments in Equity Securities

5.9 Parent Company purchases 25% of the outstanding 50,000 shares of Subsidiary Company on January 1, 19X1, for $75,000. During 19X1, Subsidiary Company earns $100,000 net income and distributes a dividend of $1.00 per share. Assume Parent has "significant influence" over Subsidiary. Prepare the necessary journal entries and show the investment account.

SOLUTION

The equity method must be used, as follows:

Investment in Long-term Equity Securities	75,000	
Cash		75,000
Investment in Long-term Equity Securities	25,000	
Investment Revenue		25,000*

*$100,000 × 25%

Cash	12,500	
Investment in Long-term Equity Securities		12,500†

†50,000 × 25% × $1.00

Investment in Long-term Equity Securities		
75,000	12,500	
25,000		
Balance 87,500		

[Section 5.5]

5.10   Assume the same information as in the previous problem, except that Parent has no "significant influence." Prepare the entries and present the investment account.

SOLUTION

This requires the cost method, as follows:

Investment in Long-term Equity Securities	75,000	
Cash		75,000

No entry is made for the $100,000 earnings.

Cash	12,500	
Dividend Revenue		12,500

Investment in Long-term Equity Securities

75,000	

[Section 5.5]

5.11   Parent Company purchases a long-term equity investment representing 25% of Subsidiary Company's outstanding shares. During the first year, Subsidiary incurs a loss of $100,000. What entry should Parent make under (*a*) the equity method; (*b*) the cost method (no significant influence)?

SOLUTION

(*a*)

Investment Loss	25,000	
Investment in Long-term Equity Securities		25,000

(*b*) No entry.

[Section 5.5]

5.12   Parent Company purchases as a long-term investment, 20% of Subsidiary Company's outstanding shares on January 1, 19X1, for $100,000. It does not have significant influence, thus requiring the use of the cost method. On December 31, 19X1, the market price of this stock is $90,000.
(*a*)   What entry, if any, should be made December 31?
(*b*)   If an entry is to be made, what is the nature of each account in this entry? How is this entry different from a similar entry made for short-term equity securities?
(*c*)   If Parent had significant influence and the equity method was used, how would this entry be different?

SOLUTION

(*a*)

Unrealized Loss Due to Market Decline	10,000	
Allowance to Reduce Cost to Market		10,000

(*b*)   The debit is a contra-capital account which bypasses the income statement. The credit is a contra to the investment account. For short-term equity securities, the debit is an expense account which *would* appear on the income statement.
(*c*)   The lower-of-cost-or-market entry is *not* made under the equity method.   [Section 5.5]

5.13   Company A buys 25% of the outstanding stock of Company B on January 1, 19X1, for $45,000. The book value of Company B's stock is $100,000.

During 19X1, Company B distributed a *total* dividend of $80,000 and earned net income of $150,000.

Any difference between the cost of the investment and book value is due equally to an understatement of the plant building and to unrecorded goodwill. The life of the building is 5 years; the life of the goodwill is unknown. Prepare all necessary journal entries.

SOLUTION

Investment in Long-term Equity Securities	45,000	
Cash		45,000
Investment in Long-term Equity Securities	37,500	
Investment Revenue		37,500
(.25 × $150,000)		
Cash	20,000	
Investment in Long-term Equity Securities		20,000
(.25 × $80,000)		
Investment Revenue	2,250*	
Investment in Long-term Equity Securities		2,250

*Investment cost = $45,000
Book value   =   25,000   (.25 × $100,000)
Excess cost   = $20,000

Building understatement: $\frac{1}{2}$ × $20,000 = $10,000

Unrecorded goodwill: $\frac{1}{2}$ × $20,000 = $10,000

Building depreciation: $10,000 ÷ 5 = $2,000

Goodwill amortization: $10,000 ÷ 40 =   250

Reduction of investment revenue   = $2,250

(When the life of goodwill is unknown, a maximum life of up to 40 years may be used.)

[Section 5.5]

Stock Dividends

5.14 A company purchases 1,000 shares of stock at $12 per share. It sells 100 shares at $11, receives a 10% stock dividend, and then sells another 100 shares at $11. Prepare all the required entries. Assume the investment is short-term.

SOLUTION

Investment in Short-term Equity Securities	12,000	
Cash		12,000
Cash	1,100	
Loss on Sale of Securities	100	
Investment in Short-term Equity Securities		1,200*

*100 × $12

There is no entry for the stock dividend, but the new cost per share is:

$$\frac{\$10,800}{900 + .10(900)} = \$10.91$$

For the second sale:

Cash	1,100	
Investment in Short-term Equity Securities		1,091*
Gain on Sale		9

*$10.91 × 100   [Section 5.6]

Stock Rights

5.15 A corporation purchases a short-term stock investment of 1,000 shares at $75 each. It then receives 1 right per share (1,000 rights) to purchase additional shares at $60. Five rights are needed to purchase

1 share. At the time the rights are received, the market value per share is $65 and per right, $5. Prepare the required journal entries, and determine the cost per right.

SOLUTION

Investment in Short-term Equity Securities	75,000	
Cash		75,000
Investment in Stock Rights	5,357*	
Investment in Short-term Equity Securities		5,357

*Stock $65 $\dfrac{65}{70} \times \$75{,}000 = \$69{,}643$ (rounded)

Rights $\dfrac{5}{\$70}$ $\dfrac{5}{70} \times \$75{,}000 = \$\ 5{,}357$ (rounded)

The cost per right is $5.36 ($5,357 ÷ 1,000). [Section 5.7]

5.16 In the previous problem, assume that the company exercises 200 of the rights to buy shares, and sells 600 rights at $6.00 each. Prepare the journal entries.

SOLUTION

Investment in Short-term Equity Securities	3,472	
Cash		2,400*
Investment in Stock Rights		1,072†

*(200 ÷ 5) × $60
†200 × $5.36

Cash	3,600	
Investment in Stock Rights		3,216*
Gain on Sale		384

*600 × $5.36   [Section 5.7]

5.17 In the previous example, if the remaining 200 rights are allowed to expire, what would be the journal entry?

SOLUTION

Loss on Expiration	1,069	
Investment in Stock Rights		1,069*

*5,357 − 1,072 − 3,216 = 1,069   [Section 5.7]

Life Insurance Policies

5.18 Prepare the journal entry for a life insurance premium of $5,000 if the cash surrender value increased during the year from $500 to $900.

SOLUTION

Life Insurance Expense	4,600	
Cash Surrender Value	400	
Cash		5,000

[Section 5.8]

5.19 A corporation receives a $50,000 life insurance settlement when its vice-president dies. At that time, the cash surrender value is $3,000. What journal entry should be made?

SOLUTION

Cash	50,000		
Cash Surrender Value		3,000	
Gain on Settlement		47,000	[Section 5.8]

Supplementary Problems

5.20 Corporation A purchases 70 shares of General Motors stock at $50 per share as a short-term investment, and pays a broker's fee of $350. It later sells these shares at $80 per share and pays a broker's fee of $550. Prepare entries for the purchase and the sale.

5.21 On February 1, 19A, Corporation B purchases 200 shares of stock as a short-term investment at $60 per share. On December 31, 19A, and December 31, 19B, the market price of these shares is $55 and $68 per share, respectively. Prepare the necessary entries for each December 31. Show how the investment would be presented on the December 31, 19A, balance sheet.

5.22 On April 15, 19A, Corporation C transfers its investment in stock from long-term status to short-term status. The cost of this investment is $20,000; the market value on this date is $18,000. Prepare the necessary entry.

5.23 A short-term bond dated January 1, 19A, is purchased on May 1, 19A at its par of $80,000. The bond pays interest on December 31 of 10%. Prepare the entries for May 1 and December 31.

5.24 Corporation F purchases a $130,000 par, 10% bond at 104 on January 1, 19A. The interest is payable annually on December 31 and the bond matures in 5 years.
  (a) Prepare the required entries on January 1 and December 31.
  (b) Determine the net interest revenue for the year.
  (c) Show how this bond would be presented on the balance sheet on December 31, 19A.

5.25 A 4-year, $170,000 bond is purchased at 104 on January 1, 19A. After 3 years elapse, the bond is sold at par. Prepare the entry for the sale.

5.26 Parent Company purchases 40% of Subsidiary Company's 200,000 shares for $240,000. During the year, Subsidiary earns net income of $40,000 and distributes cash dividends of 20 cents per share. This purchase is considered a long-term investment. If no significant influence was acquired, then prepare the necessary journal entries and show the investment account.

5.27 Assume the same information as in the previous problem except that significant influence *has* been acquired. Prepare the entries and determine the balance in the investment account.

5.28 Company G purchases 250 shares of stock at $20 per share. It then receives a 15% stock dividend. Several months later it decides to sell 50 shares at $18 per share.
  (a) After the stock dividend, what was the new cost per share?
  (b) Prepare any necessary journal entries for these transactions.

5.29 Company H engaged in the following stock transactions during 19A:
  (a) Purchased 200 shares General Motors stock at $125 per share.
  (b) Received 1 right per share to purchase 100 new shares at $115 per share. At this time, the market values per share and per right are $120 and $4, respectively.
  Prepare the entries for the stock purchase and the receipt of the rights and determine the cost per right.

5.30   Use the same information as in the previous example and assume that 50 of the rights are exercised to purchase new shares. Prepare the entry for this purchase.

5.31   Company H has an insurance policy for which it pays an annual premium of $1,000. During 19B, the cash surrender value increased from $300 to $400. Prepare an entry for the payment of the insurance premium.

5.32   When the chief executive officer of Corporation K died, the company received insurance benefits of $500,000. At this time, the cash surrender value was $150,000. Prepare an entry for the receipt of the insurance benefits.

Chapter 6

Revenue Recognition Issues

6.1 INTRODUCTION

A company's periodic income statement consists essentially of two components: revenue and expense. Revenue for the period is generally determined by applying the revenue recognition principle. According to Concepts Statement No. 5, this principle provides that revenue be recognized when it is both realized and earned. *Realization* takes place when goods or services are exchanged for cash or receivables. Revenue is considered to be *earned* when the company has substantially done what it must do to be entitled to payment; i.e., the earnings process is virtually complete. Under this principle, revenue from the sale of a product would be recognized upon delivery of the product, while service revenue would be recognized when the service has been performed.

In certain cases, revenue recognition problems arise because the ultimate collection of the selling price is not reasonably assured, or because it is difficult to determine when the earning process has been completed. In these cases, companies may wish to delay recognition of the revenue until after delivery. On the other hand, if there is a high degree of certainty regarding the earnings, companies may wish to recognize the revenue before delivery.

This chapter will discuss three approaches to revenue recognition: at point of delivery, before delivery, and after delivery.

6.2 REVENUE RECOGNITION AT DELIVERY

According to FASB Concepts Statement No. 5, revenue is recognized when both realized and earned. In most situations, both of these conditions are met upon delivery of the goods, or in the case of services, when the services are rendered. Thus the revenue recognition will be at this time.

A special problem arises when a right of return exists and the company has experienced a high ratio of returns to sales. Should the company not record the sale until all the return privileges have expired? Should it record the sale, but reduce it by an estimate of future returns? Or should it account for the returns in future periods when they occur? The FASB has concluded that revenue should be recognized at sale time only if *all* of the following six conditions have been met:

1. The seller's price to the buyer is substantially fixed at the date of sale.
2. The buyer has paid the seller, or is obligated to pay the seller, and the obligation is not contingent on the resale of the product.
3. The buyer's obligation would not be changed in the event of theft or damage to the product.
4. The buyer has economic substance apart from that provided by the seller.
5. The seller does not have significant obligations for future performance to directly bring about resale of the product by the buyer.
6. The amount of future returns can be reasonably estimated.

If these conditions have not been met, no revenue should be recognized until the return privilege has expired, or until all the conditions have been met (whichever comes first).

6.3 REVENUE RECOGNITION BEFORE DELIVERY — INTRODUCTION

In the construction industry, two accounting approaches have developed over the years regarding the recognition of revenue. The first approach — the *completed-contract method* — does not recognize any profit until the construction project is complete. The second approach — the *percentage-of-completion method* — recognizes profit on a piecemeal basis.

The logic behind the percentage-of-completion method is that both the buyer and seller have obtained enforceable rights. The buyer has the right to require specific performance on the contract; the seller has the right to require progress payments. Thus the facts seem to indicate that a continuous "sale" is in progress.

According to Statement of Position 81-1, the percentage method should be used if estimates of progress toward completion, revenues, and costs are reasonably dependable, and all the following conditions exist:

1. The contract clearly specifies the rights regarding goods or services to be provided, and the consideration to be exchanged.

2. The buyer can be expected to satisfy all the contractual obligations.

3. The seller can be expected to perform the contractual obligations.

If these conditions have not been met, then the completed-contract method should be used.

It should be emphasized that the *total* profit on the construction project is the same under *both* methods. The difference between methods is simply a question of timing—the percentage method recognizes profit little by little over time, while the completed-contract method defers the entire profit until completion.

6.4   THE COMPLETED-CONTRACT METHOD

This method defers all the profit on the construction project until the completion date. During the construction period, all costs incurred are debited to an inventory account called Construction in Process. This is similar to the Work in Process account used in cost accounting. Billings are debited to Accounts Receivable and credited to an account called Billings on Construction. This is *not* a revenue account since this method does not recognize any revenue or profit until completion. Rather, it is a contra asset to the Construction in Process Account. Finally, at completion, the construction and billings accounts are closed, and the difference between them is recognized as gross profit.

EXAMPLE 1

Construction Corporation enters into a contract on January 1, 19A, with the Department of Defense to build a small ship for $100,000. The project is estimated to take 3 years. The following information presents the transactions that took place over this time:

	19A	19B	19C	Total
Construction costs	$20,000	$25,000	$25,000	$ 70,000
Billings	25,000	35,000	40,000	100,000
Cash collections	20,000	20,000	60,000	100,000
Estimated completion costs as of year-end	45,000	25,000	—	—

Notice that the final profit is $30,000 ($100,000 − $70,000). Also notice that the estimate of what the final profit would be changed between 19A and 19B. In 19A it was $35,000 (selling price of $100,000 − $20,000 of costs incurred so far − $45,000 of estimated completion costs). In 19B it changed to $30,000 ($100,000 − $20,000 − $25,000 − $25,000).

The entries for the three years are as follows:

	19A		19B		19C	
Construction in Process	20,000		...25,000		...25,000	
Miscellaneous*		20,000		25,000		25,000
Accounts Receivable	25,000		...35,000		...40,000	
Billings on Construction		25,000		35,000		40,000
Cash	20,000		...20,000		...60,000	
Accounts Receivable		20,000		20,000		60,000
No entry for profit recognition			No entry for profit recognition.			

*Cash or manufacturing-type accounts such as materials or labor.

By the end of 19C, the billings account and the Construction in Process account appear as follows:

Billings on Construction	Construction in Process
25,000	20,000
35,000	25,000
40,000	25,000
100,000	70,000

The entry in 19C to close these accounts and recognize profit is:

Billings on Construction	100,000	
Construction in Process		70,000
Income on Construction		30,000

The information given regarding estimated completion costs was not needed in this problem. However, it is relevant if the percentage-of-completion method is used instead of the completed-contract method.

The account Billings on Construction is a contra to the construction account and is shown on the balance sheet as such. If its balance is less than the balance in the construction account, the net amount is shown as a current asset; if it is more, the net amount is shown as a current liability.

EXAMPLE 2

In the previous example, the balance sheets for 19A and 19B would appear as follows:

	19A	19B
Current Liabilities:		
Billings on Construction	$ 25,000	$ 60,000
Less Construction in Process	(20,000)	(45,000)
	$ 5,000	$ 15,000

The income statements for 19A and 19B would not show any revenue or profit since these items are deferred until completion.

EXAMPLE 3

If in 19X1 Corporation X has construction costs of $50,000 and billings of $38,000, its balance sheet would show:

Current Assets:	
Construction in Process	$ 50,000
Less Billings on Construction	(38,000)
	12,000

6.5 THE PERCENTAGE-OF-COMPLETION METHOD

This method recognizes a portion of the gross profit each year based upon the following formula:

$$\text{Recognized profit} = \frac{\text{costs incurred so far}}{\text{total expected project costs}} \times \text{estimated profit} - \text{previous years' profit}$$

The entries each year would be the same as under the completed-contract method, with one additional annual entry to recognize profit. This entry debits the construction account (the profit is placed "into" the inventory) and credits a profit account.

EXAMPLE 4

Let's use the same information as in Example 1. The entry in 19A for profit recognition is:

Construction in Process	10,769	
Income from Construction		10,769

The calculation is:

$$\frac{20,000}{20,000 + 45,000} \times 35,000 - 0 = \$10,769 \text{ (rounded)}$$

At this point, the expected profit is \$35,000 (selling price of \$100,000 − past costs of \$20,000 − future costs of \$45,000).

The \$10,769 would be shown on the 19A income statement. In 19B the profit recognized is:

$$\frac{20,000 + 25,000}{20,000 + 25,000 + 25,000} \times 30,000 - 10,769 = \$8,517$$

Notice that the total expected profit has changed from \$35,000 to \$30,000 due to changes in anticipated costs. This happens often in the construction industry.

The \$30,000 total expected profit is computed as follows:

\$100,000	selling price
(45,000)	past costs
(25,000)	future costs
\$ 30,000	

The 19B income statement would show profit of \$8,517 and the journal entry would be:

Construction in Process	8,517	
Income from Construction		8,517

In 19C:

$$\frac{20,000 + 25,000 + 25,000}{20,000 + 25,000 + 25,000} \times 30,000 - 10,769 - 8,517 = \$10,714$$

A journal entry would be made for this amount.

An examination of the accounts at the end of 19C reveals the following:

	Construction in Process		Billings on Construction
Cost	20,000		25,000
Profit	10,769		35,000
Cost	25,000		40,000
Profit	8,517		100,000
Cost	25,000		
Profit	10,714		
	100,000		

Notice that the balances of these two accounts are equal (\$100,000) under this method. This is because the construction account contains both cost and profit.

One final entry would be made at the end of 19C to close these two accounts:

Billings on Construction	100,000	
Construction in Process		100,000

If at any time during the construction period it is estimated that a loss will occur on the project (because the estimated total costs are expected to be higher than the selling price), it should be recognized by a debit to a loss account and a credit to the inventory account. Furthermore, if in previous years profit was recognized under the percentage-of-completion method, it should now be nullified via a reversing entry.

EXAMPLE 5

A company used the completed-contract method for a 5-year construction project. Thus no profit would be recognized until the fifth year. During the third year the company realizes that the total project will result in a net loss of \$50,000. The company should immediately make the following entry:

Loss on Construction	50,000	
Construction in Process		50,000

EXAMPLE 6

In the previous example, assume the company used the percentage-of-completion method and recognized profit of $10,000 and $20,000, respectively, in the first 2 years. In the third year, upon discovery of the $50,000 loss, an entry must be made to both recognize this loss, and to nullify the previous profit. The entry is:

Loss on Construction	80,000*	
Construction in Process		80,000

*10,000 + 20,000 + 50,000

6.6 THE COMPLETION-OF-PRODUCTION METHOD

There is one method that recognizes revenue before delivery. It is called the *completion-of-production* method and it recognizes revenue upon completion of the production process even though no sale has been made. Examples of these situations would be agricultural products or precious metals that have assured market prices. Revenue would be recognized when the metals are mined and the crops are harvested since their sale prices are reasonably assured, thus meeting the criteria set forth in Concepts Statement No. 5 of the revenue being realizable and earned.

6.7 REVENUE RECOGNITION AFTER DELIVERY — THE INSTALLMENT METHOD

If the collection of the selling price is not reasonably assured and there is no reasonable basis for estimating the degree of collectibility, the installment method of revenue recognition may be used. Under this method, the recognition of gross profit on the sale is deferred until cash collections take place, rather than being recognized at the time of sale. Other expenses, however, such as selling and administrative expenses, are recognized as incurred. In APB Opinion No. 10 the board concluded that except in the special circumstances just mentioned, this method should not be used since it is a violation of the concept of accrual accounting.

The procedures to be used for this method are as follows: When installment sales take place, an entry is made debiting Accounts Receivable and crediting Sales. An entry is also made for the cost of goods sold. Both the Sales account and the Cost of Goods Sold account are closed at period-end and the margin is placed into an account called Deferred Gross Profit. Part of this profit is recognized when cash is collected, based upon the gross profit percentage. These procedures are illustrated in the following example.

EXAMPLE 7

The Greenfield Corporation had the following data relating to its installment sales for 19A and 19B:

	19A	19B
Installment sales	$100,000	$200,000
Cost of goods sold	70,000	150,000
Gross profit	$ 30,000	$ 50,000
Gross profit percentage	$\frac{30,000}{100,000} = 30\%$	$\frac{50,000}{200,000} = 25\%$
Collections on 19A sales	$ 60,000	$ 40,000
Collections on 19B sales	None	$140,000

The entries for 19A are:

Accounts Receivable	100,000	
Sales		100,000
Cost of Goods Sold	70,000	
Merchandise Inventory		70,000

At this point we have a revenue account (Sales) showing $100,000 and an expense account (Cost of Goods Sold) showing $70,000, resulting in a profit of $30,000. We do not want to recognize this profit at this time. Accordingly, we close these two accounts at period-end:

Sales	100,000	
Cost of Goods Sold		70,000
Deferred Gross Profit		30,000

Many companies consider the Deferred Gross Profit to be a liability account similar to unearned revenue. However, the FASB has indicated that it should be considered a contra asset to the Accounts Receivable account. We will, therefore, treat it as such.

For the cash collection:

Cash	60,000	
Accounts Receivable		60,000

On the $60,000 collection we may now recognize profit according to the gross profit percentage. Thus the profit recognized is $60,000 \times 30\% = \$18,000$ and the entry for this:

Deferred Gross Profit	18,000	
Realized Gross Profit		18,000

The Realized Gross Profit is a revenue (profit) account. Thus the income statement for 19A will show profit of $18,000, and the balance sheet will appear as follows:

Accounts Receivable	$40,000	(100,000 − 60,000)
Less Deferred Gross Profit	12,000	(30,000 − 18,000)
Net Receivable	$28,000	

The entries for 19B are:

Accounts Receivable	200,000		
Sales		200,000	
Cost of Goods Sold	150,000		
Merchandise Inventory		150,000	
Cash	40,000		(for 19A sales having
Accounts Receivable		40,000	a profit % of 30%)
Cash	140,000		(for 19B sales having
Accounts Receivable		140,000	a profit % of 25%)
Sales	200,000		
Cost of Goods Sold		150,000	
Deferred Gross Profit		50,000	
Deferred Gross Profit	47,000		
Realized Gross Profit		47,000*	

_____

*$(.30 \times 40,000) + .25(140,000)$

The income statement for 19B will show profit on installment sales of $47,000, and the balance sheet will appear as follows:

Accounts Receivable	$60,000
Less Deferred Gross Profit	(15,000)
	$45,000

If the buyer defaults on the installment payments, and the merchandise is repossessed by the seller, an entry should be made closing the Accounts Receivable and Deferred Gross Profit accounts, recording the merchandise at its fair market value, and recognizing a gain or loss for the difference.

EXAMPLE 8

The Accounts Receivable account and its related Deferred Gross Profit account appeared as follows right before a customer defaulted:

Accounts Receivable		Deferred Gross Profit	
1,000			300

The merchandise has a fair market value of $600 and was repossessed. The entry is:

Repossessed Merchandise	600	
Deferred Gross Profit	300	
Loss on Repossession	100	
Accounts Receivable		1,000

Because the profit component of the $1,000 receivable was $300, the cost component must have been $700. Since only $600 of this cost is now being recovered, there is a $100 loss.

Until now, we have simplified matters by not including interest in our discussion. In reality, however, there is interest on installment sales balances, and each payment consists partially of principal and partially of interest. Thus the interest portion should be recognized as interest revenue, and a part of the principal portion should be recognized as profit, according to the gross profit percentage.

EXAMPLE 9

A company makes a sale of $5,000 payable over 3 years (one installment per year) including interest of 10%. Using present values, each payment will be $2,010.45 based upon the following calculation:

$$\frac{\$5,000}{\text{Present value annuity of \$1, three periods, 10\%}} = \frac{\$5,000}{2.48685} = \$2,010.58$$

(For a review of present value concepts, see the appendix on interest concepts).

If the cost of goods sold is $4,000, there is a profit of $1,000 on the $5,000 selling price, which equals 20%.

The following table indicates the journal entry to be made for each payment and the realized gross profit.

Date	Cash (Dr.)	Interest Revenue (Cr.)	Accounts Receivable (Cr.)	Balance	Realized Gross Profit
At sale	—	—	—	$5,000	—
End of year 1	$2,010.58	$500.00*	$1,510.58†	$3,489.42‡	$302.12§
End of year 2	2,010.58	348.94	1,661.64	1,827.80	332.33
End of year 3	2,010.58	182.78	1,827.80	—	365.56

*This is the Accounts Receivable balance × 10%.
†This is the cash minus the interest revenue.
‡This is the previous Accounts Receivable balance minus the current credit to Accounts Receivable.
§This is 20% of the credit to Accounts Receivable.

6.8 THE COST RECOVERY METHOD

If there is a very high degree of uncertainty regarding the collectibility of receivables, the cost recovery method may be used. Under this method, *no* profit is recognized until the entire cost has been recovered. The entries are the same as under the installment method.

EXAMPLE 10

A company sells goods costing $10,000 for $22,000, payable in installments of $7,000, $10,000, and $5,000, respectively, over 3 years. In the first year, no profit would be recognized since the cost has not yet been fully recovered. In the second year, once $3,000 is collected the cost has been recovered, and, thus the remaining collection of $7,000 ($10,000 − $3,000) is recognized as profit. In the third year, the full $5,000 collection is considered profit.

Professional judgment must be exercised to determine when the degree of uncertainty regarding collectibility is high enough to permit the use of this method.

Summary

1. Revenue is generally recognized when it has been both *realized* and *earned*. Realization takes place when goods and services are exchanged for cash or receivables. The earnings process takes place when the company has substantially done what it must do to be entitled to payment. Under these guidelines, revenue would be recognized upon delivery of a product, or performance of a service.

2. When a right of return exists and the company experiences a high ratio of returns to sales, revenue should *not* be recognized at sale time unless six conditions have been met. If they have not been met, the revenue should not be recognized until the return privilege has expired.

3. In the construction industry, two approaches have been taken regarding the timing of revenue recognition. Under the *completed-contract* method, no profit is recognized until project completion; under the *percentage-of-completion* method, the profit is recognized on a piecemeal basis.

4. The percentage method should be used *only* if estimates of degree of completion, revenue, and costs are reasonably dependable and all the following conditions have been fulfilled:
   (*a*) The contract clearly specifies the rights regarding goods to be provided, and the consideration to be exchanged.
   (*b*) The buyer can be expected to satisfy all the contractual obligations.
   (*c*) The seller can be expected to perform all the contractual obligations.

5. The *total* profit on the construction project is the *same* under both methods. The only difference between the two methods is timing. The percentage method recognizes the profit on a piecemeal basis; the completed-contract method defers the entire profit until completion.

6. Under the completed contract method, all costs incurred are debited to the inventory account Construction in Process. Billings are credited to an account called Billings on Construction and debited to Accounts Receivable. The billings account is not a revenue account, but, rather, a contra asset to the construction account. At project completion, both the billings and construction accounts are closed, and the difference is recognized as profit.

7. The percentage-of-completion method recognizes a portion of the profit each year using the following formula:

$$\text{Recognized profit} = \frac{\text{costs incurred so far}}{\text{total expected project costs}} \times \frac{\text{estimated}}{\text{profit}} - \text{previous years' profit}$$

8. This method makes the same entries as the completed contract method, plus one additional entry for profit recognition. This entry debits the construction account and credits a profit account.

9. If at any time during the construction period it is estimated that a loss will occur, it should immediately be recognized by a debit to a loss account and a credit to the construction account. If in previous years profit was recognized under the percentage method, this profit should be nullified via a reversing entry.

10. For agricultural products or precious metals that have assured market prices, the accounting profession allows revenue recognition before delivery; i.e., when the crops are harvested and the metals are mined. This approach is called the *completion-of-production* method.

11. If the collection of the selling price is not reasonably assured and there is no reasonable basis for estimating the degree of collectibility, the installment method should be used. Recognition of the gross profit would be deferred until cash collections take place, rather than being recognized at sale time. However, selling and administrative expenses would be recognized as incurred.

12. Under this method, entries are made at the time of sale for the sale and the cost of goods sold. These accounts are closed at period-end and the margin is placed into an account called Deferred Gross Profit. This account is a contra asset to Accounts Receivable. As cash collections take place, profit is recognized on a piecemeal basis using the gross profit percentage.

13. If the buyer defaults on the installment payments and the merchandise is repossessed by the seller, an entry should be made to close the Accounts Receivable and Deferred Gross Profit accounts, record the merchandise at its fair market value, and recognize a gain or loss for the difference.

14. If there is interest on the installment sale balance, each payment consists partially of principal and partially of interest. The interest portion should be recognized as interest revenue; the principal portion should be recognized *in part* as profit, according to the gross profit percentage.

15. If there is a very high degree of uncertainty regarding the collectibility of the receivable, the cost recovery method may be used. Under this method, no profit is recognized until the entire cost has been recovered.

Rapid Review

1. Generally, revenue from the sale of a product should be recognized upon _____, while revenue from the sale of services should be recognized at _____.

2. In order for revenue to be recognized, it must be both _____ and _____.

3. The two methods of accounting for construction projects are the _____ method and the _____ method.

4. No matter which method is used, the *total* profit recognized over the life of the project is _____.

5. The inventory account in construction projects is called _____.

6. The nature of the billings account is that of a _____.

7. Under the percentage-of-completion method, the annual profit is debited to the _____ account.

8. Under both methods, any anticipated losses would be recognized _____.

9. For precious metals and agricultural products, revenue may be recognized before _____.

10. Under the installment method, a portion of each cash collection is considered profit based upon the _____ percentage.

11. If a buyer defaults on installment payments, the repossessed merchandise is recorded at _____.

12. If the degree of uncertainty regarding collections is very high, it is then permissible to use the _____ method.

Answers: 1. delivery; performance 2. realized; earned 3. completed contract; percentage-of-completion 4. the same 5. construction-in-process 6. contra asset 7. inventory 8. immediately 9. delivery 10. gross profit 11. fair market value 12. cost recovery

Solved Problems

Accounting for Construction Contracts

6.1 The following information relates to a long-term construction project of the Feldbrand Corporation:

	19A	19B	19C	Total
Construction costs	$ 50,000	$70,000	$ 80,000	$200,000
Billings	40,000	90,000	120,000	250,000
Cash collections	40,000	80,000	130,000	250,000
Estimated completion costs as of year-end	140,000	80,000	—	—

Assume a contract price of $250,000. Prepare the journal entries and show what a partial balance sheet would look like for each year, under the completed-contract method.

SOLUTION

	19A		19B		19C	
Construction in Process	50,000		...70,000		...80,000	
Miscellaneous		50,000		70,000		80,000
Accounts Receivable	40,000		...90,000		...120,000	
Billings		40,000		90,000		120,000
Cash	40,000		...80,000		...130,000	
Accounts Receivable		40,000		80,000		130,000
No entry for profit			No entry for profit			
Billings					250,000	
Construction in Process						200,000
Income on Construction						50,000

The partial balance sheets would appear as follows:

19A
Current Assets:
Construction in Process		$ 50,000
Less Billings		40,000
		$ 10,000

19B
Current Liabilities:
Billings		$130,000
Less Construction in Process		120,000
		$ 10,000

19C

The billings and construction in process accounts have been closed and would therefore not appear on the balance sheet.   [Section 6.4]

6.2   Prepare journal entries and partial income statements for the preceeding problem using the percentage-of-completion method.

SOLUTION

The entries will be the same as those under the completed-contract method, with one additional entry each year for profit recognition, as follows:

19A
Construction in Process	15,789	
Income on Construction		15,789

The computation is:

$$\frac{50,000}{50,000 + 140,000} \times 60,000^* = \$15,789 \text{ (rounded)}$$

*($250,000 − $190,000)

19B

$$\frac{50,000 + 70,000}{50,000 + 70,000 + 80,000} \times 50,000^\dagger - 15,789 = \$14,211$$

†($250,000 − $200,000)

$$\text{Construction in Process} \qquad 14,211$$
$$\text{Income on Construction} \qquad\qquad 14,211$$

19C

$$\frac{50,000 + 70,000 + 80,000}{50,000 + 70,000 + 80,000} \times 50,000 - (15,789 + 14,211) = 20,000$$

$$\text{Construction in Process} \qquad 20,000$$
$$\text{Income on Construction} \qquad\qquad 20,000$$

There would be one more entry in 19C to close the following T-accounts:

Construction in Process		Billings	
50,000			40,000
15,789			90,000
70,000			120,000
14,211			250,000
80,000			
20,000			
250,000			

$$\text{Billings} \qquad 250,000$$
$$\text{Construction in Process} \qquad\qquad 250,000$$

For 19A, the income statement would show profit on construction of $15,789; for 19B it would show $14,211; for 19C it would show $20,000.   [Section 6.5]

6.3   The Green Company uses the completed-contract method for construction projects. During the third year of a project, construction costs rose unexpectedly, and the company realized it would incur a loss on this project of $100,000. Prepare the necessary journal entry.

SOLUTION

$$\text{Loss on Construction} \qquad 100,000$$
$$\text{Construction in Process} \qquad\qquad 100,000 \qquad \text{[Section 6.5]}$$

6.4   The Brown Company uses the percentage-of-completion method of accounting for construction projects. During years 19A, 19B, and 19C of a particular project, it recognized profits of $50,000, $70,000, and $60,000, respectively. In 19D it realized it would incur a total loss of $100,000 on this project. Prepare the necessary journal entry.

SOLUTION

$$\text{Loss on Construction} \qquad 280,000$$
$$\text{Construction in Process} \qquad\qquad 280,000*$$

_____

*50,000 + 70,000 + 60,000 + 100,000   [Section 6.5]

6.5   The White Company uses the completed-contract method of accounting for construction and has the following data relating to a 3-year project:

	19A	19B	19C	Total
Construction costs	$50,000	$25,000	$35,000	$110,000
Billings	50,000	25,000	25,000	100,000
Collections	50,000	20,000	30,000	100,000
Estimated completion costs as of year-end	40,000	35,000	—	—

The contract price is $100,000.

In 19B the company realized it would incur a $10,000 loss, as follows:

Costs so far	$ 75,000
Estimated remaining costs	35,000
Estimated total costs	$110,000
Selling price	100,000
Loss	$ 10,000

Prepare the journal entries for all 3 years.

SOLUTION

	19A		19B		19C	
Construction in Process	50,000		...25,000		...35,000	
Miscellaneous		50,000		25,000		35,000
Accounts Receivable	50,000		...25,000		...25,000	
Billings		50,000		25,000		25,000
Cash	50,000		...20,000		...30,000	
Accounts Receivable		50,000		20,000		30,000

In 19B an additional entry would be made recognizing the $10,000 loss:

Loss on Construction	10,000	
Construction in Process		10,000

In 19C an entry would also be made to close the billings and construction accounts, as follows:

Billings	100,000		
Construction in Process		100,000	[Section 6.5]

Installment Sales

6.6   The Widget Corporation had the following data relating to its installment sales for 19X1 and 19X2:

	19X1	19X2
Installment sales	$50,000	$80,000
Cost of goods sold	35,000	60,000
Gross profit	$15,000	$20,000
Collections on 19X1 sales	$25,000	$25,000
Collections on 19X2 sales	—	60,000

Assume that collections on these sales are not reasonably assured, and therefore the use of the installment method is appropriate. Prepare journal entries for both years.

SOLUTION

The gross profit percentages are:

$$19X1: \quad \frac{15,000}{50,000} = 30\%$$

$$19X2: \quad \frac{20,000}{80,000} = 25\%$$

		19X1		19X2	
Accounts Receivable		50,000		...80,000	
	Sales		50,000		80,000
Cost of Goods Sold		35,000		...60,000	
	Merchandise Inventory		35,000		60,000
Cash		25,000		...85,000	
	Accounts Receivable		25,000		85,000
Dec. 31	Sales	50,000		...80,000	
	Costs of Goods Sold		35,000		60,000
	Deferred Gross Profit		15,000		20,000
Deferred Gross Profit		7,500*		...22,500†	
	Realized Gross Profit		7,500		22,500

*.30 × $25,000
†.30 × $25,000 = $ 7,500
+ .25 × $60,000 =   15,000
                  $22,500

[Section 6.7]

6.7   In the previous problem, show partial balance sheets for each year.

SOLUTION

    19X1

Accounts Receivable	$25,000 ($50,000 − $25,000)
Less Deferred Gross Profit	− 7,500 ($15,000 − $7,500)
Net Receivable	$17,500

    19X2

Accounts Receivable	$20,000 ($50,000 − $25,000 + $80,000 − $85,000)
Less Deferred Gross Profit	− 5,000 ($15,000 − $7,500 + $20,000 − $22,500)
Net Receivable	$15,000

[Section 6.7]

6.8   At the time a customer defaulted on the installment payments, the Accounts Receivable and Deferred Gross Profit accounts had balances of $15,000 and $3,000, respectively. The merchandise fair market value at this point was $10,000, and was repossessed. Prepare the required journal entry.

SOLUTION

Repossessed Merchandise	10,000	
Deferred Gross Profit	3,000	
Loss on Repossession	2,000	
Accounts Receivable		15,000

[Section 6.7]

6.9   A customer's Accounts Receivable balance is $30,000 and the gross profit percentage is 20% on sales. The customer defaults and the merchandise, having a fair market value of $27,000, is repossessed.
(1)   What is the balance of the Deferred Gross Profit account?
(2)   Show what the Accounts Receivable and Deferred Gross Profit accounts look like.
(3)   Prepare the entry for the repossession.

SOLUTION

(1) $6,000 (.20 \times $30,000)$

(2)

Accounts Receivable		Deferred Gross Profit	
30,000			6,000

(3)

Repossessed Merchandise	27,000	
Deferred Gross Profit	6,000	
Accounts Receivable		30,000
Gain on Repossession		3,000

[Section 6.7]

6.10 A company sells goods for $10,000, payable in one installment per year for 3 years, including interest at 12%. The cost of these goods is $8,000.
  (1) Determine the gross profit percentage on selling price.
  (2) Determine the amount of each installment payment.
  (3) Prepare a table showing the journal entry and the realized gross profit for each payment.

SOLUTION

(1)

$$\frac{2,000^*}{10,000} = 20\%$$

$$^*(\$10,000 - \$8,000)$$

(2)

$$\frac{10,000}{\text{Present value annuity \$1, 3 periods, 12\%}} = \frac{10,000}{2.40183} = \$4,163.49$$

Date	Cash (Dr.)	Interest Revenue (Cr.)	Accounts Receivable (Cr.)	Accounts Receivable Balance	Realized Gross Profit
At sale	—	—	—	$10,000	—
End of year 1	$4,163.49	$1,200*	$2,963.49†	7,036.51‡	$592.70§
End of year 2	4,163.49	844.38	3,319.11	3,717.40	663.82
End of year 3	4,163.49	446.09	3,717.40	—	743.48

*This is 12% of the Accounts Receivable balance.
†This is the cash (Dr.) minus the interest revenue.
‡This is the previous Accounts Receivable balance minus the current credit.
§This is 20% of the Accounts Receivable credit.

[Section 6.7]

The Cost Recovery Method

6.11 The Very Poor Company is involved in making installment sales whose probability of collection is extremely low. Accordingly, it has elected to use the cost recovery method. Information regarding the years 19A and 19B is as follows:

	19A	19B
Installment sales	$50,000	$80,000
Cost of goods sold	35,000	60,000
Gross profit	$15,000	$20,000
Collections on 19A sales	$25,000	$15,000
Collections on 19B sales	—	40,000

Prepare entries for both years.

SOLUTION

	19A		19B	
Accounts Receivable	50,000		...80,000	
Sales		50,000		80,000
Cost of Goods Sold	35,000		...60,000	
Merchandise Inventory		35,000		60,000
Cash	25,000		...55,000	
Accounts Receivable		25,000		55,000
Sales	50,000		...80,000	
Cost of Goods Sold		35,000		60,000
Deferred Gross Profit		15,000		20,000

No profit recognition since the cost has not yet been recovered.

Deferred Gross Profit	5,000*	
Realized Gross Profit		5,000

---

*5,000 of $15,000 collection on 19A Sales. Nothing on the 19B collection since the cost has not yet been recovered.

[Section 6.8]

Supplementary Problems

6.12　Company A has the following information regarding a construction project whose selling price is $400,000:

	19A	19B	19C	Total
Costs incurred	$100,000	$150,000	$ 60,000	$310,000
Billings	100,000	170,000	130,000	400,000
Collections	100,000	120,000	180,000	400,000
Expected completion costs	250,000	50,000	—	—

　　　Prepare entries for each year under the completed-contract method. In addition, present a partial balance sheet and income statement.

6.13　For the previous problem, prepare entries for each year under the percentage-of-completion method and show a partial balance sheet and income statement.

6.14　Company C uses the percentage-of-completion method for construction projects. During 19A and 19B it incurred construction costs of $10,000 and $20,000 respectively, and it expects to incur another $40,000 additional costs in the future. In 19A, it recognized $5,000 profit. The total contract price is $100,000. How much profit should Company C recognize in 19B?

6.15　In the previous problem, if Company C used the completed-contract method, how much profit should it recognize in 19B? In 19A? Why?

6.16　In 19C Company D determines it will incur a $50,000 loss on a construction project. Prepare the required journal entry if:
　(a)　the company uses the completed-contract method;
　(b)　the company uses the percentage-of-completion method and recognized profits of $10,000 and $15,000, respectively, in 19A and 19B.

6.17   S & W Metals, Inc. had the following information regarding its installment sales for 19A and 19B:

	19A	19B
Installment sales	$300,000	$500,000
Cost of goods sold	180,000	350,000
Gross profit	$120,000	$150,000
Gross profit %	?	?
Collections on 19A sales	$140,000	$160,000
Collections on 19B sales	None	$400,000

Prepare all necessary entries for both years.

6.18   For the previous problem, show partial balance sheets and income statements for each year.

6.19   Company K had an account receivable on an installment sale in the amount of $10,000. At the time the related deferred gross profit was $4,000, the customer defaulted and the merchandise was repossessed, with a fair market value of $3,000. Prepare the required journal entry.

6.20   Company L makes a sale of $12,000 which is payable over 3 years (one installment payment per year) including interest of 10%.
   (*a*)   How much is each installment payment?
   (*b*)   Prepare a table that indicates for each year the necessary journal entry and the amount of realized gross profit.

6.21   Company M uses the cost recovery method. During 19A, it sells goods with a cost of $15,000 for $25,000, payable in installments of $10,000, $10,000 and $5,000, respectively, beginning in 19A. How much profit should be recognized each year?

Examination II

Chapters 4, 5, 6

A. True-False Questions. Place the Letter T or F next to the question.

1. _____ Basic EPS is determined by dividing the net income (less preferred dividends) by common shares outstanding and common stock equivalents.

2. _____ For primary EPS, the interest rate on convertible bonds must be at least two-thirds of the Aa rate.

3. _____ If preferred stock is cumulative, its dividend must be subtracted in the numerator regardless of whether or not declared.

4. _____ For fully diluted EPS and stock options, the average market price of the stock is used to determine the number of shares repurchased for the treasury.

5. _____ The exercise of stock options only affects the denominator of EPS, not the numerator.

6. _____ Preferred stock conversions affect the denominator but not the numerator.

7. _____ For primary EPS, the bond conversion privilege must be exercisable *after* 5 years; for fully diluted EPS, *after* 10 years.

8. _____ If convertible bonds were outstanding for only a fraction of the year rather than for a whole year, this must be taken into account in the denominator, but not in the numerator.

9. _____ An investment is considered temporary if it is readily marketable, *or* the intention is to convert it to cash within 1 year (or the operating cycle).

10. _____ Broker's fees on the purchase of securities are considered to be expenses.

11. _____ If the market price falls below cost, the difference is considered a *realized* loss.

12. _____ Both debt securities and equity securities receive the LCM treatment.

13. _____ Discounts and premiums on short-term debt securities are *not* amortized.

14. _____ If a bond is purchased between interest dates, the increase in the bond price for accrued interest increases interest revenue to the buyer.

15. _____ The equity method should be used if 20 to 50% of the subsidiary's stock is purchased.

16. _____ Stock dividends increase cost per share.

17. _____ The cash surrender value of life insurance is considered to be an expense.

18. _____ Under the percentage-of-completion method, the annual profit is debited to the Billings account.

19. _____ The billings account is considered to be a contra asset.

20. _____ Under the installment method, the entire revenue is recognized when the last installment has been collected.

21. _____ If merchandise is repossessed, it is recorded at its fair market value.

B. Completion Questions. Fill in the blanks.

22. When bonds are converted into stock, the stock is recorded at _____ value rather than at _____ value.

23. Rights to purchase shares of stock at a fixed price are called stock _____ or stock _____ .

24. A stock option plan that does not meet the four special conditions is considered to be a _____ plan.

25. On the date of the grant for a stock option plan, the account to be debited is _____ .

26. Special rights that grant the holder to receive cash based on the difference between the grant price of the stock and the market price are called _____ .

27. The three types of earnings per share are _____ , _____ , and _____ .

28. For one type of earnings per share, the interest rate on convertible bonds must be less than _____ the _____ rate.

29. For basic earnings per share, if the preferred stock is noncumulative, then its dividends are subtracted in the numerator only if _____ .

30. For fully diluted earnings per share, convertible bonds or preferred stock must be convertible within _____ years.

31. Short-term stock investments that can easily be sold and whose intention is to sell them within 1 year (or the operating cycle) are called _____ .

32. If short-term stock or bond investments are transferred to the long-term category, they should be transferred at the _____ value, and a _____ loss should be recognized.

33. The two methods of accounting for long-term investments in equity securities are the _____ method and the _____ method.

34. The three possible courses of action one can take with stock rights are: _____ , _____ , or _____ .

35. Revenue is usually recognized when it is both _____ and _____ .

36. The two methods of accounting for long-term construction contracts are the _____ method and the _____ method.

37. The billings account is not a _____ account; rather it is a _____ to the construction account.

38. The method of revenue recognition that recognizes revenue piecemeal based upon the gross profit percentage is called the _____ method.

39. Under the above method, each year's profit is temporarily placed into an account called _____ .

40. A revenue recognition method that recognizes revenue only after the total cost has been received is called the _____ method.

C. Problems

41. During 19X9, GX Corporation had net income of $100,000, 1,000 shares of common stock outstanding, and 1,000 shares of 5%, $100 par, cumulative preferred stock outstanding. The preferred shares are con-

vertible into 500 shares of common stock in 3 years. GX also had a $100,000 par bond, 10%, convertible into 1,000 shares of common stock in 3 years. This bond was outstanding only from July 1. The Aa bond rate is 12%; the tax rate is 20%. Find:

(*a*)   Basic earnings per share

(*b*)   Primary earnings per share

(*c*)   Fully diluted earnings per share

Assume both the bonds and preferred stock were issued at par.   [Chapter 4]

42.   Corporation A purchased 25% of Corporation B's 100,000 shares of outstanding stock at a price of $1.00 per share. During the first year after acquisition, Corporation B incurred a net loss of $10,000 and distributed a dividend of 50 cents per share. On December 31, the market price per share was 90 cents. Prepare entries for these transactions using:

(*a*)   The cost method (assume no significant influence).

(*b*)   The equity method.

Assume these shares are a long-term investment.   [Chapter 5]

43.   Corporation D purchases 1,000 shares of stock for $100,000. It then receives 1,000 stock rights enabling it to purchase 500 additional shares (two rights are needed per share) at $60 per share. At this time the market price per share and per right are $80 and $15, respectively. It then exercises 500 rights, sells 250 rights at $20 each, and allows the remaining 250 rights to expire.

Prepare journal entries for all the foregoing.   [Chapter 5]

44.   The following data relate to a construction project of Construction Corporation that has a contract price of $200,000:

	19A	19B	Total
Costs incurred	$ 60,000	$ 90,000	$150,000
Billings	100,000	100,000	200,000
Collections	80,000	120,000	200,000
Estimated remaining costs at year-end	80,000	—	—

Prepare entries for this information using the percentage-of-completion method.   [Chapter 6]

45.   Foolish Corporation had the following information relating to its installment sales for 19X1 and 19X2, for which it uses the installment method of accounting:

	19X1	19X2
Installment sales	$50,000	$80,000
Cost of goods sold	35,000	60,000
Gross profit	$15,000	$20,000
Collections on 19X1 sales	$25,000	$25,000
Collections on 19X2 sales	—	70,000

Prepare journal entries for these transactions.   [Chapter 6]

Answers to Examination II

A.   True-False Questions

1. F   2. F   3. T   4. F   5. T   6. F   7. F   8. F   9. F   10. F   11. F   12. T   13. T
14. F   15. T   16. F   17. F   18. F   19. T   20. F   21. T

B. Completion Questions

22. book; market   **23.** options; warrants   **24.** compensatory   **25.** deferred compensation cost   **26.** stock appreciation rights   **27.** basic; primary; fully diluted   **28.** 2/3; Aa   **29.** declared   **30.** 10   **31.** marketable equity securities   **32.** LCM; realized   **33.** cost; equity   **34.** sale; exercise; lapse   **35.** realized; earned   **36.** completed-contract; percentage-of-completion   **37.** revenue; contra asset   **38.** installment   **39.** deferred gross profit   **40.** cost recovery

C. Problems

41. (a) $\dfrac{Basic \text{ earnings}}{\text{per share}} = \dfrac{100,000 - 5,000}{1,000} = \$95$

(b) $\dfrac{Primary \text{ earnings}}{\text{per share}} = \dfrac{100,000}{1,000 + 500} = \$66.67$

(The preferred stock is considered a common stock equivalent; the bond is not)

(c) $\dfrac{Fully\ diluted \text{ earnings}}{\text{per share}} = \dfrac{100,000 + .80(.5 \times 10,000)}{1,000 + 500 + .5(1,000)} = \$52$

42. (a) Cost Method

Investment in Long-term Equity Securities	25,000	
Cash		25,000
25,000 shares × $1.00		
No entry for the net loss		
Cash	12,500	
Dividend Revenue		12,500 (.50 × 25,000)
Unrealized Loss Due to Market Decline	2,500	
Allowance to Reduce Long-term Securities to Market		2,500

(b) Equity Method

Investment in Long-term Equity Securities	25,000	
Cash		25,000
Investment Loss	2,500	
Investment in Long-term Equity Securities		2,500
Cash	12,500	
Investment in Long-term Equity Securities		12,500
No entry for lower-of-cost-or market		

43.

Investment in Equity Securities	100,000	
Cash		100,000
Investment in Stock Rights	15,789.47	
Investment in Equity Securities		15,789.47*

$$*\frac{15}{95} \times \$100,000$$

The cost per right is 15,789.47 ÷ 1,000 = $15.79
For the exercise:

Investment in Equity Securities	22,895	
Cash		15,000*
Investment in Stock Rights		7,895†

*250 shares × $60
†500 × $15.79

For the sale:

Cash	5,000		
Investment in Stock Rights*		3,947.50	
Gain on Sale of Rights		1,052.50	

*$15.79 × 250

For the expiration:

Loss on Expiration of Stock Rights	3,947.50	
Investment in Stock Rights		3,947.50

44.

	19A		19B	
Construction in Process	60,000		...90,000	
Miscellaneous Credits		60,000		90,000
Accounts Receivable	100,000		...100,000	
Billings on Construction		100,000		100,000
Cash	80,000		...120,000	
Accounts Receivable		80,000		120,000
Construction in Process	25,714		...24,286	
Profit on Construction		25,714*		24,286†

$$* \quad \frac{60,000}{60,000 + 80,000} \times (200,000 - 140,000)$$

$$†\frac{150,000}{150,000} \times (200,000 - 150,000) - 25,714$$

There is one additional entry in 19B:

Billings on Construction	200,000	
Construction in Process		200,000

45. The gross profit percentages for 19X1 and 19X2 are 30% and 25%, respectively (15/50 and 20/80).

	19X1		19X2	
Accounts Receivable	50,000		...80,000	
Sales		50,000		80,000
Cost of Goods Sold	35,000		...60,000	
Merchandise Inventory		35,000		60,000
Cash	25,000		...95,000	
Accounts Receivable		25,000		95,000
Sales	50,000		...80,000	
Cost of Goods Sold		35,000		60,000
Deferred Gross Profit		15,000		20,000
Deferred Gross Profit	7,500		...25,000	
Realized Gross Profit		7,500		25,000
	(.30 × $25,000)		(.30 × $25,000 + .25 × $70,000)	

Chapter 7

Accounting for Leases

7.1 INTRODUCTION

In a lease arrangement, the owner-lessor agrees to rent an asset (machinery, equipment, land, or building) to the tenant-lessee for a set number of periods at a fixed rental fee per period.

Leases can be broadly classified as either operating leases or capital leases. If the lease agreement transfers a "material ownership interest" from the lessor to the lessee, it is a *capital lease*. If not, it is an *operating lease*. Material ownership interests, operating leases, capital leases, and sales-leaseback arrangements are the subjects of this chapter and will be discussed in detail in the following pages.

7.2 OPERATING LEASES

Operating leases are the simplest type of lease arrangement from an accounting viewpoint. The rentals are considered to be revenue to the owner-lessor and expenses to the tenant-lessee. If rentals are received in advance, they should be recorded as unearned rent (a liability) by the lessor and as prepaid rent (an asset) by the lessee. As time goes by, adjusting entries should be made to slowly recognize these items as revenue and expense, respectively. In addition, the lessor should be the one to record the annual depreciation entry since the asset still belongs to him or her.

EXAMPLE 1

On January 1, 19X1, Lessor rents a building for 3 years to Lessee at a fixed rental of $6,000 per year. The total rental of $18,000 is received immediately. The building cost Lessor $25,000 and has a life of 5 years with no salvage value. The entries for year 1 are:

		Lessor				*Lessee*		
Jan.	1	Cash	18,000		Prepaid Rent	18,000	
		Unearned Rent		18,000	Cash		18,000
Dec.	31	Unearned Rent	6,000		Rent Expense	6,000	
		Rent Revenue		6,000	Prepaid Rent		6,000
Dec.	31	Depreciation Expense	5,000				
		Accumulated Depreciation		5,000	No entry		

On December 31, 19X2 and 19X3, entries would once again be made by both parties to recognize $6,000 as revenue and expense, respectively.

If there are any initial direct costs incurred by the lessor in consummating the lease agreement, they should be debited to an intangible asset account and then gradually be amortized and matched against the annual revenue. Such costs include legal fees, credit report fees, accounting fees, and commissions.

EXAMPLE 2

If in the previous example Lessor incurred $600 of initial direct costs, then Lessor would make the following entry:

Lease Initiation Fees	600	
Cash		600

In addition, Lessor would also make the following entry each December 31:

Lease Initiation Expense	200	
Lease Initiation Fees		200*

---

*600 ÷ 3

7.3 CAPITAL LEASES

If a lease agreement fulfills certain conditions that indicate that a transfer of a "material ownership interest" has taken place, the lease requires special accounting treatment. *Material ownership interest* has been defined as a transfer of most of the risks and rewards of ownership.

Fulfillment of *any* one of the following conditions indicates a material ownership interest:

1. The lease agreement transfers title to the lessee at the end of the lease term.

2. The lessee has the option of buying the asset at a bargain price ("bargain purchase option" or "BPO") at the end of the lease term.

3. The present value of the annual annuity of rentals is greater than, or equal to, 90% of the fair market value of the lease at the lease inception date.

4. The lease term is equal to 75% or more of the asset's life.

What is the "special accounting treatment" required if any one of these conditions is fulfilled? The answer is that we "make-believe" the lessor *sold* this asset to the lessee instead of *renting* it to the lessee. Each annual rental payment is thus not a "rental" but an installment payment on the selling price. Even though the *legal form* of this agreement is that of a *rental*, the *economic substance* of this agreement is that of a *sale*. This is one more example of a situation where the accounting profession has chosen to emphasize a transaction's substance over its form. Because this transaction transfers a material ownership interest and so closely resembles a sale, not to recognize it as such would make this company's financial statements incomparable to the statements of a company that actually made a "real" sale.

In addition to the four conditions mentioned earlier, two additional conditions must both be met for the *lessor* to treat this transaction as a sale. They are:

1. Collectibility of the lease payments must be reasonably assured.

2. No important uncertainties surround the amount of unreimbursable costs yet to be incurred by the lessor under the lease agreement.

If these conditions have not been met, then the *lessor* would *not* consider the transaction to be a sale, while the *lessee would*. The result is ironic: Two parties to the same agreement treat this agreement in two different accounting ways.

Leases that meet any one of the four conditions mentioned (and the two additional conditions for the lessor) are referred to as *capital leases*. There are two types of capital leases: direct financing and sales-type. In a *direct financing* lease, the lessor does not make a profit at the time of sale; in a *sales-type* the lessor does.

EXAMPLE 3

Lessor rents a building with a life of 4 years to Lessee for 3 years. Let's assume that the two special conditions for the lessor have been met. This is considered a capital lease since the lease life is 75% of the building's life.

EXAMPLE 4

Lessor rents a building with a life of 4 years to Lessee for 2 years. Thus the 75% test has not been met. However, the fair market value of the building is $100,000 and the present value of the rentals is $92,000. Since the present value is greater than or equal to 90% of the fair market value, this is a capital lease.

EXAMPLE 5

Lessor rents a building to Lessee that has a cost to Lessor of $100,000. If the present value of the lease payments is greater than $100,000, then Lessor has made a profit and the lease is thus considered to be a sales-type lease.

7.4 DIRECT FINANCING LEASES

As mentioned previously, if the lease agreement meets the necessary conditions for a capital lease and the lessor does not make a profit on the sale, the lease is a direct financing lease, and the asset is considered to have been sold. Each annual payment on the lease is not a rental payment, but a partial payment of the purchase price obligation. Interest accrues annually on this obligation and must be recorded. Annual depreciation is recorded by the lessee since he or she is now considered to be the owner.

The annual lease payment is determined by the lessor using the following formula:

$$\frac{\text{Selling price}}{\text{Present value of annuity, at rate } i, \text{ for } n \text{ periods}}$$

EXAMPLE 6

Lessor leases a building to Lessee for 4 years starting January 1, 19A. Both the cost to Lessor and the selling price are $50,000. There will be four lease payments, with the first one starting immediately on January 1, 19A. (Thus we are dealing with an annuity due situation). The building has a 4-year life with no salvage value. Lessor's target rate of return is 10%. This lease meets the 75% test (the lease term is at least 75% of the life — here it is 100% of the life) and is therefore, a capital lease. Using the above formula, the annual lease payment is:

$$\frac{\$50,000}{\text{present value annuity due, 10\%, 4 periods}} = \frac{\$50,000}{3.48685} = \$14,339.59$$

Both the lessor and lessee will make entries on their books indicating that a sale/purchase has taken place. The lessor will credit the asset and debit a receivable; the lessee will debit the asset and credit a payable for the present value of the annuity of lease payments.

If the lessee is *not* aware of the target rate used by the lessor, then the lessee should use his or her own "incremental borrowing rate" — the rate the lessee would pay to borrow funds in the market. If the lessee *is* aware of the lessor's target rate, then he or she should use the lower of the two rates.

EXAMPLE 7

Let's assume in the previous example that both rates are 10%. The following entries will be made by both parties for 19A:

	Lessor				*Lessee*		
Jan. 1, 19A	Lease Receivable	50,000			Building	50,000	
	Building		50,000		Lease Payable		50,000
Jan. 1, 19A	Cash	14,339.59			Lease Payable	14,339.59	
	Lease Receivable		14,339.59		Cash		14,339.59
Dec. 31, 19A	Lease Receivable	3,566.04*			Interest Expense	3,566.04	
	Interest Revenue		3,566.04		Lease Payable		3,566.04

*($50,000 − 14,339.59) × 10%

Dec. 31, 19A	No entry				Depreciation Expense	12,500†	
					Accumulated Depreciation		12,500

†$50,000 ÷ 4 years

The entries for the following years would be the same except that the amount for the interest entry would change. It is helpful to prepare an amortization table to determine the annual interest and Lease Receivable/Payable balances.

EXAMPLE 8

If we use the same information as in the previous examples, the amortization table would appear as follows:

(1) Date	(2) Payment	(3) Interest	(4) Change in Receivable/Payable	(5) Balance of Receivable/Payable
Jan. 1, 19A	—	—	—	$50,000.00
Jan. 1, 19A	$14,339.59	—	$(14,339.59)	35,660.41
Dec. 31, 19A	—	$3,566.04	3,566.04	39,226.45
Jan. 1, 19B	14,339.59	—	(14,339.59)	24,886.86
Dec. 31, 19B	—	2,488.69	2,488.69	27,375.55
Jan. 1, 19C	14,339.59	—	(14,339.59)	13,035.96
Dec. 31, 19C	—	1,303.60	1,303.60	14,339.56
Jan. 1, 19D	14,339.59	—	(14,339.59)	−0−
				(rounded)

Column 3 is the balance of column 5 multiplied by 10%. To column 5 we add the interest accrual, and subtract the lease payment.

In addition to annual lease payments, a lease agreement may require the lessee to pay the annual costs of maintaining the asset. These costs include insurance, security, maintenance, etc. Such costs should *not* be capitalized by the lessee as part of the cost of the asset but should be considered an expense of the period. These costs are called *executory costs*.

7.5 SALES-TYPE LEASES

In a sales-type lease the lessor sets a selling price above the asset cost, thus recognizing an immediate profit at the inception of the lease. Accordingly, the selling price, not the cost, will be used in the numerator in determining the annual rentals, and the amortization table will be based on this price as well.

EXAMPLE 9

Lessor leases a machine having a 3-year life to Lessee for a 3-year lease period. The cost to Lessor was $20,000; the selling price is $25,000. The annual rentals begin immediately on January 1, 19A.

Lessor's target rate of return is 10% and this rate is known to Lessee. However Lessee's own incremental rate is 12%. Because Lessor's rate of 10% is the lower of the two rates, it must also be used by Lessee.

The annual rental is computed as follows:

$$\frac{\$25,000}{\text{Present value annuity due, 10\%, 3 periods}} = \frac{\$25,000}{2.73554} = \$9,138.96$$

The entries for 19A are:

	Lessor				Lessee		
Jan. 1	Lease Receivable	25,000			Machine	25,000	
	Machine		20,000		Lease Payable		25,000
	Profit on Lease		5,000				
Jan. 1	Cash	9,138.96			Lease Payable	9,138.96	
	Lease Receivable		9,138.96		Cash		9,138.96
Dec. 31	Lease Receivable	1,586.10			Interest Expense	1,586.10	
	Interest Revenue		1,586.10		Lease Payable		1,586.10
Dec. 31	No entry				Depreciation Expense	8,333.33*	
					Accumulated Depreciation		8,333.33

*25,000 ÷ 3

The amortization table would appear as follows:

Date	Payment	Interest	Change in Receivable/Payable	Balance of Receivable/Payable
Jan. 1, 19A	—	—	—	$25,000.00
Jan. 1, 19A	$9,138.96	—	$(9,138.96)	15,861.04
Dec. 31, 19A	—	$1,586.10	1,586.10	17,447.14
Jan. 1, 19B	9,138.96	—	(9,138.96)	8,308.18
Dec. 31, 19B	—	830.82	830.82	9,139.00
Jan. 1, 19C	9,138.96	—	(9,138.96)	–0–
				(rounded)

For both direct financing and sales-type leases, the lease agreement may specify that under certain conditions the lease terminates early and the asset reverts back to the lessor. In these cases, the lessor will debit the asset at the lower of its original cost or present fair market value, remove the lease receivable, and recognize any gain or loss. The lessee will also remove the lease payable from his or her books and recognize a loss or gain as well.

EXAMPLE 10

In the previous example assume that the lease terminates on December 31, 19A, when the balance of the lease receivable/payable is $17,447.14. The fair market value of the machine at this point is $15,000. The entries are:

Lessor			*Lessee*		
Machine	15,000		Lease Payable	17,447.14	
Loss on Lease Termination	2,447.14		Accumulated Depreciation	8,333.33	
Lease Receivable		17,447.14	Gain on Lease Termination		780.47
			Machine		25,000

7.6 BARGAIN PURCHASE OPTIONS

In all the previous examples, the asset had no salvage value at the end of the lease term. If it *does* have a salvage value, the lease agreement may sometimes specify that the lessee has the option of either returning the asset at that date or purchasing the salvage value at a bargain price. This is called a *bargain purchase option* (*BPO*).

When such an option exists, the lessor assumes that the lessee will indeed take advantage of this bargain and purchase the asset (because few people pass up a bargain!). Thus the lessor expects two types of cash flows from this lease agreement:

1. The annuity of annual rentals
2. The purchase price at lease termination (not an annuity)

Accordingly, in the determination of the annual rental, the lessor must first subtract the present value of the bargain payment.

EXAMPLE 11

Lessor enters into an agreement with Lessee on January 1, 19A, for the 3-year rental of a machine. The machine has a 4-year life with a salvage value of $7,000 after 3 years and zero at the end of 4 years. Lessor's cost and selling price are both $30,000. The interest rate for both parties is 10%. Lessee has an option to purchase this machine after 3 years for a bargain price of $5,000. There are no uncertainties regarding collection of rentals or future costs, and the first payment is due on January 1, 19A.

This lease qualifies as a capital lease for both parties (direct financing type) since there are no cost uncertainties and it meets two of the four conditions mentioned earlier, namely:

1. The lease term is 75% of the asset life.
2. There is a bargain purchase option.

Lessor calculates the annual rental as follows:

Selling price	$30,000.00
Less Present value of $5,000, 3 periods, 10%:	
.75131 × $5,000	3,756.55
Amount to be recovered from annual rentals	$26,243.45

This amount is now divided by the present value of an annuity for 3 periods at 10%, as follows:

$$\text{Annual rental} = \frac{\$26,243.45}{2.73554} = \$9,593.52$$

The entries for both parties in 19A are:

		Lessor			*Lessee*		
Jan.	1	Lease Receivable	30,000		Machine	30,000	
		Machine		30,000	Lease Payable		30,000
Jan.	1	Cash	9,593.52		Lease Payable	9,593.52	
		Lease Receivable		9,593.52	Cash		9,593.52
Dec. 31		Lease Receivable	2,040.65		Interest Expense	2,040.65	
		Interest Income		2,040.65	Lease Payable		2,040.65
		No entry			Depreciation Expense	7,500*	
					Accumulated Depreciation		7,500

*$30,000 ÷ 4

Notice that Lessee uses a 4-year life for depreciation purposes because we assume that the bargain purchase option will be exercised.

The amortization table is as follows:

Date	Payment	Interest	Change in Receivable/Payable	Balance of Receivable/Payable
Jan. 1, 19A	—	—	—	$30,000.00
Jan. 1, 19A	$9,593.52	—	$(9,593.52)	20,406.48
Dec. 31, 19A	—	$2,040.65	2,040.65	22,447.13
Jan. 1, 19B	9,593.52	—	(9,593.52)	12,853.61
Dec. 31, 19B	—	1,285.36	1,285.36	14,138.97
Jan. 1, 19C	9,593.52	—	(9,593.52)	4,545.45
Dec. 31, 19C	—	454.55	454.55	5,000.00

Notice the $5,000 balance in the Lease Receivable/Payable account at this point. This is the bargain purchase option. If Lessee now exercises this option, the entries are:

Lessor			Lessee		
Dec. 31, 19C Cash	5,000		Lease Payable	5,000	
Lease Receivable		5,000	Cash		5,000

If not, the asset reverts back to Lessor, who would record it at its fair market value of $7,000, and the entries would be:

Lessor			Lessee		
Machine	7,000		Lease Payable	5,000	
Lease Receivable		5,000	Loss on Lapse of		
Gain on Lapse of			Lease Option	2,500	
Lease Option		2,000	Accumulated Depreciation	22,500	
			Machine		30,000

7.7 SALVAGE VALUE—UNGUARANTEED

If the asset has a salvage value at the end of the lease term, this value may either be purchased at a bargain price (a BPO), kept by the lessee "for free," or returned to the lessor. The BPO situation has already been discussed. In the situation where the salvage value is kept by the lessee, no special recognition is given to this salvage except for the depreciation calculation. The lessee would depreciate the asset over its life rather than over the lease life, and would also subtract the salvage existing at the end of the *asset's life,* rather than the salvage value at the end of the *lease life.*

A different situation arises where the salvage value must be returned to the lessor. In this case, such salvage value may be either guaranteed or unguaranteed by the lessee. If it is guaranteed, the lessee agrees to pay any difference between the guaranteed value and the actual value at the end of the lease term.

EXAMPLE 12

If the guaranteed salvage value is $10,000 but due to a lack of proper care the actual value is only $9,000, the lessee must pay the $1,000 difference in cash.

Let's first discuss the situation of an unguaranteed salvage value. In this case, the lessor (perhaps naively so!) assumes that he or she will get this salvage value back at lease termination, and thus takes this value into account in determining the annual rental. The lessee, on the other hand, does not make this assumption. We thus have an ironic situation in which the amount capitalized by the lessee will *not* be equal to the selling price of the lessor, the amortization tables will *not* be the same, and the journal entries will be *asymmetrical.*

EXAMPLE 13

Lessor rents a machine, cost of $60,000, to Lessee for 3 years. The salvage value at that time is $10,000, which is *unguaranteed.* The interest rate, known to both parties, is 10% and the lease meets all the requirements needed to qualify as a capital lease.

Lessor would calculate the annual rental as follows (assume the selling price is also $60,000):

Cost and selling price	$60,000.00
Less present value of $10,000, 3 periods, 10%:	
.75131 × $10,000	7,513.10
Amount to recover from annual rentals	$52,486.90
Divided by present value of annuity	÷
due, 3 periods, 10%	2.73554
Annual rental	$19,187.03

Lessee, however, would capitalize this machine for only $52,486.90 — the present value of the rentals, not for the full $60,000. Thus the respective amortization tables and annual interest will differ.

Lessor's table would appear as follows:

Date	Payment	Interest	Change in Receivable/Payable	Balance of Receivable/Payable
Jan. 1, 19A	—	—	—	$60,000.00
Jan. 1, 19A	$19,187.03	—	$(19,187.03)	40,812.97
Dec. 31, 19A	—	$4,081.30	4,081.30	44,894.27
Jan. 1, 19B	19,187.03	—	(19,187.03)	25,707.24
Dec. 31, 19B	—	2,570.72	2,570.72	28,277.96
Jan. 1, 19C	19,187.03	—	(19,187.03)	9,090.93
Dec. 31, 19C	—	909.09	909.09	10,000.00
				(rounded)

Notice the $10,000 balance at the end representing the salvage value.

Lessee's table would differ, as follows:

Date	Payment	Interest	Change in Receivable/Payable	Balance of Receivable/Payable
Jan. 1, 19A	—	—	—	$52,486.90
Jan. 1, 19A	$19,187.03	—	$(19,187.03)	33,299.87
Dec. 31, 19A	—	$3,329.99	3,329.99	36,629.86
Jan. 1, 19B	19,187.03	—	(19,187.03)	17,442.83
Dec. 31, 19B	—	1,744.28	1,744.28	19,187.11
Jan. 1, 19C	19,187.03	—	(19,187.03)	–0–
				(rounded)

Notice the zero balance at the end.

The entries for the first year would be:

	Lessor				Lessee		
Jan.	1	Lease Receivable	60,000		Machine	52,486.90	
		Machine		60,000	Lease Payable		52,486.90
Jan.	1	Cash	19,187.03		Lease Payable	19,187.03	
		Lease Receivable		19,187.03	Cash		19,187.03
Dec.	31	Lease Receivable	4,081.30		Interest Expense	3,329.99	
		Interest Revenue		4,081.30	Lease Payable		3,329.99
		No entry			Depreciation Expense	17,495.63*	
					Accumulated Depreciation		17,495.63

*$52,486.90 ÷ 3 years

Notice that Lessee ignores the salvage value in the depreciation calculation.

At the end of 19C, Lessee would return the machine to Lessor, and the entries would be:

Lessor			*Lessee*		
Machine	10,000		Accumulated Depreciation	52,486.90	
Lease Receivable		10,000	Machine		52,486.90

If the fair market value at this time is less than $10,000, then Lessor would debit a loss for the difference.

7.8   SALVAGE VALUE—GUARANTEED

In order to motivate the lessee to take better care of the asset, the lease agreement may require the lessee to *guarantee* a certain salvage value at lease termination. In this case, the lessee will capitalize the asset at the same selling price used by the lessor (by adding together the present value of both the annual rentals and the guaranteed salvage value). In addition, both tables will be the same, and the journal entries on the two sets of books will be symmetrical.

EXAMPLE 14

If we use the same information as in the previous example but assume that the salvage value is guaranteed, then both parties would capitalize the lease at $60,000, both amortization tables would appear as was shown for Lessor, and the journal entries for everyone will also be as shown for Lessor. Thus at the end of 19C, the table will show a balance of $10,000.

In this case, because the salvage value of $10,000 is guaranteed, it must be taken into account in the depreciation calculation. Thus annual depreciation will be $16,666.67 [($60,000 − 10,000) ÷ 3].

At the end of the lease term the lessee returns the asset to the lessor. If the salvage value is less than the guaranteed value, the lessee must pay the difference in cash and recognize a loss on this difference.

EXAMPLE 15

We once again refer back to the previous two examples. At the end of the lease term, the Lease Receivable/Payable account has a balance of $10,000. Let's assume the actual value is only $9,000. The entries are:

Lessor			*Lessee*		
Machine	9,000		Lease Payable	10,000	
Cash	1,000		Loss on Lease Termination	1,000	
Lease Receivable		10,000	Accumulated Depreciation	50,000	
			Cash		1,000
			Machine		60,000

7.9   SALE AND LEASEBACKS

If the owner of an asset sells it and then immediately leases it back from the buyer, this is referred to as a *sale-leaseback,* and the seller then continues to use the property without interruption.

The accounting profession has ruled that in this situation any gain on the sale should be deferred and recognized piecemeal over the life of the lease. If not for this restriction, the seller-lessee could sell the asset to the buyer-lessor for an unrealistic price in order to report a large gain on the sale. The seller-lessee could then lease the asset back at annual rentals whose present value is equal to the original selling price. The result is the reporting by the seller-lessee of a large "phantom" gain, despite his or her being in the same economic position as before. In order to prevent this, FASB No. 13 requires that the two transactions (sale and leaseback) be treated as a single transaction with the gain deferred.

If the lease meets the necessary criteria to be considered a capital lease, the gain is recognized gradually as a reduction of the annual depreciation expense. If not, it is considered a reduction of the annual rent expense.

EXAMPLE 16

Seller-Lessee sells an asset to Buyer-Lessor on January 1, 19A, for $100,000, and immediately leases it back for a 3-year period at a 10% interest rate. Seller-Lessee's original cost was $80,000 (thus the gain on the sale is $20,000) and the asset has no salvage value. Let's assume the criteria for a capital lease are *not* met and, accordingly, the lease is an operating lease.

The annual lease payment is:

$$\frac{\$100,000}{2.73554} = \$36,556 \text{ (rounded)}$$

The entries in the first year for both parties are:

	Seller-Lessee				Buyer-Lessor		
Jan. 1	Cash	100,000			Asset	100,000	
	Asset		80,000		Cash		100,000
	Unearned Gain on Sale-Leaseback*		20,000				
Jan. 1	Rent Expense	36,556			Cash	36,556	
	Cash		36,556		Rent Revenue		36,556
Dec. 31	No entry				Depreciation Expense	33,333.33[†]	
					Accumulated Depreciation		33,333.33

[†]$(100,000 \div 3)$

	Seller-Lessee				Buyer-Lessor		
Dec. 31	Unearned Gain on Sale-Leaseback	6,667.67			No entry		
	Rent Expense		6,667.67				
	$(20,000 \div 3)$						

*This is a liability account similar to other unearned accounts.

EXAMPLE 17

In the previous example, if the lease qualified as a capital lease, the entries would be:

	Seller-Lessee				Buyer-Lessor		
Jan. 1	Cash	100,000			Asset	100,000	
	Asset		80,000		Cash		100,000
	Unearned Gain on Sale-Leaseback		20,000				
Jan. 1	Asset	100,000			Lease Receivable	100,000	
	Lease Payable		100,000		Asset		100,000
Jan. 1	Lease Payable	36,556			Cash	36,556	
	Cash		36,556		Lease Receivable		36,556
Dec. 31	Interest Expense*	6,344.40			Lease Receivable	6,344.40	
	Lease Payable		6,344.40		Interest Revenue		6,344.40

*$(100,000 - 36,556).10$

	Seller-Lessee				Buyer-Lessor		
Dec. 31	Depreciation Expense	33,333.33			No entry		
	Accumulated Depreciation		33,333.33				
Dec. 31	Unearned Gain on Sale-Leaseback	6,667.67			No entry		
	Depreciation Expense		6,667.67				

Summary

1.   Leases can be broadly classified as either operating leases or capital leases. If there is a transfer of a "material ownership interest," it is a *capital lease*. Otherwise, it is an *operating lease*.

2. For operating leases the rentals are considered to be revenue to the owner-lessor and expenses to the tenant-lessee. If the rentals are paid in advance, they are recorded as unearned rent by the lessor and as prepaid rent by the lessee. These are then gradually amortized to revenue and expense, respectively. The annual depreciation should be recorded by the lessor since the asset still belongs to him or her.

3. Any initial direct costs incurred by the lessor in consummating the lease should be debited to an intangible asset account and then gradually be amortized and matched against revenue. Such costs include legal fees, accounting fees, and commissions.

4. Fulfillment of any one of the following conditions indicates a transfer of a material ownership interest and thus requires the lease to be treated as a capital lease:

    (1) The agreement transfers title to the lessee at the end of the lease term.

    (2) There is a bargain purchase option.

    (3) The present value of the rental annuity is greater than, or equal to, 90% of the asset's fair market value.

    (4) The lease term is equal to 75% or more of the asset's life.

5. Two additional conditions must both be met for the lessor to consider the lease a capital lease. They are:

    (1) Collectibility of the lease payments must be reasonably assured.

    (2) No important uncertainties surround the amount of unreimbursable costs yet to be incurred by the lessor.

    If these conditions have not been met, the lessee would consider this lease to be a capital lease; the lessor would not.

6. There are two types of capital leases: *direct financing* and *sales-type*. In a direct financing lease, the lessor does not make a profit at the time of sale, while in a sales-type lease, he or she does.

7. For capital leases, the annual lease payment is determined by the lessor under the following formula:

$$\frac{\text{Selling price}}{\text{Present value of annuity, at rate } i, \text{ for } n \text{ periods}}$$

8. For capital leases, the lessor and lessee will make entries on their respective books indicating that a sale/purchase has taken place. The lessor will credit the asset and debit a receivable; the lessee will debit the asset and credit a payable. Depreciation will be recorded by the lessee.

9. If the lessee is not aware of the interest rate used by the lessor, then the lessee should use his or her own incremental borrowing rate. If the lessee is aware of both rates, he or she should use the lower of the two rates.

10. Annual costs of insurance, security, and maintenance are referred to as *executory costs*. These costs, if paid by the lessee, should not be capitalized but expensed.

11. In the case of a *bargain purchase option (BPO)*, there are two types of cash flows: the rental annuity and the bargain price at lease termination. Both of these flows must be taken into account by the lessor in determining the annual rental fee.

12. If the asset has a salvage value at the end of the lease term which is kept by the lessee, then the depreciation period would be the asset life rather than the lease life, and the amount to subtract for salvage would be the salvage existing at the end of the *asset's life,* rather than at the end of the *lease life*.

13. If the asset has a salvage value at the end of the lease term which must be returned and is also *guaranteed* by the lessee, then the lessee should capitalize the asset for the sum of the present value of the annual rentals and the guaranteed salvage value.

14. In a *sale-leaseback* situation, the owner of an asset sells the asset and then immediately leases it back from the buyer. Any gain on such sale must be deferred and recognized piecemeal over the life of the lease. If the lease meets the required criteria for a capital lease, the gain is recognized gradually as a reduction of the annual depreciation expense. If not, it is considered a reduction of the annual rent expense.

Rapid Review

1. The two broad classifications of leases are _____ leases and _____ leases.

2. The original owner of the asset is called the _____; the new owner is called the _____.

3. The two types of capital leases are: _____ leases and _____ leases.

4. For the lessee, only _____ of _____ conditions need to be met for a lease to qualify as a capital lease; for the lessor, an additional _____ conditions are required.

5. The right to purchase the asset at the end of the lease term at a low price is called a _____.

6. If the lessor makes a profit at the time of the sale, the lease is a _____ lease.

7. If a lease qualifies as a capital lease, the party that records the depreciation is the _____.

8. The amount the lessee will debit the asset for is the _____.

9. If the lessee's interest rate is different from the lessor's rate, the _____ one should be used by the lessee.

10. In a BPO situation, the depreciation period to be used is the life of the _____ rather than the life of the _____.

11. If an asset is sold and then immediately leased back, this is a _____ situation.

12. In the above situation, the gain on sale must be _____.

13. Annual insurance and maintenance costs are called _____.

Answers: 1. operating; capital 2. lessor; lessee 3. direct finance; sales-type 4. one; four; two 5. bargain purchase option 6. sales-type 7. lessee 8. present value of the rentals 9. lower 10. asset; lease 11. sale and leaseback 12. deferred 13. executory costs

Solved Problems

Operating Leases

7.1   On January 1, 19A, Lessor rents a machine having a 5-year life to Lessee for a 3-year lease period. The lease agreement does not meet the necessary conditions for a capital lease.

On this date, Lessee pays the entire rental of $15,000 ($5,000 per year) and Lessor incurs initial direct costs of $1,200 in consummating the lease. This machine has a cost to Lessor of $25,000. Prepare the necessary entries for both parties for 19A.

SOLUTION

	Lessor			Lessee		
Jan. 1	Cash	15,000		Prepaid Rent	15,000	
	Unearned Rent		15,000	Cash		15,000
	Lease Initiation Fees	1,200		No entry		
	Cash		1,200			
Dec. 31	Lease Initiation Expense	400		No entry		
	Lease Initiation Fees		400			
	($1,200 ÷ 3)					
	Unearned Rent	5,000		Rent Expense	5,000	
	Rent Revenue		5,000	Prepaid Rent		5,000
	Depreciation Expense	5,000		No entry		
	Accumulated Depreciation		5,000			
	($25,000 ÷ 5)				[Section 7.2]	

Capital Leases

7.2 Lessor rents a building to Lessee for 5 years at an annual rental of $20,000. Lessor's cost of this building was $90,000 and the building has a life of 6 years. The applicable interest rate is 10%. There are no uncertainties regarding costs and collections.

(a) Is this a capital lease or operating lease? Why? Assume the annuity is an annuity due.

(b) If the rentals were only $12,000 per year, would your answer to part (a) be any different?

(c) If the life of the building was 9 years, the annual rental was $12,000, and there was a BPO option, how would your answer to part (a) change?

SOLUTION

(a) This is a capital lease because the present value of the annuity of $20,000 is $83,397, which is greater than 90% of the $90,000 cost.

(b) It would still be a capital lease because the lease life of 5 years is at least 75% of the building life of 6 years.

(c) Even though the lease life is now less than 75% of the building life, the lease is still a capital lease because of the BPO.   [Section 7.3]

7.3 Lessor rents a piece of equipment to Lessee for 9 years with annual rentals to begin immediately. The life of the equipment is 18 years and the target rate for Lessor is 8%. Lessor's cost was $100,000 and his or her selling price is $150,000. There are no uncertainties regarding collections or expenses.

(a) What is the amount of the annual rental?

(b) What type of lease is this to Lessee? To Lessor? Why?

SOLUTION

(a) $$\frac{\$150,000}{\text{Present value annuity due, 9 periods, 8\%}} = \frac{\$150,000}{6.74664} = \$22,233 \text{ (rounded)}$$

(b) It is a capital lease to Lessee because the present value of the rentals is at least 90% of the fair market value (it is 100%). It is also a capital lease to Lessor, for this reason plus the fact that there are no uncertainties regarding collections and expenses. This capital lease is a sales-type since Lessor has made a profit at the inception date.   [Sections 7.4, 7.5]

7.4 Lessee rents a building for a 3-year period at an annual rental of $10,000 beginning immediately. In addition, Lessee also agrees to pay annual maintenance and insurance fees of $1,000.

The building has a 3-year life with no salvage value at the end of its life. Lessor's interest rate is 10%, which is known to Lessee.

(a) What kind of costs are these maintenance and insurance fees?

(b) What type of lease is this to Lessee?

(c)   Should Lessee capitalize this lease? If yes, for how much?

(d)   What entries would Lessee prepare for the first year?

SOLUTION

(a)   They are an expense called "executory costs."

(b)   Capital lease (meets 75% test)

(c)   Yes, for $27,355.40 ($10,000 × 2.73554)

(d)

Jan.	1	Building	27,355.40	
		Lease Payable		27,355.40
Jan.	1	Lease Payable	10,000	
		Cash		10,000
Dec. 31		Interest Expense	1,735.54	
		Lease Payable		1,735.54
		($27,355.40 − $10,000) × 10%		
Dec. 31		Depreciation Expense	9,118.47	
		Accumulated Depreciation		9,118.47
		$27,355.40 ÷ 3		
Dec. 31		Executory Expense	1,000	
		Cash		1,000 [Section 7.4]

7.5   Lessor rents a building to Lessee for 3 years starting on January 1, 19A. Both the cost and the selling price to Lessor are $25,000. There will be three lease payments beginning January 1, 19A. The building has a 3-year life with no salvage value. Lessor's target rate of return is 8% and Lessee is aware of this rate. There are no uncertainties regarding costs or collections.

(a)   What type of lease is this? Why?

(b)   Compute the annual rental.

(c)   Prepare entries for both Lessor and Lessee for 19A.

(d)   Prepare an amortization table.

SOLUTION

(a)   It is a capital lease (direct financing type—no profit made at inception) to both parties because the lease life is at least 75% of the building life and there are no uncertainties.

(b)
$$\frac{\$25,000}{2.78326} = \$8,982.27$$

(c)   *Lessor*

Jan.	1	Lease Receivable	25,000	
		Building		25,000
		Cash	8,982.27	
		Lease Receivable		8,982.27
Dec. 31		Lease Receivable	1,281.42	
		Interest Revenue		1,281.42
		No entry		

Lessee

Building	25,000	
Lease Payable		25,000
Lease Payable	8,982.27	
Cash		8,982.27
Interest Expense	1,281.42	
Lease Payable		1,281.42
Depreciation Expense	8,333.33	
Accumulated Depreciation		8,333.33
($25,000 ÷ 3)		

(d)

Date	Payment	Interest (8%)	Change in Receivable/Payable	Balance of Receivable/Payable
Jan. 1, 19A	—	—	—	$25,000.00
Jan. 1, 19A	$8,982.27	—	$(8,982.27)	16,017.73
Dec. 31, 19A	—	$1,281.42	1,281.42	17,299.15
Jan. 1, 19B	8,982.27	—	(8,982.27)	8,316.88
Dec. 31, 19B	—	665.35	665.35	8,982.23
Jan. 1, 19C	8,982.27	—	(8,982.27)	–0–
				(rounded)

[Section 7.4]

7.6 Let's use the same information as in the previous problem except that the selling price is $35,000.
(a) What type of lease is this to Lessor?
(b) Compute the annual rental.
(c) Prepare entries for both Lessor and Lessee for 19A.

SOLUTION

(a) It is a capital lease, sales-type, since a profit is being made at inception.

(b)
$$\frac{\$35,000}{2.78326} = \$12,575.18$$

(c)

	Lessor				*Lessee*		
Jan. 1	Lease Receivable	35,000			Building	35,000	
	Building		25,000		Lease Payable		35,000
	Profit on Lease		10,000				
	Cash	12,575.18			Lease Payable	12,575.18	
	Lease Receivable		12,575.18		Cash		12,575.18
Dec. 31	Lease Receivable	1,793.99*			Interest Expense	1,793.99	
	Interest Revenue		1,793.99		Lease Payable		1,793.99

*($35,000 − $12,575.18) × 8%

No entry			Depreciation Expense	11,666.67	
			Accumulated Depreciation		11,666.67
			$35,000 ÷ 3		

[Section 7.5]

7.7 As a result of certain conditions specified in the lease agreement, a 3-year lease is terminated at the end of 2 years. At this time, the balance in the Lease Receivable/Payable account is $20,000, the fair market value of the asset is $17,000, and the accumulated depreciation is $30,000. The selling price was originally $45,000.

Prepare the entries on the books of both Lessor and Lessee for the termination.

SOLUTION

Lessor				*Lessee*		
Asset	17,000			Lease Payable	20,000	
Loss on Termination	3,000			Accumulated Depreciation	30,000	
Lease Receivable		20,000		Asset		45,000
				Gain on Termination		5,000

[Section 7.5]

Bargain Purchase Options

7.8   Lessor enters into an agreement with Lessee on January 1, 19A, for a 3-year rental of a machine. The machine has a 4-year life with a salvage value of $5,000 after 3 years and zero at the end of 4 years. Lessor's cost and selling price are both $25,000. Lessor's interest rate is 8%; Lessee's rate is 10%, and Lessee is aware of Lessor's rate.

Lessee has an option to purchase this machine after 3 years at a bargain price of $4,000. There are no uncertainties regarding costs or collections.

(*a*)   What type of lease is this? Why?
(*b*)   What interest rate should be used by Lessor? By Lessee?
(*c*)   Calculate the annual rental.

SOLUTION

(*a*)   It is a capital lease because it contains a BPO and also because the lease term is 75% of the asset life.
(*b*)   8% for both Lessor and Lessee.

(*c*)

Selling price	$25,000.00
Less present value of $4,000, 3 periods, 8%:	
.79383 × $4,000	(3,175.32)
	$21,824.68
Divide by present value of annuity due,	÷
3 periods, 8%	2.78326
Annual rental	$7,841.41 [Section 7.6]

7.9   For the previous problem, prepare the journal entries for 19A and also prepare an amortization table.

SOLUTION

	Lessor			*Lessee*		
Jan. 1	Lease Receivable	25,000		Machine	25,000	
	Machine		25,000	Lease Payable		25,000
	Cash	7,841.41		Lease Payable	7,841.41	
	Lease Receivable		7,841.41	Cash		7,841.41
Dec. 31	Lease Receivable	1,372.69		Interest Expense	1,372.69	
	Interest Revenue		1,372.69	Lease Payable		1,372.69
	No entry			Depreciation Expense	6,250	
				Accumulated Depreciation		6,250
				($25,000 ÷ 4)		

Date	Payment	Interest	Change in Receivable/Payable	Balance of Receivable/Payable
Jan. 1, 19A	—	—	—	$25,000.00
Jan. 1, 19A	$7,841.41	—	$(7,841.41)	17,158.59
Dec. 31, 19A	—	$1,372.69	1,372.69	18,531.28
Jan. 1, 19B	7,841.41	—	(7,841.41)	10,689.87
Dec. 31, 19B	—	855.19	855.19	11,545.06
Jan. 1, 19C	7,841.41	—	(7,841.41)	3,703.65
Dec. 31, 19C	—	296.29	296.29	4,000.00 (BPO) (rounded)

[Section 7.6]

7.10   In the previous problem, prepare the necessary journal entry if:

(a)   Lessee exercises the BPO on December 31, 19C.

(b)   Lessee does not exercise the BPO, but returns the machine to Lessor.

SOLUTION

(a)   **Lessor**

Cash	4,000	
Lease Receivable		4,000

(b)   Machine   5,000*

Lease Receivable		4,000
Gain on Lapse of		
Lease Option		1,000

*Salvage value

Lessee

Lease Payable	4,000	
Cash		4,000
Lease Payable	4,000	
Accumulated Depreciation	18,750	
Loss on Lapse of		
Lease Option	2,250	
Machine		25,000

[Section 7.6]

Salvage Values

7.11   On January 1, 19A, Lessor rents a machine to Lessee for 3 years. Both the cost and the selling price are $30,000. The salvage value at the end of the 3-year period is $5,000, which is *unguaranteed* by Lessee. The interest rate, which is known to both parties, is 10%, and the lease meets all the conditions required to be a capital lease.

(a)   Calculate the annual rental.

(b)   Determine the amount to be capitalized by Lessor.

(c)   Determine the amount to be capitalized by Lessee.

SOLUTION

(a)

Selling price	$ 30,000.00
Less present value of salvage, $5,000,	
3 periods, 10%: .75131 × $5,000	− 3,756.55
Amount to recover from annual rentals	$ 26,243.45
Divide by present value of annuity due,	÷
3 periods, 10%	2.73554
Annual rental	$ 9,593.52

(b) $30,000

(c) $26,243.45 (the present value of the rentals)   [Section 7.7]

7.12   In the previous problem, prepare the first year's journal entries and the amortization table for Lessor.

SOLUTION

Jan.	1	Lease Receivable	30,000	
		Machine		30,000
Jan.	1	Cash	9,593.52	
		Lease Receivable		9,593.52
Dec. 31		Lease Receivable	2,040.65	
		Interest Revenue		2,040.65
Dec. 31		No entry for depreciation		

Amortization Table

Date	Payment	Interest	Change in Receivable/Payable	Balance of Receivable/Payable
Jan. 1, 19A	—	—	—	$30,000.00
Jan. 1, 19A	$9,593.52	—	$(9,593.52)	20,406.48
Dec. 31, 19A	—	$2,040.65	2,040.65	22,447.13
Jan. 1, 19B	9,593.52	—	(9,593.52)	12,853.61
Dec. 31, 19B	—	1,285.36	1,285.36	14,138.97
Jan. 1, 19C	9,593.52	—	(9,593.52)	4,545.45
Dec. 31, 19C	—	454.55	454.55	5,000.00

[Section 7.7]

7.13   In the previous problem, prepare Lessee's journal entries for 19A, and also an amortization table.

SOLUTION

Jan.	1	Machine	26,243.45	
		Lease Payable		26,243.45
Jan.	1	Lease Payable	9,593.52	
		Cash		9,593.52
Dec.	31	Interest Expense	1,664.99	
		Lease Payable		1,664.99
Dec.	31	Depreciation Expense	8,747.82	
		Accumulated Depreciation		8,747.82
		$26,243.45 ÷ 3		

Amortization Table

Date	Payment	Interest	Change in Receivable/Payable	Balance of Receivable/Payable
Jan. 1, 19A	—	—	—	$26,243.45
Jan. 1, 19A	$9,593.52	—	$(9,593.52)	16,649.93
Dec. 31, 19A	—	$1,664.99	1,664.99	18,314.92
Jan. 1, 19B	9,593.52	—	(9,593.52)	8,721.40
Dec. 31, 19B	—	872.14	872.14	9,593.54
Jan. 1, 19C	9,593.52	—	(9,593.52)	–0–
				(rounded)

[Section 7.7]

7.14   In the previous problem, assume that the machine is worth only $4,000 when it is returned by Lessee to Lessor at the end of the 3-year period. Prepare the entry for the return by both Lessor and Lessee.

SOLUTION

Lessor				*Lessee*		
Machine	4,000			Accumulated Depreciation	26,243.45	
Loss on Lease Termination	1,000			Machine		26,243.45
Lease Receivable		5,000				

[Section 7.7]

7.15   On January 1, 19A, Lessor rents a machine to Lessee for 3 years, with the annual rentals beginning immediately. Lessor's cost and selling price are both $30,000. The salvage value at the end of the 3-year period is expected to be $5,000, which is *guaranteed* by Lessee. The interest rate, known to both parties, is 10%, and the lease meets the required conditions to qualify as a capital lease.

(a) Calculate the annual rental.
(b) Determine the amount to be capitalized by Lessor.
(c) Determine the amount to be capitalized by Lessee.

SOLUTION

(a)

Selling price		$30,000.00
Less present value of salvage, $5,000, 3 periods, 10%: .75131 × $5,000		− 3,756.55
Amount to recover from annual rentals		$26,243.45
Divide by present value of annuity due, 3 periods, 10%		÷ 2.73554
Annual rental		$ 9,593.52

(b) $30,000
(c) $30,000 (present value of both the guaranteed salvage value and the annual rentals)   [Section 7.8]

7.16 In the previous problem, prepare Lessor's journal entries for 19A and an amortization table.

SOLUTION

Jan.	1	Lease Receivable	30,000	
		Machine		30,000
Jan.	1	Cash	9,593.52	
		Lease Receivable		9,593.52
Dec. 31		Lease Receivable	2,040.65	
		Interest Revenue		2,040.65
Dec. 31		No entry for depreciation		

Amortization Table

Date	Payment	Interest	Change in Receivable/Payable	Balance of Receivable/Payable
Jan. 1, 19A	—	—	—	$30,000.00
Jan. 1, 19A	$9,593.52	—	$(9,593.52)	20,406.48
Dec. 31, 19A	—	$2,040.65	2,040.65	22,447.13
Jan. 1, 19B	9,593.52	—	(9,593.52)	12,853.61
Dec. 31, 19B	—	1,285.36	1,285.36	14,138.97
Jan. 1, 19C	9,593.52	—	(9,593.52)	4,545.45
Dec. 31, 19C	—	454.55	454.55	5,000.00 (salvage)

[Section 7.8]

7.17 In the previous problem, prepare Lessee's journal entries for 19A, and also an amortization table.

SOLUTION

The amortization table would be the same as for Lessor. The entries are:

Jan.	1	Machine	30,000	
		Lease Payable		30,000
Jan.	1	Lease Payable	9,593.52	
		Cash		9,593.52
Dec. 31		Interest Expense	2,040.65	
		Lease Payable		2,040.65
Dec. 31		Depreciation Expense	8,333.33	
		Accumulated Depreciation		8,333.33
		($30,000 − $5,000) ÷ 3		

[Section 7.8]

7.18 In the previous example, assume the machine is worth only $3,000 upon return by Lessee at the end of 19C. Prepare the entries for both Lessor and Lessee.

SOLUTION

Lessor				*Lessee*		
Cash	2,000			Lease Payable	5,000	
Machine	3,000			Accumulated Depreciation	25,000	
Lease Receivable		5,000		Loss on Lease Termination	2,000	
				Machine		30,000
				Cash		2,000

[Section 7.8]

Sale and Leasebacks

7.19 Seller-Lessee sells a machine to Buyer-Lessor on January 1, 19A, for $70,000 and immediately leases it back for a 3-year period at a 10% interest rate. Seller-Lessee's original cost was $40,000 and the machine has no salvage value.

(*a*)   Compute the annual rental.

(*b*)   Prepare the entries for both parties for 19A assuming the lease does not qualify as a capital lease—i.e., it is an operating lease.

(*c*)   Prepare the entries assuming it *does* qualify as a capital lease.

SOLUTION

(*a*) $70,000 \div 2.73554 = \$25,589.10$

(*b*)

	Seller-Lessee			*Buyer-Lessor*		
Jan. 1	Cash	70,000		Machine	70,000	
	Machine		40,000	Cash		70,000
	Unearned Gain on					
	Sale-Leaseback		30,000			
Jan. 1	Rent Expense	25,589.10		Cash	25,589.10	
	Cash		25,589.10	Rent Revenue		25,589.10
Dec. 31	No entry			Depreciation Expense	23,333.33	
				Accumulated Depreciation		23,333.33
Dec. 31	Unearned Gain on			No entry		
	Sale-Leaseback	10,000				
	Rent Expense		10,000			
	$30,000 \div 3$					

(*c*)

	Seller-Lessee			*Buyer-Lessor*		
Jan. 1	Cash	70,000		Machine	70,000	
	Machine		40,000	Cash		70,000
	Unearned Gain on					
	Sale-Leaseback		30,000			
Jan. 1	Machine	70,000		Lease Receivable	70,000	
	Lease Payable		70,000	Machine		70,000
Jan. 1	Lease Payable	25,589.10		Cash	25,589.10	
	Cash		25,589.10	Lease Receivable		25,589.10
Dec. 31	Interest Expense	4,441.09		Lease Receivable	4,441.09	
	Lease Payable		4,441.09	Interest Revenue		4,441.09
	($70,000 − $25,589.10) × 10%					
Dec. 31	Depreciation Expense	23,333.33		No entry		
	Accumulated Depreciation		23,333.33			
Dec. 31	Unearned Gain on			No entry		
	Sale-Leaseback	10,000				
	Depreciation Expense		10,000			

[Section 7.9]

Supplementary Problems

7.20 What are the four conditions (of which only one need be met) for a lease to be considered a capital lease? What are the two additional conditions to be met for the *lessor* to consider the lease a capital lease?

7.21 Lessor rents a building to Lessee for a 3-year period beginning on January 1, 19A. The annual rental is $7,000 and the total rent is payable in advance on January 1, 19A. The lease does *not* meet any of the conditions necessary to be considered a capital lease. In order to consummate the lease, Lessor pays $1,000 in legal fees. Assume the building has a 10-year life and Lessor's original cost was $60,000. Prepare entries for both Lessor and Lessee for the first year.

7.22 In a capital lease situation, if the selling price is $100,000, the number of rental payments is five, and the target rate of return is 12%, what is the annual rental? Assume the rentals are payable at the beginning of each period.

7.23 If the annual rental is $3,000, the number of rental payments is 5, and the target rate is 9%, find the selling price. (Assume the payments are made at the beginning of each period.)

7.24 A building with a life of 5 years is leased for a 3-year period. The selling price is $200,000; the present value of the rental payments is $180,000. There is no BPO at the end of the lease term. Does this qualify as a capital lease to Lessee? Why?

7.25 Lessor's target rate of return (known to Lessee) is 10%. Lessee's incremental borrowing rate is 9%. What rates should Lessor and Lessee use to capitalize this lease?

7.26 Lessor leases a building for 3 years to Lessee. The building has a life of 3 years and no salvage value at the end. Lessor's cost and selling price are both $30,000 and Lessor has a target rate of return of 12%. Lessee, who is aware of this rate, has an incremental rate of 15%. There are no uncertainties regarding collections or expenses and the rentals are payable at the beginning of each period.
(*a*) What type of lease is this to Lessor? To Lessee? Why?
(*b*) Determine the annual rental.
(*c*) Prepare an amortization table.
(*d*) Prepare entries for both parties for the first year.

7.27 Assume the same information as in the previous problem, except that the selling price is $50,000. What type of lease is this to Lessor? Do requirements (*b*), (*c*), and (*d*).

7.28 Lessor enters into an agreement with Lessee on January 1, 19A, for the 3-year rental of a machine. The machine has a 4-year life with a salvage value of $9,000 after 3 years and zero at the end of 4 years. Lessor's cost and selling price are both $75,000, and the interest rate for both parties is 12%. Lessee has the option to purchase this machine after 3 years at a bargain price of $6,000. There are no uncertainties regarding collections or future costs. The first rental payment is due on January 1, 19A.
(*a*) What type of lease is this to Lessor and Lessee? Why?
(*b*) What is the annual rental?
(*c*) Prepare an amortization table.
(*d*) Prepare entries for all 3 years for both parties. Assume lessee exercises the bargain purchase option.

7.29 Lessor rents a machine with a cost and selling price of $50,000 to Lessee for 3 years. At that time the salvage value is expected to be $7,000, which is *unguaranteed*. The interest rate, known to both parties, is 10%, and the lease meets all the requirements needed to qualify as a capital lease. Assume the annual rentals are payable at the beginning of each period.
(*a*) Determine the annual rental.
(*b*) Prepare an amortization table for each party. Would they both be the same?
(*c*) Prepare entries for each party for the first year.

7.30   Assume the same information as in the previous problem except that the salvage value is *guaranteed*. Do requirements (*a*), (*b*), and (*c*). In addition, assume that when Lessee returns the machine after 3 years, the machine is only worth $6,000. Prepare an entry for the return.

7.31   Seller-Lessee sells a machine to Buyer-Lessor on January 1, 19A, for $150,000 and immediately leases it back for a 3-year period at a rate of 10%. Seller-Lessee's original cost was $120,000 and the machine has no salvage value. Assume the lease qualifies as a capital lease. Prepare entries for the first year on the books of both parties.

Chapter 8

The Statement of Cash Flows

8.1 INTRODUCTION

In our discussion of intermediate accounting up to this point, both in volume I and volume II, we have focused on three financial statements: the balance sheet, the income statement, and the statement of retained earnings. In this chapter we introduce and discuss in detail a fourth statement: the statement of cash flows. The statement of cash flows became mandatory under FASB No. 95 (November 1987) for fiscal years ending after July 15, 1988.

The essence and purpose of this statement is to provide information about a company's cash receipts and cash payments during the accounting period. According to FASB No. 95, such information should help investors and creditors assess a company's ability to generate positive future cash flows, assess a company's ability to pay liabilities and dividends, and explain the reasons for the difference between net income and the net change in cash for the period.

The statement of cash flows comprises three sections: cash from operating activities, cash from investment activities, and cash from financing activities. These sections illustrate the various transactions that took place during the period causing increases and decreases in cash. The net result of these transactions should be equal to the change in the cash balance on the balance sheet from a year ago to the present.

The first section — cash from operating activities — can be prepared under two possible methods: the direct method and the indirect method. The FASB has encouraged the use of the direct method. Because the indirect method is easier to understand and apply, we will discuss it first; later in the chapter we will discuss the direct method.

8.2 CASH FROM OPERATING ACTIVITIES — INDIRECT METHOD

The cash from operating activities section shows the net increase (or decrease) in cash resulting from a company's operations. It thus includes cash *inflows* from sales of goods and services, interest income, and dividend income. It also includes cash *outflows* for merchandise inventory, employee wages, taxes, interest expense, and other expenses. The difference between the inflows and outflows represents the *net* change in cash resulting from operations.

It would seem at first glance that this net change in cash is also the *net income* for the period. Unfortunately, this is not the case. Under the accrual method of accounting (which must be used under GAAP and which we have been using all along), revenue is recognized when earned, not when received. Similarly, expenses are recognized when incurred, not when paid. The net income figure may thus include certain revenue and expense items for which no actual cash has been received or paid. For example, if sales on account were made at the end of 19A, these sales would be included in the 19A net income even though no cash was received until 19B. Similarly, if expenses were incurred at the end of 19A, they would reduce 19A income even though payment didn't actually take place until 19B. Furthermore, there are several expenses that do not involve the payment of cash altogether, such as depreciation expense and amortization of intangible assets. These items do not affect cash; they affect the property, plant, equipment, and intangible assets accounts.

Accordingly, the net income figure cannot represent the net cash flow from operations. It represents only a starting point which must be "refined" in order to arrive at the net cash flow. The refinement process uses the following formula:

Net Income
+ Depreciation Expense
+ Amortization Expense of Intangibles
+ Amortization of Bond *Discount*
+ Loss on Sale of Plant Assets or Investments
+ Decrease in Accounts Receivable
+ Decrease in Merchandise Inventory
+ Decrease in Prepaid Expenses (insurance, rent, supplies)
+ Increase in Accounts Payable (except dividends payable)
+ Increase in Accrued Liabilities (taxes payable, interest, payable, wages payable, expenses payable)
+ Decrease in Investment in Subsidiary (equity method)
+ Increase in Deferred Tax Liability

= Net Cash Flow from Operations

Depreciation expense and amortization expense must be added back to the net income since they do not involve an outlay of cash. The same reasoning applies to the amortization of bond discount — its entry was:

Interest Expense	xx	
Bond Discount		xx

Since this entry reduced net income without affecting cash, we must add this amount back into the net income. If we are dealing with a bond *premium* instead of a bond discount, the amortization must be *subtracted* instead of *added*.

Changes in an ownership interest of a subsidiary as a result of the equity method and changes in deferred tax liabilities also do not affect cash. Therefore, adjustments must be made for these items. It should be noted that increases in deferred tax assets receive the opposite treatment — they should be subtracted. (The topic of deferred taxes will be discussed in a later chapter).

For the same reason, any loss on the sale of plant assets or investments must also be added back. If there was a *gain* on the sale, it must be *subtracted*.

The remaining items must be taken into account in order to convert from accrual accounting to cash accounting. Thus *decreases* in accounts receivable, merchandise inventory, and prepaid items must be *added*. If there are *increases,* they should be *subtracted. Increases* in accounts payable and accrued liabilities (taxes, wages, utilities, interest, etc.) should be *added. Decreases* should be *subtracted.*

Notice that dividends payable are not part of the formula. This is due to the fact that dividends are not an expense and thus do not enter into the net income figure.

EXAMPLE 1

Company A wishes to determine its net cash flow from operations for 19B. Partial balance sheets for the years ending December 31, 19A, and December 31, 19B, indicate the following:

	12/31/19A	12/31/19B
Accounts Receivable	$1,000	$800
Merchandise Inventory	700	600
Prepaid Insurance	900	400
Accounts Payable	350	500
Dividends Payable	80	100
Wages Payable	400	850
Taxes Payable	200	375

The income statement reveals the following information:

Net Income:	5,000
Depreciation Expense:	(2,000)
Loss on Sale of Equipment:	(1,000)
Amortization of Patent:	(400)

Based on the foregoing, the net cash flow from operations would be calculated as follows:

Net Income	$5,000
+ Depreciation Expense	2,000
+ Loss on Sale of Equipment	1,000
+ Amortization of Patent	400
+ Decrease in Accounts Receivable	200
+ Decrease in Merchandise Inventory	100
+ Decrease in Prepaid Insurance	500
+ Increase in Accounts Payable	150
+ Increase in Wages Payable	450
+ Increase in Taxes Payable	175
Net Cash Flow from Operations	$9,975

Dividends payable is ignored because it is a debit to Accounts RETAIN EARNINGS not an expense account.

Notice that dividends payable were ignored.

EXAMPLE 2

Partial balance sheets of Company B appear as follows:

	12/31/19A	12/31/19B
Accounts Receivable	$5,000	$7,000
Merchandise Inventory	2,000	4,000
Prepaid Rent	7,000	3,000
Supplies	1,000	3,000
Accounts Payable	1,500	2,000
Utilities Payable	2,000	1,400

The income statement discloses the following:

Net Income	$2,000
Depreciation Expense	(400)
Gain on Sale of Land	900
Amortization of Bond Premium	500
Amortization of Goodwill	(200)

Net cash flow from operations for 19B would thus be calculated as follows:

Net Income	$2,000
+ Depreciation Expense	400
− Gain on Sale of Land	(900)
− Amortization of Bond Premium	(500)
+ Amortization of Goodwill	200
− Increase in Accounts Receivable	(2,000)
− Increase in Merchandise Inventory	(2,000)
+ Decrease in Prepaid Rent	4,000
− Increase in Supplies	(2,000)
+ Increase in Accounts Payable	500
− Decrease in Utilities Payable	(600)
Net Cash Flow from Operations	$ (900)

8.3 CASH FROM INVESTMENT ACTIVITIES

The next section of the statement of cash flows deals with cash inflows and outflows from investment activities. *Cash inflows* include cash from:

1. Sales of property, plant, and equipment
2. Sales of stock or bond investments
3. Collection of principal on loans to other entities (but *not* interest)

Cash outflows include cash outlays for:

1. Purchase of property, plant, and equipment

2. Purchases of stock or bond investments

3. Making of loans to other entities

Notice that collection of interest on loans to other entities is *not* included in this section. The reason is that interest, being a revenue item, has already been included in the net income in the section on cash from operations. The same reasoning also applies to dividend collections. *but not payment of Dividend*

EXAMPLE 3

Company C engaged in the following investment activities during 19X1:

1. Purchased equipment for $10,000.

2. Sold land for $4,000.

3. Sold its investment in Xerox stock for $9,000.

4. Collected $5,000 on a loan.

5. Collected $250 interest on a loan.

6. Lent $1,500 to Company Y.

The net cash flow from investments is:

Equipment purchase	$(10,000)
Land sale	4,000
Investment sale	9,000
Loan collection	5,000
Lent cash	(1,500)
	$ 6,500

EXAMPLE 4

A company's beginning balance in its Land account was $10,000; its ending balance was $17,000, and during the period it sold land with a cost of $7,000 for $11,000. How much cash did the company spend for the purchase of new land? How do we treat the gain of $4,000 on the sale of the land?

An analysis of the Land T-account reveals the following:

Land

Beginning balance	10,000	7,000	sold
Purchases	X		
Ending balance	17,000		

$$\$10,000 + X - \$7,000 = \$17,000$$
$$\$3,000 + X \qquad = \$17,000$$
$$X \qquad = \$14,000 = \text{purchase}$$

The entry for the sale is as follows:

Cash	11,000	
Land		7,000
Gain on Sale of Land		4,000

In the investment section, this company would show $-\$14,000$ for the land purchase, and $+\$11,000$ for the land sale. Since the $11,000 includes the $4,000 gain, and this gain is also included in the net income, we must subtract it in the *cash flow from operations section* in order to avoid double counting. It now should be clear why we stated in Section 8.2 that gains on the sale of plant, equipment, and land must be *subtracted* from the net income.

8.4 CASH FROM FINANCING ACTIVITIES

The third section of the statement of cash flows is cash from financing activities.
Cash inflows include:

1. Cash from issuance of the company's own stock

2. Cash from issuance of the company's own bonds or notes

    Cash outflows include:

1. Cash paid to purchase treasury stock

2. Cash paid to pay up bonds and notes

3. Cash dividends paid (but not *stock* dividends)

EXAMPLE 5

Company D had the following finance and investment activities during 19C:

1. Bought treasury stock for $9,000.

2. Sold a machine for $18,000.

3. Bought General Motors stock for $15,000.

4. Lent $3,000 to Company W.

5. Issued $4,000 par of its own stock at $4,500.

6. Paid up a $10,000 bond.

7. Paid cash dividends of $2,000.

8. Issued 100 shares, $50 par common stock as a stock dividend.

The *finance* section would show:

Treasury Stock	$(9,000)
Stock Issuance	4,500
Paid Up Bond	(10,000)
Cash Dividend	(2,000)
Total	($16,500)

The *investments* section would show:

Machine Sale	$18,000
Stock Purchase	(15,000)
Made Loan	(3,000)
Total	–0–

8.5 COMPLETE STATEMENT OF CASH FLOWS—INDIRECT METHOD

We will now tie together the three sections of the statement—cash from operations, investments, and financing—in order to present a complete statement of cash flows.

In order to prepare the statement, we must have two balance sheets in front of us—today's balance sheet and the balance sheet from a year ago. We must also have this year's income statement and additional information from the general ledger.

EXAMPLE 6

Company E had the following balance sheets for years 19A and 19B:

	12/31/19A	12/31/19B
Cash	$ 30,000	$ 60,000
Accounts Receivable	50,000	60,000
Merchandise	63,000	81,000
Buildings	115,000	155,000
Accumulated Depreciation	(40,000)	(55,000)
Land	30,000	45,000
Total Assets	$248,000	$346,000
Accounts Payable	$ 52,000	$ 60,000
Preferred Stock	150,000	200,000
Premium on Preferred Stock	—	10,000
Retained Earnings	46,000	76,000
Total Equities	$248,000	$346,000

The T-accounts in the general ledger reveal that no buildings or land were disposed of during the year, stock issuances were for cash, and the entries in the Retained Earnings account were for net income of $55,000 and dividends paid of $25,000.

From the balance sheets we see that cash went up by $30,000 over the year. Let's now prepare a complete statement of cash flows based upon all this information.

First, the section dealing with cash flow from operations. Using the formula from Section 8.2 we have:

Net Income	$55,000
Depreciation Expense	15,000*
Increase in Accounts Receivable	(10,000)
Increase in Merchandise	(18,000)
Increase in Accounts Payable	8,000
Net Cash Flow from Operations	$50,000

---

*Because no buildings were disposed of, the only entry in Accumulated Depreciation during the year was for depreciation expense in the amount of $15,000 ($55,000 − $40,000).

We now proceed down the remainder of the balance sheet, one account at a time, analyze the account, and determine if its transactions belong in the investment section or the finance section. We thus have the following:

CASH FROM INVESTMENT ACTIVITIES

Purchased Building	$(40,000)	($155,000 − $115,000)
Purchased Land	(15,000)	($45,000 − $30,000)
Net Cash Flow from Investments	$(55,000)	

CASH FROM FINANCING ACTIVITIES

Issued Stock	$ 50,000	($200,000 − $150,000 par)
Premium on Stock	10,000	
Paid Dividends	(25,000)	
Net Cash Flow from Financing	$ 35,000	

The final step in the statement is to summarize the three cash flows and see if they yield the same figure as the cash change on the balance sheet, $30,000 ($60,000 − $30,000):

Net Cash Flow from Operations	$ 50,000
Net Cash Flow from Investments	(55,000)
Net Cash Flow from Financing	35,000
Total Net Cash Flow	$ 30,000

We indeed have arrived at a final figure that matches the change in the Cash account on the balance sheet.

Let's take a look at another complete statement of cash flows.

EXAMPLE 7

Zinner Corporation had the following balance sheets for 19A and 19B:

	12/31/19A	12/31/19B	
Cash	$ 3,000	$ 5,000	
Accounts Receivable	15,000	11,300	+
Merchandise	25,000	11,500	+
Prepaid Insurance	1,000	1,200	−
Land	40,000	34,000	+
Machinery	60,000	95,000	−
Accumulated Depreciation	(20,000)	(23,000)	
Accounts Payable	15,000	9,500	−
Bonds Payable (Long-term)	6,000	13,500	@ +
Common Stock	80,000	80,000	
Retained Earnings	23,000	32,000	

Additional information from the income statement and T-accounts indicate the following:

1. Net income was $20,000.
2. Dividends paid were $11,000 (cash).
3. Land carried at $6,000 was sold at a gain of $1,000 for $7,000.
4. Depreciation expense was $6,500.
5. Machinery was purchased for $40,000; machinery with a cost of $5,000 and accumulated depreciation of $3,500 was sold at its book value of $1,500.
6. Bonds were issued for cash.

The change in cash for the year according to the balance sheet was $2,000. Let's do a complete statement and see if we come up with this figure.

CASH FROM OPERATIONS

Net Income	$ 20,000	
Depreciation Expense	6,500	
Gain on Land Sale	(1,000)	
Accounts Receivable	3,700	
Merchandise	13,500	
Prepaid Insurance	(200)	
Accounts Payable	(5,500)	
Net Cash Flow from Operations		$ 37,000

CASH FROM INVESTMENT ACTIVITIES

Sale of Land	$ 7,000	
Sale of Machinery	1,500	
Purchase of Machinery	(40,000)	
Net Cash Flow from Investments		(31,500)

CASH FROM FINANCE ACTIVITIES

Cash Dividends	$(11,000)	
Bond Proceeds	7,500	
Net Cash Flow from Financing		(3,500)
Total Change in Cash		$ 2,000

EXAMPLE 8

The Berko Corporation had the following balance sheets for 19A and 19B:

	12/31/19A	12/31/19B
Cash	$ 16,000	$ 29,000
Accounts Receivable	10,000	19,000
Prepaid Rent	30,000	35,000
Equipment	55,000	56,000
Accumulated Depreciation	(10,000)	(12,000)
Total Assets	$101,000	$127,000
Accounts Payable	$ 20,000	$ 22,000
Dividends Payable	3,000	4,000
Preferred Stock	50,000	60,000
Retained Earnings	28,000	41,000
Total Liabilities and Stockholders' Equity	$101,000	$127,000

The following information was gleaned from the T-accounts in the general ledger and from the income statement:

1. Net income $17,000
2. Depreciation expense   5,000
3. Sold equipment, cost $7,000,
   accumulated depreciation $3,000,
   for a price of   4,000   (no gain or loss)
4. Purchased new equipment   ?
5. Issued preferred stock for cash   10,000
6. *Declared* dividends   4,000

First, let's do the cash flow from operations section:

Net Income	$17,000
Depreciation Expense	5,000
Accounts Receivable	(9,000)
Prepaid Rent	(5,000)
Accounts Payable	2,000
Net Cash Flow from Operations	$10,000

In order to determine equipment purchases, let's draw the Equipment T-account:

Equipment			
Beginning 55,000	7,000		Sold
Purchases			
End 56,000			

Thus:

$$\$55,000 + X - 7,000 = \$56,000$$

$$X = \$8,000 = \text{purchases}$$

Let's use the same type of analysis to determine dividends *paid*:

	Dividends Payable		
Paid	X	3,000	Beginning
		4,000	Declarations
		4,000	End

Thus:

$$\$3,000 + \$4,000 - X = \$4,000$$

$$X = \$3,000 = \text{payments}$$

Now let's do the investment and finance sections:

CASH FROM INVESTMENT ACTIVITIES

Sale of Equipment	$ 4,000
Equipment Purchase	(8,000)
Net Cash Flow from Investments	$ (4,000)

CASH FROM FINANCE ACTIVITIES

Issuance of Stock	$ 10,000
Paid Dividends	(3,000)
Net Cash Flow from Financing	$ 7,000

Summary

Cash from Operations	$10,000
Cash from Investment Activities	(4,000)
Cash from Finance Activities	7,000
Total Net Cash Flow	$13,000

This matches the change in cash on the balance sheet.

8.6 CASH FROM OPERATING ACTIVITIES — DIRECT METHOD

Up until this point we have been using the indirect method to determine cash flows from operations. Under this method we work backward — we take the final net income figure (which is based upon accrual accounting) and refine it via a formula in order to determine the net cash flow. Under the direct method, however, the procedure is more straightforward — we try to *directly* determine how much cash was received from operations and how much was paid out.

Cash receipts from operations include cash received from customers for goods and services, cash interest and dividends, and other operating receipts, if any. Cash payments include cash paid to employees and suppliers of goods and services, cash interest and income tax payments, and other operating payments, if any. We must search through the accounts to find these cash receipts and payments.

Let us now take a look at the various T-accounts that play a role in the cash receipts and payments relating to operating activities. By dissecting these accounts, we will learn how to search for and find these cash transactions.

The accounts that relate to sales and collections are Accounts Receivable and Sales, as follows:

Accounts Receivable		Sales	
Beginning balance	Collections on account		Sales on account
Sales on account			
Ending balance			

We are making an assumption that the Sales account is used *exclusively* for sales *on account* and the Accounts Receivable account is used *exclusively* for receivables relating to sales.

The accounts that relate to merchandise purchases and payments (assuming a perpetual inventory system) are Merchandise Inventory and Accounts Payable as follows:

Merchandise Inventory			Accounts Payable	
Beginning balance Purchases	Cost of goods sold		Payments	Beginning balance Purchases on account
Ending balance				Ending balance

We assume that Accounts Payable is used strictly for purchases of *merchandise,* and that all purchases are made *on account.*

The accounts that relate to wages, interest, and taxes are as follows:

Wages Expense			Wages Payable	
Wages accrued			Wages paid	Beginning balance Wages accrued
				Ending balance

(As a reminder, the entry to accrue wages is:

Wages Expense	xx	
Wages Payable		xx)

Interest Expense			Interest Payable	
Interest accrued			Interest paid	Beginning balance Interest accrued
				Ending balance

Income Tax Expense			Income Tax Payable	
Taxes accrued			Taxes paid	Beginning balance Taxes accrued
				Ending balance

Another item affecting cash from operations is the purchase of various prepaid items such as insurance, rent, and supplies. The expiration of such items often appears on the income statement in the selling and administrative expense category. The T-account for prepaid items is structured as follows:

Prepaid Items	
Beginning balance Purchases	Expirations
Ending balance	

For cash purposes it is not the expiration that concerns us; it is the purchases.

EXAMPLE 9

Company A reports $800,000 of sales on its income statement. On its balance sheet it reports beginning and ending balances for Accounts Receivable in the amounts of $68,000 and $60,000 respectively. Its cash from collections on sales would be determined as follows:

Accounts Receivable			
Beginning balance	68,000	X	(Collections)
Sales	800,000		
Ending balance	60,000		

$$68,000 + 800,000 - X = 60,000$$
$$868,000 - 60,000 = X$$
$$X = 808,000$$

EXAMPLE 10

Company B had beginning and ending inventories of $40,000 and $35,000 respectively, and beginning and ending balances in Accounts Payable of $20,000 and $17,000, respectively. On its income statement it reported cost of goods sold of $169,000. The amount of cash paid for merchandise purchases would be calculated as follows:

Merchandise Inventory

Beginning balance	40,000	169,000	Cost of goods sold
Purchases on account			
Ending balance	35,000		

$$40,000 + X - 169,000 = 35,000$$
$$X - 129,000 = 35,000$$
$$X = 164,000^*$$

Accounts Payable

Payments	Y	20,000	Beginning balance
		164,000*	Purchases (From above)
		17,000	Ending balance

$$20,000 + 164,000 - Y = 17,000$$
$$184,000 - Y = 17,000$$
$$Y = 167,000$$

EXAMPLE 11

Company C reports beginning and ending balances in its Wages Payable account of $10,000 and $50,000 respectively, while on its income statement it shows wages expense of $70,000. Its cash payments for wages this year was $30,000, determined as follows:

Wages Payable

Payments	X	10,000	Beginning balance
		70,000	Wages expense accrual
		50,000	Ending balance

$$\$10,000 + \$70,000 - X = \$50,000$$
$$X = \$30,000$$

EXAMPLE 12

Company D reports interest expense of $30,000 on its 19X1 income statement. On its comparative balance sheets it shows $40,000 and $50,000 as its beginning and ending respective balances for interest payable. Its cash payments in 19X1 for interest would be calculated as follows:

Interest Payable

Payments	X	40,000	Beginning balance
		30,000	Interest expense
		50,000	

$$\$40,000 + \$30,000 - X = \$50,000$$
$$\$70,000 - X = \$50,000$$
$$X = \$20,000$$

EXAMPLE 13

Company E reports insurance expense on its income statement of $60,000, while its comparative balance sheets show beginning and ending balances for prepaid insurance in the amounts of $70,000 and $35,000, respectively. The amount it paid for insurance is:

Prepaid Insurance

Beginning balance	70,000	60,000	Insurance expense
Prepayments	X		
Ending balance	35,000		

$$\$70,000 + X - \$60,000 = \$35,000$$
$$X + \$10,000 = \$35,000$$
$$X = \$25,000$$

It should be noted that under FASB requirements, even if a company chooses to use the direct method, it must also present a reconciliation of its net income to its cash from operations, using the formula we discussed in Section 8.2 above.

8.7 COMPLETE STATEMENT OF CASH FLOWS—DIRECT METHOD

Let's now use the information discussed in the previous section to prepare a statement of cash flows under the direct method.

EXAMPLE 14

Company F had the following comparative balance sheets for 19X1 and 19X2:

	12/31/19X1	12/31/19X2
Cash	$ 28,900	$ 46,000
Accounts Receivable	45,000	41,000
Merchandise	51,000	48,000
Prepaid Rent	3,700	4,100
Plant Assets	835,000	970,000
Accumulated Depreciation	(400,000)	(356,000)
Total Assets	$ 563,600	$ 753,100
Accounts Payable	$ 37,000	$ 32,500
Salaries Payable	7,500	4,500
Taxes Payable	5,000	7,000
Notes Payable (Long-term)	—	100,000
Preferred Stock	350,000	400,000
Paid-in Capital in Excess of Par	45,000	55,000
Retained Earnings	119,100	154,100
Total Equities	$ 563,600	$ 753,100

Its income statement for 19X2 reported the following:

Sales	$ 810,000	
Cost of Goods Sold	(460,000)	
Gross Profit		350,000
Expenses:		
Depreciation Expense	(30,000)	
Administrative Expenses	(175,500)	
Tax Expense	(69,500)	
Total Expenses		(275,000)
Net Income		$ 75,000

Other data:

1. All sales and purchases were made on account.

2. Dividends of $40,000 were paid during the year.

3. Preferred stock with a par of $50,000 was issued for $60,000 cash.

4. Plant assets with an original cost of $80,000 and accumulated depreciation of $74,000 were sold for $6,000 in cash.

5. Plant assets were purchased for $100,000 cash.

6. Other plant assets were purchased at a price of $115,000. Payment terms were $15,000 cash, plus a long-term note payable for $100,000.

Company F
Statement of Cash Flows
For the Year Ended December 31, 19X2

CASH FROM OPERATIONS

Cash Inflows:

Cash Received from Customers		$ 814,000

Cash Outflows:

Cash Paid for Merchandise	(461,500)	
Cash Paid for Taxes	(67,500)	
Cash Paid for Administrative Expenses	(175,500)	
Cash Paid for Rent	(400)	
Cash Paid for Salaries	(3,000)	
Total Cash Outflows		(707,900)
Net Cash Flow from Operations		$ 106,100

CASH FROM INVESTMENT ACTIVITIES

Sale of Plant Assets	$ 6,000	
Purchase of Plant Assets	(115,000)*	
Net Cash Flow from Investment Activities		$(109,000)

CASH FROM FINANCE ACTIVITIES

Issuance of Preferred Stock	$ 60,000	
Dividend Payments	(40,000)	
Net Cash Flow from Finance Activities		$20,000
Net Change in Cash		$17,100

*Plant assets of $215,000 were purchased for cash of $115,000 and a long-term note payable of $100,000.

The cash inflows and outflows from operations were determined as follows:
Cash collections:

Accounts Receivable

45,000	X
(Sales) 810,000	
41,000	

$$\$45,000 + \$810,000 - X = \$41,000$$
$$X = \$814,000$$

Cash paid for merchandise:

Merchandise

51,000	460,000
P	
48,000	

$$\$51,000 + P - \$460,000 = \$48,000$$
$$P = \$457,000 = \text{purchases}**$$

Accounts Payable

Y	37,000
	457,000** (From above)
	32,500

$$\$37,000 + \$457,000 - Y = \$32,500$$
$$Y = \$461,500 = \text{purchase payments}$$

Cash paid for taxes:

Taxes Payable

X	5,000
	69,500
	7,000

$$\$5,000 + \$69,500 - X = \$7,000$$
$$X = \$67,500$$

The Administrative Expense title on the income statement includes salaries, expiration of prepaid rent, and other administrative items. Since the Prepaid Rent account increased by $400 over the year, this implies that the amount of prepaid insurance purchased exceeded the amount expired in the amount of $400. Similarly, since Salaries Payable decreased by $3,000, this implies that salaries paid exceeded salaries incurred by $3,000. Since the Administrative Expense account only includes expirations and accruals (rather than purchases and payments), we must include these amounts as additional cash outflows from operations.

8.8 SPECIAL ISSUES RELATING TO THE STATEMENT OF CASH FLOWS

We mentioned earlier in this chapter that under the indirect method increases in Accounts Receivable are subtracted from the net income and decreases are added. What happens if the Accounts Receivable has a related contra account for bad debts (allowance for doubtful accounts)? In these cases, we compare the *net* receivable from year beginning to year end, and then add or subtract this amount.

EXAMPLE 15

Company H shows the following Accounts Receivable information for 19X1 and 19X2:

	12/31/19X1	12/31/19X2
Accounts Receivable	$10,000	$20,000
Allowance for Doubtful Accounts	(1,000)	(800)
	$ 9,000	$19,200

The *net* increase of $10,200 (19,200 − 9,000) would be subtracted.

If the *direct* method is used, we must analyze the Accounts Receivable account (as we did previously) to determine cash collections on sales. However, we must also bear in mind that Accounts Receivable will contain credit(s) for write-offs that took place during the year.

EXAMPLE 16

Accounts Receivable had beginning and ending balances of $10,000 and $20,000, respectively, during 19X1. Sales on account were $500,000, bad debt expense (on the income statement) was $50,000, and write-offs were $60,000. Cash collections on account would be calculated as follows:

Accounts Receivable		
10,000	60,000	
	X	(collections)
500,000		
20,000		

$$\$10,000 + \$500,000 - \$60,000 - X = \$20,000$$
$$X = \$430,000$$

Transactions that do not affect cash do not appear in the statement of cash flows. Nevertheless, the FASB had decided that if these transactions are significant, they should be included in a footnote or supplementary schedule to the statement. Such transactions include:

1. Acquisition of assets by assuming liabilities or through the issuance of equity securities
2. Exchanges of nonmonetary assets
3. Refinancing of long-term debt
4. Conversion of debt or preferred stock to common stock
5. Issuance of equity securities to retire debt

Summary

1. The statement of cash flows helps investors and creditors assess a company's ability to generate positive cash flows and its ability to pay liabilities and dividends. It is required under FASB Statement No. 95.

2. This statement has three sections: cash from operating activities, cash from investment activities, and cash from financing activities. Cash from operating activities can be determined under either the direct method or the indirect method.

3. Under the indirect method, the net income (accrual basis) is converted into cash flow from operations by *adding* to it the following items: depreciation expense; amortization of intangibles; amortization of bond discount; losses on sales of plant assets or investments; *decreases* in accounts receivable, inventory, and prepaid expenses; *increases* in accounts payable and accrued liabilities; *decreases* in the Investment in Subsidiary account under the equity method; and *increases* in the Deferred Tax Liability account.

4. Under the direct method, cash from operating activities is determined *directly* by calculating cash received from customers and cash paid for merchandise, wages, interest, and other expenses. This is done via an analysis of the T-accounts.

5. Cash from investment activities includes cash received from the sale of plant assets; sales of stock or bond investments, and collection of principal on loans. Cash outflows include cash spent for purchases of plant assets; purchases of stock or bond investments, and the making of loans.

6. Cash from financing activities includes cash received from the issuance of stock or bonds. Cash outflows include purchases of treasury stock, bond retirements, and *cash* dividends.

7. The steps to be taken in preparing a statement of cash flows are as follows: First, we determine the cash from operations by using either the direct method or the indirect method. We then proceed down the bal-

ance sheet, one account at a time, analyzing the account for its effect on cash and placing this effect in the appropriate section (investment activity or finance activity). We then combine the *net* cash change of each section — operating, investment, and finance — to arrive at the *net* change in cash for the period. This figure should be equal to the change in the Cash account from beginning of year to year-end.

8. Under the indirect method, the Accounts Receivable and its related allowance account should be netted and the change from beginning of year to year-end should be added (or subtracted if there was an increase) to the net income to determine cash from operations. Under the direct method, however, this should not be done. Instead, an analysis of the Accounts Receivable account is made to determine cash collections from customers.

9. Significant noncash transactions such as the acquisition of assets via the issuance of equity securities or the issuance of equity securities to retire debt should be disclosed in a footnote or supplementary schedule.

Rapid Review

1. The three sections of the statement of cash flows are: cash from _____, cash from _____, and cash from _____ .

2. The two methods of determining cash from operations are the _____ method and the _____ method.

3. Amortization of bond premium must be *Sub/Racted* from the net income.

4. *Increases* in accounts receivable, merchandise, and prepaid items must be *Subtracted* to (from) net income.

5. *Decreases* in accounts payable and accrued liabilities must be *Sub/Racted*.

6. *Decreases* in the investment in a subsidiary under the equity method should be *added* .

7. Gains on sales of plant assets should be *Sub/Racted*.

8. Collection of principal on loans belongs in the *Investment* section.

9. Purchases of stock of other companies belong in the *Investment* section.

10. Collection of *interest* on loans belong in the *and Operating* section.

11. Cash paid to purchase treasury stock belongs in the *Financing* section.

12. Cash dividends paid belongs in the *Financing* section.

13. Cash dividends declared but *not* paid should be shown in the *not Shown* section.

14. To prepare the statement of cash flows, we must have comparative *Bal.S* and an *Income* statement.

15. Under the direct method we are not concerned with the *expiration* of prepaid items but rather with the *Purchase* of these items.

16. Under the indirect method, Accounts Receivable and its related allowance should be *2 netted* .

17. Significant noncash transactions should be disclosed in a *footnotes* .

Answers: 1. operations; investments; finance 2. direct; indirect 3. subtracted 4. subtracted 5. subtracted 6. added 7. subtracted 8. investment 9. investment 10. operating 11. finance 12. finance 13. *not* shown 14. balance sheets; income 15. purchase 16. netted 17. footnote

Solved Problems

Cash from Operating Activities—Indirect Method

8.1 Use the following balance sheet information and other data to determine net cash from operating activities:

	Dec. 31, 19X1	Dec. 31, 19X2
Accounts Receivable	$ 4,000	$ 7,000
Merchandise Inventory	10,000	8,000
Prepaid Insurance	1,000	700
Accounts Payable	12,000	6,000
Rent Payable	9,000	16,000
Dividends Payable	2,000	2,500
Bonds Payable	50,000	40,000

Other Data:

(1)	Net income	$25,000
(2)	Depreciation expense	5,000
(3)	Amortization of goodwill	3,000
(4)	Amortization of bond premium	900
(5)	Amortization of patent	1,400
(6)	Gain on sale of plant	4,400

SOLUTION

Net Income	$25,000
Depreciation Expense	5,000
Goodwill Amortization	3,000
Bond Premium Amortization	(900)
Patent Amortization	1,400
Gain on Plant Sale	(4,400)
Accounts Receivable	(3,000)
Merchandise Inventory	2,000
Prepaid Insurance	300
Accounts Payable	(6,000)
Rent Payable	7,000
Net Cash from Operations	$29,400

[Section 8.2]

Cash from Operating, Investment, and Finance Activities

8.2 Classify the following list of items by operating section, investment section, or finance section. Use the letter "O" for operating, the letter "I" for investment, and the letter "F" for finance.

(1) Depreciation expense

(2) Sale of equipment for cash

(3) Issuance of bonds for cash

(4) Payment of cash dividend

(5) Receipt of cash dividend

(6) Payment of interest

(7) Receipt of interest

(8) Decrease in prepaid items

(9) Net income

(10)   Issuance of stock for cash

(11)   Purchase of treasury stock for cash

(12)   Amortization of organization costs

(13)   Rent expense

(14)   Sales revenue

(15)   Retirement of bonds for cash   — *This means paid cash*

(16)   Receipt of principal on loan made to third party

SOLUTION

(1) O	(5) O	(9) O	(13) O (an element of net income)
(2) I	(6) O	(10) F	(14) O
(3) F	(7) O	(11) F	(15) F
(4) F	(8) O	(12) O	(16) I

[Sections 8.2, 8.3, 8.4]

8.3   In the previous problem, indicate for each item whether it results in an increase in cash (+), or a decrease (−).

SOLUTION

(1) +	(5) +	(9) +	(13) −
(2) +	(6) −	(10) +	(14) +
(3) +	(7) +	(11) −	(15) −
(4) −	(8) +	(12) +	(16) +

[Sections 8.2, 8.3, 8.4]

8.4   From the following information prepare the investments section of the statement of cash flows:

(1)   Purchased a building for $10,000 cash.

(2)   Sold a machine: selling price, $12,000; cost, $16,000; accumulated depreciation, $9,000.

(3)   Paid a cash dividend of $1,000.

(4)   Bought Xerox stock for $2,000.

(5)   Sold General Motors bonds for $3,500.

(6)   Accounts receivable increased by $5,000.

(7)   Lent $2,400 to a third party.

SOLUTION

Purchase of Building	$(10,000)
Sale of Machine	12,000
Bought Xerox Stock	(2,000)
Sold General Motors Stock	3,500
Loan	(2,400)
Net Cash Flow from Investments	$ 1,100

[Section 8.3]

8.5   From the following information prepare the finance section of the statement of cash flows:

(1)	Issued bonds for	$12,000
(2)	Bought treasury stock for	9,000
(3)	Purchased land for	5,000
(4)	Retired bonds for	3,000
(5)	Paid a cash dividend of	7,000
(6)	Received a cash dividend of	2,500

(7) Issued stock ($10,000 par)   13,000

(8) Paid interest   1,450

(9) Issued a stock dividend   950 (par)

SOLUTION

Issuance of Bonds	$12,000	
Purchase of Treasury Stock	(9,000)	
Retirement of Bonds	(3,000)	
Payment of Cash Dividend	(7,000)	
Issuance of Stock	13,000	
Net Cash Flow from Finance	$ 6,000	[Section 8.4]

8.6 From the following information prepare the investment and finance sections:

(1) Purchased land $20,000

(2) Issued stock   5,000

(3) Accounts receivable increase   2,500

(4) Retired bonds   4,500

(5) Paid cash dividend   1,000

(6) Bought Xerox stock   9,500

(7) Sold IBM stock (cost, $3,000; selling price, $2,500)

(8) Accounts Payable decrease   1,200

(9) Bought treasury stock   1,300

(10) Collected on a loan   10,000

SOLUTION

INVESTMENT ACTIVITIES		FINANCE ACTIVITIES	
Land Purchase	$(20,000)	Stock Issuance	$ 5,000
Stock (Xerox) Purchase	(9,500)	Bond Retirement	(4,500)
Stock (IBM) Sale	2,500	Cash Dividend	(1,000)
Loan Collection	10,000	Treasury Stock Purchase	(1,300)
Net Cash Flow	$(17,000)	Net Cash Flow	$(1,800)

[Sections 8.3, 8.4]

8.7 The Bodner Corporation sold a machine with a cost of $10,000 and accumulated depreciation of $6,000 for a selling price of (a) $7,000; (b) $2,000. How would this transaction be handled on the statement of cash flows?

SOLUTION

(a) The selling price of $7,000 would appear in the investments section as an increase in cash, and the gain of $3,000 would appear in the operations section as a subtraction from the net income.

(b) The $2,000 selling price would appear in the investments section, while the $2,000 loss would appear in the operations section as an increase to the net income.   [Sections 8.2, 8.3]

8.8 The beginning and ending balances of the Accumulated Depreciation account were $4,000 and $1,000 respectively, and during the year a piece of equipment was sold whose accumulated depreciation was $9,000. How much was depreciation expense for the year? Use a T-account to justify your answer.

SOLUTION

Accumulated Depreciation

Sold	9,000	4,000	Beginning bal.
		X	Deprec. expense
		1,000	Ending bal.

$$\$4,000 + X - \$9,000 = \$1,000$$
$$X - \$5,000 = \$1,000$$
$$X = \$6,000 \qquad \text{[Section 8.5]}$$

8.9   The beginning and ending balances of the Plant account were $12,000 and $20,000, respectively, and during the period a building with a cost of $6,000 and accumulated depreciation of $3,000 was sold for $9,000. How much in plant purchases were made during the period? Show a T-account for your analysis.

SOLUTION

Plant

Beginning Bal.	12,000	6,000	Plant sold
Purchases	X		
Ending Bal.	20,000		

$$\$12,000 + X - \$6,000 = \$20,000$$
$$X + \$6,000 = \$20,000$$
$$X = \$14,000 \qquad \text{[Section 8.5]}$$

8.10   The Dividends Payable account had beginning and ending balances of $50,000 and $40,000, respectively, and cash dividends of $35,000 were declared during the period. Determine how much in cash dividends were paid. (Assume this account is used solely for *cash* dividends.)

SOLUTION

Dividends Payable

Paid	X	50,000	Beginning bal.
		35,000	Declared
		40,000	Ending bal.

$$\$50,000 + \$35,000 - X = \$40,000$$
$$\$85,000 - X = \$40,000$$
$$X = \$45,000 \qquad \text{[Section 8.5]}$$

Complete Cash Flow Statements — Indirect Method

8.11   The Bodner Corporation had the following balance sheets for 19A and 19B:

	12/31/19A	12/31/19B
Cash	$ 48,000	$ 77,000
Accounts Receivable	66,000	60,000
Inventory	112,000	100,000
Supplies	8,000	9,000
Buildings	240,000	312,000
Accumulated Depreciation	(41,000)	(66,000)
Goodwill	40,000	30,000
Total Assets	$473,000	$522,000

Accounts Payable	105,000	85,000
Expenses Payable	63,000	68,000
Long-term Notes Payable	70,000	—
Common Stock	—	100,000
Paid-in Capital in Excess of Par — Common	—	25,000
Preferred Stock	200,000	200,000
Retained Earnings	35,000	44,000
Total Liabilities and Stockholders' Equity	$473,000	$522,000

The only entries in the Retained Earnings account were for net income and dividends of $29,000 and $20,000, respectively. No buildings were sold during the period and stock was issued for cash. Prepare a statement of cash flows using the indirect approach.

SOLUTION

Bodner Corporation
Statement of Cash Flows
For the Year Ended December 31, 19B

CASH FROM OPERATING ACTIVITIES

Net income	$ 29,000	
Depreciation expense	25,000	(66,000 − 41,000)
Amortization of goodwill	10,000	
Change in Accounts Receivable	6,000	
Change in inventory	12,000	
Change in supplies	(1,000)	
Change in Accounts Payable	(20,000)	
Change in expenses payable	5,000	
Net Cash Flow from Operations	$ 66,000	

CASH FROM INVESTING ACTIVITIES

Building purchase	$ (72,000)	

CASH FROM FINANCE ACTIVITIES

Payment of Note Payable	$(70,000)	
Issuance of common stock	125,000	(par + premium)
Payment of dividends	(20,000)	
Net Cash Flow from Finance Activities	$ 35,000	

Summary

Net Cash Flow from Operations	$ 66,000	
Net Cash Flow from Investment Activities	(72,000)	
Net Cash Flow from Finance Activities	35,000	
Change in Cash	$ 29,000	[Section 8.5]

8.12 From the following balance sheet information and other data, prepare a statement of cash flows for Brown Company, using the indirect method:

	12/31/19A	12/31/19B
Cash	$ 1,800	$ 2,830
Accounts Receivable	3,050	2,950
Prepaid Insurance	4,310	5,490
Investment in Green Company (equity method)	600	730
Investment in Blue Company (cost method)	1,000	1,000
Land	2,000	3,500
Machinery	6,060	6,240
Accumulated Depreciation	(1,070)	(1,390)
Patents	200	160
Total Assets	$17,950	$21,510
Wages Payable	$ 5,630	$ 6,040
Note Payable (Long-term)	—	1,500
Bonds Payable	2,100	1,600
Deferred Taxes Payable	300	410
Common Stock	1,000	1,000
Preferred Stock	4,000	4,300
Paid-in Capital in Excess of Par — Preferred	1,750	2,260
Retained Earnings	3,340	4,400
Treasury Stock (cost method)	(170)	—
Total Liabilities and Stockholders' Equity	$17,950	$21,510

Other data:

(1) Net income $1,490

(2) Depreciation expense   530

(3) Equity in Green Company net income   130

(4) Loss on sale of machinery   50

(5) Amortization of patents   40

(6) Dividends paid (cash)   430

(7) Machinery with a cost of $450 and a book value of $240 was sold for $190.

(8) Machinery was purchased for $630.

(9) Treasury stock was sold for $250 cash.

(10) Land with a fair market value of $1,500 was purchased by the issuance of a long-term note payable.

(11) Preferred stock was issued for $230 cash.

(12) The remaining changes in the Preferred Stock account and in the Paid-in-Capital in Excess of Par account resulted from the issuance of preferred stock to retire $500 of bonds payable.

SOLUTION

Brown Company
Statement of Cash Flows
For the Year Ended December 31, 19B

CASH FROM OPERATING ACTIVITIES

Net Income	$ 1,490
Depreciation Expense	530
Increase in Equity of Green Company	(130)
Loss on Sale of Machinery	50
Amortization of Patents	40
Change in Accounts Receivable	100
Change in Prepaid Insurance	(1,180)
Change in Wages Payable	410
Change in Deferred Tax Liability	110
Net Cash Flow from Operations	$ 1,420

Taxes are dealt with in the operating Activities

CASH FROM INVESTMENT ACTIVITIES

Sale of machinery	$ 190
Purchase of machinery	(630)
Net Cash Flow from Investment Activities	$ (440)

CASH FROM FINANCE ACTIVITIES

Cash dividends paid	$ (430)
Sale of treasury stock	250
Issuance of preferred stock	230
Net Cash Flow from Finance Activities	$ 50

Summary

Net Cash Flow from Operations	$ 1,420
Net Cash Flow from Investment Activities	(440)
Net Cash Flow from Finance Activities	50
Change in Cash	$ 1,030

(A footnote disclosure would be made of the conversion of the bonds payable into stock, and of the issuance of the long-term note for the purchase of the land.) [Section 8.5]

Cash from Operating Activities — Direct Method

8.13 The Weinbaum Corporation had beginning and ending balances of $40,000 and $30,000, respectively, in its Wages Payable account during 19X1, and wages expense of $60,000 on its income statement. It also had in its Interest Payable account a beginning balance of $100,000, an ending balance of $125,000, and interest expense of $50,000. Determine the amounts paid for wages and interest.

SOLUTION

Wages Payable			Interest Payable		
X	40,000		Y	100,000	
	60,000			50,000	
	30,000			125,000	

$$\$40,000 + \$60,000 - X = \$30,000 \qquad \$100,000 + \$50,000 - Y = \$125,000$$
$$\$100,000 - X = \$30,000 \qquad\qquad \$150,000 - Y = \$125,000$$
$$X = \$70,000 \qquad\qquad Y = \$25,000 \qquad \text{[Section 8.6]}$$

8.14 The Feiner Corporation showed sales (on account) on its income statement of $200,000 for 19X1. Its beginning 19X1 balance in Accounts Receivable was $100,000; its ending balance was $150,000. Determine cash received on collections of sales.

SOLUTION

Accounts Receivable	
100,000	X
200,000	
150,000	

$$\$100,000 + \$200,000 - X = \$150,000$$
$$\$300,000 - X = \$150,000$$
$$X = \$150,000 \qquad \text{[Section 8.6]}$$

8.15 The beginning and ending balances of the Merchandise Inventory account were $70,000 and $120,000, respectively. The beginning and ending balances of Accounts Payable were $18,000 and $11,000, respectively. Cost of goods sold on the income statement was $140,000. Determine the amount paid for merchandise purchases.

SOLUTION

Merchandise Inventory	
70,000	140,000
X	
120,000	

$$\$70,000 + X - \$140,000 = \$120,000$$
$$X - \$70,000 = \$120,000$$
$$X = \$190,000 = \text{purchases}$$

Accounts Payable	
Y	18,000
	190,000 (purchases)
	11,000

$$\$18,000 + \$190,000 - Y = \$11,000$$
$$\$208,000 - Y = \$11,000$$
$$Y = \$197,000 = \text{payments}$$
$$\text{[Section 8.6]}$$

8.16 From the following information determine net cash flow from operations using the direct method:

INCOME STATEMENT

Service Revenue	$500,000
Wages Expense	(50,000)
Insurance Expense	(10,000)
Net Income	$440,000

BALANCE SHEETS

	12/31/19X0	12/31/19X1
Accounts Receivable	$30,000	$36,000
Prepaid Insurance	5,000	6,000
Wages Payable	7,000	4,000

SOLUTION

Accounts Receivable

30,000	X
500,000	
36,000	

$$\$30,000 + \$500,000 - X = \$36,000$$
$$\$530,000 - X = \$36,000$$
$$X = \$494,000$$
$$= \text{cash collections}$$

Prepaid Insurance

5,000	10,000
Y	
6,000	

$$\$5,000 + Y - \$10,000 = \$6,000$$
$$Y - \$5,000 = \$6,000$$
$$Y = \$11,000$$
$$= \text{cash paid for insurance}$$

Wages Payable

P	7,000
	50,000
	4,000

$$\$7,000 + \$50,000 - P = \$4,000$$
$$57,000 - P = \$4,000$$
$$P = \$53,000$$
$$= \text{cash paid for wages}$$

Cash Collections	$494,000
Insurance Payments	(11,000)
Wage Payments	(53,000)
Net Cash Flow from Operations	$430,000

[Section 8.6]

8.17   The income statement of Company J contained the following data:

Sales	$ 800,000
Cost of Goods Sold	(500,000)
Gross Profit	$ 300,000

Partial balance sheets revealed the following:

	Dec. 31, 19X5	Dec. 31, 19X6
Accounts Receivable	$40,000	$30,000
Inventory	80,000	95,000
Accounts Payable	39,000	34,000

Determine cash received from customers and cash paid for inventory purchases. Assume Accounts Payable relates solely to inventory purchases.

SOLUTION

Accounts Payable

40,000	X
800,000	
30,000	

$$\$40,000 + \$800,000 - X = \$30,000$$
$$\$840,000 - X = \$30,000$$
$$X = \$810,000$$
$$= \text{cash received from customers}$$

Inventory

80,000	500,000
Y	
95,000	

$$\$80,000 + Y - \$500,000 = \$95,000$$
$$Y - \$420,000 = \$95,000$$
$$Y = \$515,000*$$
$$= \text{purchases on account}$$

Accounts Payable

P	39,000
	515,000* (From above)
	34,000

$$\$39,000 + \$515,000 - P = \$34,000$$
$$\$554,000 - P = \$34,000$$
$$P = \$520,000$$
$$= \text{cash paid for purchases}$$

[Section 8.6]

Complete Statement of Cash Flows — Direct Method

8.18 Company K had the following balance sheet data for 19X1 and 19X2:

	12/31/19X1	12/31/19X2
Cash	$ 11,500	$ 18,000
Accounts Receivable	13,000	17,500
Merchandise	19,000	16,000
Machinery	17,000	19,000
Accumulated Depreciation	(11,500)	(12,000)
Long-term Investments	14,000	13,000
Total Assets	$ 63,000	$ 71,500
Accounts Payable	$ 9,000	$ 12,000
Expenses Payable	3,000	2,000
Note Payable (Long-term)	15,000	14,000
Common Stock	17,000	19,000
Retained Earnings	19,000	24,500
Total Equities	$ 63,000	$ 71,500

The income statement appeared as follows:

Sales	$ 69,000
Cost of Goods Sold	(47,000)
Gross Profit	22,000
General Expenses	(11,000)
Depreciation Expense	(500)
Net Income	$ 10,500

Additional information: Cash dividends were $5,000; long-term investments were sold at book value. Prepare a statement of cash flows using the direct method.

SOLUTION

Company K
Statement of Cash Flows
For the Year Ended December 31, 19X2

CASH FROM OPERATING ACTIVITIES

Cash Received from Customers	$ 64,500	
Cash Paid for Merchandise	(41,000)	
Cash Paid for Expenses	(12,000)	
Net Cash Flow from Operations		$11,500

CASH FROM INVESTING ACTIVITIES

Purchases of Machinery	$ (2,000)	
Sale of Long-term Investment	1,000	
Net Cash Flow from Investing Activities		$ (1,000)

CASH FROM FINANCING ACTIVITIES

Payment of Notes Payable	$ (1,000)	
Issuance of Stock	2,000	
Cash Dividends Paid	(5,000)	
Net Cash Flow from Financing Activities		$ (4,000)
Net Change in Cash		$ 6,500

Explanation of cash from operating activities:

Accounts Receivable

13,000	X
69,000	
17,500	

$13,000 + $69,000 - X = $17,500
X = $64,500
= cash from customers

Merchandise

19,000	47,000
Y	
16,000	

$19,000 + Y - $47,000 = $16,000
Y = $44,000 = purchases

Accounts Payable

P	9,000
	44,000 (purchases)
	12,000

$9,000 + $44,000 - P = $12,000
P = $41,000 = purchase payments

Expenses Payable

X	3,000
	11,000 (general expenses)
	2,000

$3,000 + $11,000 - X = $2,000
X = $12,000
= payments for expenses

[Section 8.7]

Special Issues Relating to the Statement of Cash Flows

8.19 Company L showed the following data relating to its accounts receivable for 19X1 and 19X2:

	Dec. 31, 19X1	Dec. 31, 19X2
Accounts Receivable	$15,000	$18,000
Allowance for Bad Debts	(1,000)	(500)
	$14,000	$17,500

How should this information be used under the indirect method?

SOLUTION

The net increase of $3,500 should be subtracted from the net income.   [Section 8.8]

8.20 Company M had beginning and ending balances in Accounts Receivable in the amounts of $17,000 and $12,000, respectively. Sales on account were $125,000; bad debts expense was $2,000; write-offs were $9,000. How should this information be used under the direct method?

SOLUTION

It should be used to determine cash received from customers, as follows:

So the BAD debt Write offs nch the BAD debts figure is included/reflected in the ending Balance.

Accounts Receivable	
17,000	9,000
125,000	X (collections)
12,000	

$$\$17,000 + \$125,000 - \$9,000 - X = \$12,000$$
$$\$133,000 - X = \$12,000$$
$$X = \$121,000$$

[Section 8.8]

Supplementary Problems

8.21 From the following information, determine the net cash flow from operating activities for 19B:

	19A	19B
Accounts receivable	$ 5,000	$ 7,000
Merchandise	3,000	2,500
Prepaid items	2,000	2,200
Accounts Payable	4,000	3,000
Accrued expenses payable	3,000	3,500
Bonds payable	50,000	48,000
Net income		$50,000
Depreciation expense		6,000
Amortization of bond premium		2,000
Amortization of goodwill		500
Loss on sale of equipment		500

8.22 From the following information, determine the net cash flow from investment activities:
(a) Sold equipment (book value of $7,000) for $8,000.
(b) Purchased land for $6,000.
(c) Purchased treasury stock for $9,000.
(d) Collected principal on long-term loan of $50,000.
(e) Sold investment (cost of $6,000) for $4,000.
(f) Retired bond payable of $40,000.

8.23 From the following information determine the net cash flow from financing activities:
(a) Retired a bond payable for $10,000.
(b) Issued 100 shares of $100 par common stock at $110.
(c) Paid a long-term note payable of $7,000.
(d) Purchased treasury stock for $10,000.
(e) Issued 100 shares of $100 par common stock in exchange for equipment.

8.24 During 19A, the balance in the Equipment account increased by $10,000 despite the fact that equipment (cost $7,000; accumulated depreciation $4,000) was sold for $8,000. How much new equipment must have been purchased?

8.25   From the following information, determine net cash flow from investment activities during 19B:

(a)   Change in accounts receivable during 19B, $4,000.

(b)   Net income, $50,000.

(c)   Depreciation expense, $7,000.

(d)   Purchased land, $70,000.

(e)   Sold machinery (cost $50,000; accumulated depreciation $40,000), $18,000.

(f)   Issued preferred stock, $25,000.

(g)   Issued bonds, $19,000.

(h)   Lent cash to subsidiary, $75,000.

8.26   From the following information prepare a statement of cash flows under the indirect method:

	19A	19B
Cash	$150	$ 65
Accounts Receivable	70	50
Prepaid Insurance	50	60
Merchandise Inventory	40	45
Equipment (net)	500	700
Long-term Investment	800	1,000
Accounts Payable	200	250
Accrued Expenses Payable	400	380
Taxes Payable	300	340
Bonds Payable	200	300
Common Stock	400	490
Premium on Common Stock	0	10
Retained Earnings	110	150

Additional information from the income statement and general ledger is as follows:

(a)   Net income, $50.

(b)   Depreciation expense, $10.

(c)   Cash dividends paid, $10.

(d)   Purchased equipment for $300.

(e)   Sold equipment at its book value of $90.

(f)   Purchased a long-term investment for $200.

(g)   Issued bonds for cash.

(h)   Issued common stock for cash.

8.27   The balances in the Retained Earnings account of Company S at the beginning and end of 19B were $100,000 and $400,000, respectively. During 19B, Company P earned $600,000 net income. There were no other transactions involving retained earnings except for the declaration of a cash dividend. How much was this declaration? Will this amount *necessarily* appear on the statement of cash flows? Why?

8.28   Corporation P had beginning and ending balances of $50,000 and $40,000, respectively, in its Taxes Payable account during 19A. On its income statement it reported income tax expense of $70,000. Determine the amount it paid for taxes during 19A.

8.29   Corporation S showed sales (on account) on its income statement of $150,000 for 19A. Its beginning balance of Accounts Receivable was $70,000; its ending balance was $120,000. Determine cash received as collections for sales.

8.30   The beginning and ending balances of the Merchandise Inventory account during 19B were $50,000 and $100,000, respectively. The beginning and ending balances of Accounts Payable were $15,000 and $8,000, respectively. The income statement showed cost of goods sold of $120,000. Determine the amount paid for merchandise purchases.

Chapter 9

Accounting Changes and Correction of Errors

9.1 INTRODUCTION

Companies often make changes in their use of accounting principles or accounting estimates. For example, they may decide to change from one method of depreciating their plant and equipment to another. Or they may decide that an original estimate of the life of equipment was incorrect and should be revised. Such changes are referred to in accounting literature as "accounting changes."

Occasionally, a company discovers that errors were made in a previous accounting period and it now wishes to correct them. These are referred to as "error corrections." Both accounting changes and error corrections are covered by APB Opinion No. 20, and are discussed in this chapter.

According to APB No. 20, there are three types of accounting changes:

1. Changes in accounting principle

2. Changes in accounting estimate

3. Changes in reporting entity

A *change in accounting principle* involves changing from one *generally accepted* accounting principle to another. For example, a change in depreciation methods or inventory costing methods would fall under this category.

If the accounting principle previously followed was not acceptable or was incorrectly applied, it is *not* considered a change in principle but rather a correction of an error.

A *change in accounting estimate* arises as a result of new information obtained regarding certain estimations. For example, a change in the estimated useful life or residual value of a fixed asset would fall under this category.

If the original estimate was made either in bad faith or with poor judgment, the change is not considered to be a change in estimate but rather a correction of an error.

A *change in reporting entity* involves organizations whose identity has evolved from one form to another. An example would be the preparation of consolidated statements instead of individual statements for a parent and its subsidiary.

Error corrections involve the discovery of various kinds of errors that took place in prior periods. These are considered to be prior period adjustments and require correction entries.

9.2 CHANGES IN ACCOUNTING PRINCIPLE — CUMULATIVE EFFECT APPROACH

As stated previously, these changes involve a change from one generally accepted accounting principle to another. Examples would be a change in depreciation or inventory methods.

There are three types of accounting principle changes:

1. Cumulative effect–type changes

2. Retroactive effect–type changes

3. A change to the LIFO inventory method

Cumulative effect–type changes require the use of the "catch-up" approach to account for the change. This approach involves the following elements:

(a) The difference in income over past years between the old method and the new method must be shown on the income statement between the extraordinary items and the net income. This is called the "cumulative effect of the change in accounting principle." A journal entry should also be made for this amount.

(b) Financial statements for prior periods included for comparative purposes should *not* be restated but should be presented as previously reported.

(c) As supplementary information, income before extraordinary items and net income (for all periods presented) should be computed and shown on a pro forma (as if) basis. In other words, we recompute income before extraordinary items and net income *as if the newly adopted principle had been in effect all along*.

EXAMPLE 1

During the years 19X1 and 19X2, a company used the sum-of-the-years' digits (SYD) method of depreciation for its plant assets, both for book and tax purposes. At the beginning of 19X3, it decides to change to the straight-line method, both for book and tax purposes. Let's assume that a tax rate of 40% is in effect for all years, and there are 1,000 shares of common stock outstanding.

The following table shows the effect on net income for each year as a result of this change. Assume that straight-line depreciation for each year is $50,000, while SYD depreciation would be $80,000 and $70,000, respectively, for 19X1 and 19X2.

Year	Straight-line	SYD	Difference	Taxes	Net Income Change
19X1	$ 50,000	$ 80,000	$30,000	$12,000	$18,000
19X2	50,000	70,000	20,000	8,000	12,000
	$100,000	$150,000	$50,000	$20,000	$30,000

Thus, accumulated depreciation is overstated by $50,000 and the cumulative effect on the net income (after taxes) is an increase of $30,000. The journal entry for this would be:

Accumulated Depreciation	50,000	
Cumulative Effect of Change in Accounting Principle		30,000
Taxes Payable		20,000

The cumulative effect of $30,000 is similar to revenue and would thus increase net income on the income statement. If the cumulative effect had been a debit, it would be similar to an expense and would reduce the net income.

If we assume that income from continuing operations for 19X3 and 19X2 is $150,000 and $160,000, respectively, and there were no extraordinary items, the comparative income statements for 19X3 and 19X2 would appear as follows:

	19X3	19X2
Income from Continuing Operations	$150,000	$160,000
Cumulative Effect of Change in Accounting Principle (net of tax)	30,000	—
Net Income	$180,000	$160,000
Earnings Per Share:		
Continuing Operations	$150	$160
Cumulative Effect of Change in Accounting Principle	30	—
Net Income	$180	$160

Pro forma amounts assuming retroactive application of the new depreciation method are:

	19X3	19X2
Income from Continuing Operations	$150,000	$172,000*
Net Income	$150,000	$172,000
Earnings Per Share	$150	$172

*Original income reported	$160,000
Increase in net income due to change	12,000
	$172,000

9.3   CHANGES IN ACCOUNTING PRINCIPLE — RETROACTIVE APPROACH

Some changes in accounting principle do not take the cumulative effect approach but rather the retroactive approach. This approach has the following characteristics:

(a) The financial statements of all prior periods presented are restated.

(b) In the year of the change an adjustment is made to the beginning retained earnings balance in the retained earnings statement and an entry is recorded for this amount.

There are five situations that require the use of the retroactive approach. They are:

1. A change from the LIFO inventory method to another method.

2. A change in the method of accounting for long-term construction contracts.

3. A change to or from the full-cost method of accounting in the extractive industries.

4. Issuance of financial statements by a company for the first time to obtain equity capital or to register securities.

5. A professional pronouncement recommending that a change in accounting principle be applied retroactively. (For example, FASB No. 11 requires retroactive treatment for changes in accounting for contingencies.)

A major reason why the accounting profession required the retroactive approach in these cases is that the cumulative approach might have such a strong effect on the current year's net income as to possibly render the statements misleading.

Let's now take a look at an example of the retroactive approach.

EXAMPLE 2

During 19X1 and 19X2, the Weinbaum Corporation used the completed-contract method of accounting for construction contracts. At the beginning of 19X3, it decides to change to the percentage-of-completion method, for both tax and book purposes. The tax rate for all years is 40%, and there are 1,000 shares of common stock outstanding. The following table presents the relevant information for the years 19X1, 19X2, and 19X3:

	Pretax Income		Difference before Tax	Tax Effect	Difference after Tax
	Percentage Method	**Completed-Contract Method**			
19X1	$300,000	$200,000	$100,000	$40,000	$60,000
19X2	150,000	120,000	30,000	12,000	18,000
Total	$450,000	$320,000	$130,000	$52,000	$78,000
19X3	$170,000	$150,000	$ 20,000	$ 8,000	$12,000

The entry in 19X3 to record this change is:

Construction in Process	130,000	
Taxes Payable		52,000
Retained Earnings		78,000

(For a review of accounting for construction, see Chapter 6.)

Retained earnings is increased by $78,000 because the net income after taxes for 19X1 and 19X2 has risen by this amount, and net income increases retained earnings.

The 19X3 comparative income statement would show the following:

	19X3	19X2
Income before Taxes	$170,000	$150,000
Income Taxes (40%)	(68,000)	(60,000)
Net Income	$102,000	$ 90,000
Earnings Per Share (1,000 shares)	$ 102	$ 90

The above figures are based upon the new, retroactive, percentage-of-completion figures.

Let's assume the beginning retained earnings balances for 19X3 and 19X2 were $800,000 and $680,000, respectively, and that no dividends were declared during these years. The comparative retained earnings statements for these years would appear as follows:

	19X3	19X2
Beginning Balance, as previously reported	$800,000	$680,000
Adjustment Due to Change in Accounting for Construction	78,000	*60,000
Beginning Balance, as adjusted	878,000	740,000
Net Income	102,000	90,000
Ending Balance	$980,000	$830,000

*This is a result of the change (after taxes) in the *19X1* income (see the table).

9.4 CHANGES IN ACCOUNTING PRINCIPLE—CHANGE TO LIFO

A change *to* the LIFO inventory method from another inventory method gets neither the cumulative effect treatment nor the retroactive effect treatment. The cumulative effect is *not* recognized and prior years' income and retained earnings are *not* revised. The base year inventory for all subsequent LIFO calculations is the opening inventory in the year the method is adopted.

The only disclosure required is a footnote describing the effect of this change on the results of the current year operations. In addition, a justification for the change should be given.

9.5 CHANGE IN ACCOUNTING ESTIMATES

There are a number of situations in accounting that require the use of estimates. Examples include uncollectibility of accounts receivable, liabilities for estimated warranty costs, and the salvage values and lives of plant assets.

It often happens that estimates need to be revised as a result of new information. Such changes in accounting estimates are handled differently from changes in accounting principles. Prior statements are *not* revised, correction entries are *not* made, and the cumulative effect of the change is *not* recorded. Instead, the change affects only the future (and this period if the revision is made before the end of the period). In short, this change is neither retroactive nor current, but "prospective" in nature.

The reason why the accounting profession prescribed this treatment is that such changes occur frequently, and would thus require continual retroactive or catch-up entries. This would make the financial statements difficult to read and interpret.

If a change is made in the estimated useful life or residual value of a plant asset, then for the future, the new depreciation would be calculated based on the following:

$$\text{New depreciation} = \frac{\text{book value} - \text{residual value}}{\text{remaining years}}$$

No adjustment or correction entries would be made for the depreciation taken so far.

EXAMPLE 3

Smith Corporation purchased a machine on January 1, 19X1, for $100,000. At that time it was thought the machine would have a life of 10 years and a residual value of $10,000. Thus the annual depreciation taken was $9,000 [($100,000 − $10,000) ÷ 10].

Early in 19X5 the company realizes that the *total* life of the machine is only 8 years and the residual value is only $8,000. Since 4 years have already passed (19X1–19X4), there are another 4 years still remaining. The book value at this time is $64,000, as indicated by the following T-accounts:

Machine		Accumulated Depreciation	
100,000			9,000
			9,000
			9,000
			9,000
			36,000

$$\text{Book value} = \$100,000 - \$36,000 = \$64,000$$

The annual depreciation for 19X5, 19X6, 19X7, and 19X8 is:

$$\frac{\$64,000 - \$8,000}{4} = \$14,000$$

No correction entries are made to correct the depreciation of prior years.

If a change has to be made and it is unclear if it is a change in principle or a change in estimate, it should be considered a change in *estimate*.

The treatment just discussed for changes in estimates only applies if the original estimate was calculated with proper care. It does not apply if the estimate was determined without proper care or in bad faith. In such cases, the change is considered to be a correction of an error, which requires different treatment. Correction of errors is discussed later in this chapter.

9.6 CHANGES IN REPORTING ENTITY

Some accounting changes result in financial statements that are the statements of a new or different entity. Examples include presenting consolidated statements instead of statements for each individual company, changing the specific subsidiaries that make up a consolidated group, and accounting for a pooling of interests.

The financial statements in the year of the change should describe the nature of the change and the reason for the change, and the statements for all prior periods presented should be *restated* to reflect this new entity. The effect of the change on net income and earnings per share should be disclosed for all periods presented.

This topic is discussed in more detail in Advanced Accounting.

9.7 CORRECTION OF ERRORS

Mistakes due to errors in arithmetic, poor estimates, or carelessness usually require adjusting, corrective entries. Very often these entries require a debit or credit to the beginning-of-period Retained Earnings. Such entries are called *prior period adjustments*. For simplification, we will ignore taxes. Some errors affect only the balance sheet. For example, a notes payable may have been entered as an account payable, or the purchase of a machine was debited to Land instead of to Machine. Such errors require a correcting entry to reclassify these items under their proper account titles. If comparative balance sheets are prepared that include the year in which the error was made, the balance sheet for that year should be restated to reflect the correction.

EXAMPLE 4

In 19X1 a building was purchased for $100,000 and the entry was:

Machine	100,000	
Cash		100,000

The error was discovered in 19X2. The correction is:

Building	100,000	
Machine		100,000

As we know, all expense and revenue items flow into Retained Earnings at the end of each period via the closing process. Thus each period begins with a "clean slate" for the expense and revenue accounts.

Accordingly, if an error occurs that affects *only* income statement accounts, and the error is discovered in the *same* period, a correction must be made. However, if it is discovered in a future period, no correction is necessary because the original accounts have been closed.

EXAMPLE 5

In 19X1 the payment of a telephone bill was debited to Advertising Expense. If the error is discovered *this* year, the correction would be:

Telephone Expense	xx	
Advertising Expense		xx

If the error is discovered after this year, no correction would be needed since these accounts have been closed.

Let's now discuss errors that affect *both* the balance sheet and the income statement. These come in two types: counterbalancing and non-counterbalancing. *Counterbalancing* errors are self-correcting over 2 years; *non-counterbalancing* errors take more than 2 years to self-correct, and sometimes may *never* self-correct.

Most errors are counterbalancing. For example, a company fails to accrue wages on December 31, 19A, but instead records them at the time of payment in January of 19B. Thus, in 19A the company erred in *not* making the following entry:

$$\text{Wages Expense} \qquad \text{xx}$$
$$\qquad \text{Wages Payable} \qquad \text{xx}$$

In 19B the company erred by the following:

$$\text{Wages Expense} \qquad \text{xx}$$
$$\qquad \text{Cash} \qquad \text{xx}$$

This is an error because these wages are not an expense of 19B; they are an expense of 19A. Briefly put, 19B and its income statement do not "deserve" this expense.

Based upon the above analysis, we can conclude as follows:

For 19A: Expenses were understated, net income was thus overstated, retained earnings was overstated (because net income flows into retained earnings), and wages payable was understated.

For 19B: Expenses are overstated, net income is thus understated, wages payable is correct, and retained earnings is also correct.

Why is retained earnings now correct? The answer is: Last year retained earnings was *overstated* because the net income was overstated. This year net income was understated, causing an *understatement* in retained earnings. Therefore, the understatement and overstatement offset each other, thus leaving retained earnings correct. This is what we mean by "counterbalancing."

In light of the above we can now understand what corrective action, if any, need be taken for counterbalancing errors. If the error is discovered in the second period *before* closing entries have been made, an entry must be made to correct retained earnings. This is because the counterbalancing action (which would self-correct the retained earnings) takes place at closing, and we are still *before* closing. This correction entry is called a prior period adjustment. If, however, the error is discovered *after* closing, *no* corrective entry is needed — retained earnings has self-corrected via the counterbalancing action of closing, the other balance sheet accounts are correct, and the income statement accounts have zero balances due to closing.

EXAMPLE 6

On December 31, 19A, Company E failed to accrue its telephone expense because it failed to debit Telephone Expense and credit Accounts Payable. In January of 19B, when it received the phone bill, it then made the following entry:

$$\text{Telephone Expense} \qquad 100$$
$$\qquad \text{Cash} \qquad 100$$

The effect of the error on the 19A statements is as follows:

Income statement: Expenses understated, net income overstated.

Balance sheet: Liabilities understated, retained earnings overstated (because the net income was overstated).

If the error is discovered in 19B before closing, a correction entry would be made, as follows:

$$\text{Retained Earnings} \qquad 100$$
$$\qquad \text{Telephone Expense} \qquad 100$$

Retained Earnings is debited because it was overstated in 19A. Telephone Expense is credited because 19B does not "deserve" the telephone expense belonging to 19A.

If the error is discovered in 19B *after* closing, *no* correction entry is needed because the books are now correct. Retained earnings has been counterbalanced (this year's overstatement of expense causing an understatement in retained earnings offsets last year's overstatement), the other balance sheet accounts are correct, and the expense accounts have been closed. The effect on the 19B statements would be the following:

Income statement: Expenses overstated, net income understated.

Balance sheet: Correct.

Let's take a look at several additional examples involving counterbalancing errors. For simplification, we ignore taxes.

EXAMPLE 7

At the beginning of 19A, Company E bought a 2-year insurance policy for $2,000 and debited Insurance Expense and credited Cash for the full $2,000. It should have debited Prepaid Insurance. No adjusting entries were made at the end of 19A to reduce the expense to $1,000 and to recognize the asset prepaid insurance of $1,000. The effect of this error on the 19A statements would be:

Income statement: Expenses overstated, net income understated.

Balance sheet: Assets understated, retained earnings understated.

If the error is discovered in 19B *before* closing, the correction entry is:

Insurance Expense	1,000	
Retained Earnings		1,000

(Insurance Expense is debited because 19B "deserves" an expense of $1,000.)

If the error is discovered *after* closing, *no* correction is needed — retained earnings has been counterbalanced. In this case, the effect on the 19B statements is:

Income statement: Expenses understated, net income overstated.

Balance sheet: Correct.

EXAMPLE 8

On the last day of 19A, Company E received a $100,000 prepayment of 19B rent for a building it rented to a tenant. It debited Cash and credited Rent Revenue for this amount. It should have credited Unearned Rent — a liability. The effect of this error on the 19A statements is:

Income statement: Revenue overstated, net income overstated.

Balance sheet: Liabilities understated, retained earnings overstated.

If the error is discovered in 19B *before* closing, the correction is:

Retained Earnings	100,000	
Rent Revenue		100,000

(Rent Revenue is credited because 19B "deserves" this revenue.)

If the error is discovered after closing, no correction is needed — the error has been counterbalanced. In this case, the effect on the 19B statements is:

Income statement: Revenue understated, net income understated.

Balance sheet: Correct.

EXAMPLE 9

At the end of 19A, Company E failed to accrue interest of $500 on a note receivable via an entry debiting Interest Receivable and crediting Interest Revenue. At the beginning of 19B, when it received the cash, it then debited Cash and credited Interest Revenue. The effect of this error in 19A is:

Income statement: Revenue understated, net income understated.

Balance sheet: Assets understated, retained earnings understated.

If the error is discovered in 19B *before* closing, the correction is:

Interest Revenue	500	
Retained Earnings		500

(Interest Revenue is debited because 19B does not "deserve" this interest.)

If the error is discovered *after* closing, no correction is necessary — retained earnings has been counterbalanced, the other balance sheet accounts are correct, and the income statement accounts have all been closed. In this case, the effect on the 19B statements is:

Income statement: Revenue overstated, net income overstated.

Balance sheet: Correct.

EXAMPLE 10

At the end of 19A, Company E understated its ending inventory by $20,000. This also causes the beginning inventory of 19B to be understated by the same amount. As we know, when the *ending* inventory is understated, cost of goods sold will be overstated and thus net income will be understated. When the *beginning* inventory is understated, the opposite effect will occur. Thus the effect of this error on 19A is:

Income statement: Ending inventory understated, net income understated.

Balance sheet: Assets understated, retained earnings understated.

If the error is discovered in 19B *before* closing, the correction is:

Inventory	20,000	
Retained Earnings		20,000

If the error is discovered *after* closing, no correction is needed — the opposite effect that takes place this year (as discussed) counterbalances retained earnings. In this case, the effect on the 19B statements is:

Income statement: Beginning inventory understated, net income overstated.

Balance sheet: Correct.

EXAMPLE 11

Near the end of 19A, Company E purchased merchandise FOB destination for the amount of $5,000. The goods did not arrive until 19B and were thus *correctly* not included in the ending inventory of 19A. However, the company *incorrectly* recorded the purchase in 19A via the following entry:

Purchases	5,000	
Accounts Payable		5,000

This is incorrect because the purchase does not belong to 19A; it belongs to 19B. We know that when purchases are overstated, cost of goods sold is also overstated, thus causing net income to be understated (which in turn understates retained earnings).

Accordingly, the effect on the statements for 19A is:

Income statement: Purchases overstated, net income understated.

Balance sheet: Liabilities overstated, retained earnings understated.

If the error is discovered in 19B *before* closing, the correction entry is:

Purchases	5,000	
Retained Earnings		5,000

(Purchases is debited because 19B "deserves" this purchase.)

If the error is discovered *after* closing, no correction is needed — the error has counterbalanced. In this case, the effect on 19B is:

Income statement: Purchases understated, net income overstated.

Balance sheet: Correct.

Let's now take a look at *non*-counterbalancing errors. Such errors take longer than two periods to self-correct, and in certain cases, may never self-correct. Thus correction entries are needed in the second period *even* after closing entries have been made.

EXAMPLE 12

Company E purchased a machine with an estimated useful life of 5 years on January 1, 19A, for $20,000, thus requiring annual depreciation expense of $4,000. By mistake the entire $20,000 was expensed instead of capitalized, and the entry was:

Miscellaneous Expense	20,000	
Cash		20,000

Accordingly, expenses were overstated by $16,000 (20,000 instead of 4,000). The effect on the 19A statements is:

Income statement: Expenses overstated, net income understated.

Balance sheet: Assets (machine) understated by $16,000, retained earnings understated by $16,000.

If this error is discovered in 19B *before* closing, an entry will have to be made to recognize the asset machine, to recognize the related accumulated depreciation, and to correct retained earnings. The entry is:

Machine	20,000	
Accumulated Depreciation		4,000
Retained Earnings		16,000

In addition, a second entry must be made to record depreciation expense for 19B, as follows:

Depreciation Expense	4,000	
Accumulated Depreciation		4,000

If the error is discovered in 19B *after* closing, a correction entry *must still be made* because the error has not yet counterbalanced (it will take 4 years for the counterbalancing to occur.) The correction is:

Machine	20,000	
Accumulated Depreciation		8,000
Retained Earnings		12,000

(Accumulated depreciation is now $8,000, representing 2 years of depreciation. Retained earnings needs a correction of only $12,000 because its shortage has been reduced from $20,000 due to 2 years of depreciation on the machine.)

EXAMPLE 13

Early in 19A, Company E purchased a machine with a 5-year life for $20,000. By mistake the debit was to Land instead of to Machine, and no depreciation was taken. The effect on the 19A statements is:

Income statement: Depreciation expense understated, net income overstated.

Balance sheet: Assets overstated, retained earnings overstated.

If the error is discovered in 19B *before* closing, the following correction must be made:

Machine	20,000	
Retained Earnings	4,000	
Accumulated Depreciation		4,000
Land		20,000

In addition, an entry must be made for the 19B depreciation:

Depreciation Expense	4,000	
Accumulated Depreciation		4,000

If the error is discovered *after* closing, a correction *must still be made* — the error has not yet counterbalanced. The correction is:

Machine	20,000	
Retained Earnings	8,000	
Land		20,000
Accumulated Depreciation		8,000

Since the error was not discovered until *after* closing and the 19B financial statements have already been issued, they would be incorrect, as follows:

Income statement: Expenses (depreciation) understated, net income overstated.

Balance sheet: Assets overstated (because no depreciation has been taken), retained earnings overstated.

Summary

1. Accounting changes consist of three types: changes in accounting principles, changes in accounting estimates, and changes in the reporting entity.

2. *Changes in accounting principle* involve a change from one *acceptable* method of accounting to another—for example, changing from the straight-line method of depreciation to an accelerated method. If the original method was *unacceptable,* the change is considered to be a correction of an error, rather than a change in principle, and requires different treatment.

3. There are three types of changes in accounting principle: cumulative effect–type changes, retroactive effect–type changes, and a change to the LIFO inventory method.

4. Cumulative effect–type changes require the "catch-up" approach. Under this approach, the cumulative effect of the change is shown on the income statement between extraordinary items and net income, and a journal entry is made for this amount. The cumulative effect measures the difference in income over the years of the old accounting principle versus the new one. Comparative financial statements of prior periods, however, should *not* be restated, but presented as previously reported.

5. In addition, as supplementary information, income before extraordinary items and net income, for all prior periods presented, should be shown on a "pro forma" (as if) basis.

6. Some changes in accounting principle require the retroactive approach. Under this approach, no entry is made for the cumulative effect of the change, the financial statements of prior periods *are* restated, and the beginning balance of Retained Earnings for the period of the change is adjusted via a prior period adjustment entry. Changes from LIFO to another method and changes in accounting for construction contracts require this approach.

7. A change *to* the LIFO inventory method requires no recognition of the cumulative effect of the change, nor retroactive changes in net income or retained earnings. In a footnote the company should disclose the effect of this change on the current-year net income, and the reason for the change.

8. Sometimes, accounting estimates have to be revised to reflect new financial information. In such cases, prior statements are *not* revised; correction entries involving retained earnings are *not* made; and the cumulative effect of these changes is *not* recorded. Instead, the change only affects the future—the past is not changed in any way. This change is thus neither retroactive nor current, but prospective in nature.

9. If a change must be made and it is unclear as to whether it is a change in accounting principle or a change in accounting estimate, it should be treated as a change in *estimate.*

10. Some accounting changes result in financial statements of a new entity. An example would be presenting consolidated financial statements instead of separate statements for each company. This is called a *change in reporting entity.* In the year of this change, the financial statements should describe the nature of, and reason for, the change, and the statements of all prior periods presented should be restated to reflect this new entity.

11. *Prior period adjustments* involve the correction of errors or *careless* estimates of prior periods. These error corrections often affect the beginning balance of Retained Earnings.

12. If an error occurs that affects *only* income statement accounts and the error is discovered in the same period, a correction entry must be made. If the error is discovered in a future period, no correction is made because the incorrect accounts have already been closed.

13. Errors that affect *both* the income statement and the balance sheet come in two types: *counterbalancing* and *non-counterbalancing.* The former self-corrects over 2 years; the latter takes longer (and in certain cases may never self-correct).

14. For counterbalancing errors, if the error is discovered in the second year *before* closing, a correction entry must be made to Retained Earnings. If the error is discovered *after* closing, no correction is needed because the error has counterbalanced. For non-counterbalancing errors, corrections must be made *even if* the error is discovered *after* closing.

Rapid Review

1. The three types of accounting changes are: change in _____, change in _____, and change in _____ .

2. Changing from one acceptable method of depreciation to another would be a change in _____ .

3. If the change is from an unacceptable accounting method, this change is considered to be an _____ .

4. The three types of changes in accounting principle are: _____, _____, and _____ .

5. If a change requires the "catch-up" approach, it is called the _____ type change.

6. In this case, supplementary information for all prior periods presented should be shown on a _____ basis.

7. Changes from LIFO to another inventory method require the _____ approach.

8. Changes in the method of accounting for long-term construction contracts require the _____ approach.

9. If a change does not affect the past but only the future, this is a change in _____ . Such a change is neither retroactive nor _____ in nature, but _____ .

10. If an accounting change results in the financial statements of a new organization, this is called a change in _____ .

11. Errors that correct themselves within two periods are called _____ .

12. For these errors, if the error is discovered in the second year *before* closing, a _____ must be made. If the error is discovered *after* closing, _____ need be made.

Answers: 1. accounting principle; accounting estimate; reporting entity 2. accounting principle 3. error correction 4. cumulative effect–type; retroactive effect–type; change to LIFO 5. cumulative 6. pro forma 7. retroactive 8. retroactive 9. estimate; current; prospective 10. reporting entity 11. counterbalancing 12. correction; no correction

Solved Problems

Accounting Changes and Corrections — General

9.1 For the following situations, choose the description that best describes the nature of the situation. The descriptions are:

(1) Change in accounting principle — cumulative effect–type

(2) Change in accounting principle — retroactive effect–type

(3)   Change to LIFO

(4)   Change in accounting estimate

(5)   Change in reporting entity

(6)   Error correction — counterbalancing type

(7)   Error correction — non-counterbalancing type

The situations are:

(a)   Failure to record accrued salaries at year-end

(b)   Change from straight-line depreciation to double-declining balance depreciation

(c)   Change from LIFO to FIFO

(d)   Change from FIFO to LIFO

(e)   Changed estimated useful life of a machine

(f)   Change in realizability of receivables

(g)   Change in accounting for construction contracts

(h)   Purchase of a machine with a 5-year life recorded as a debit to land

(i)   Addition of a new subsidiary to the consolidated group

SOLUTION

(a) 6   (b) 1   (c) 2   (d) 3   (e) 4   (f) 4   (g) 2   (h) 7   (i) 5

[Sections 9.2, 9.3, 9.7]

Cumulative Effect–Type Changes

9.2   During 19A and 19B, the Metro Corporation used the straight-line method of depreciation to depreciate a truck. This method was used both for book purposes and for tax purposes, and the depreciation each year was $30,000. Early in 19C, the corporation decided to switch over to the sum-of-the-years' digits method, for both book and tax purposes. The tax rate for all years is 30%. If the company had used SYD in 19A and 19B, depreciation for those years would have been $50,000 and $40,000, respectively.

(1)   Prepare a table indicating the effect of this change on 19A and 19B, both before and after taxes.

(2)   What type of change is this?

(3)   What journal entry, if any, is necessary?

SOLUTION

(1)

Year	Straight-line	SYD	Difference	Taxes	Net Difference
19A	$30,000	$50,000	$20,000	$6,000	$14,000
19B	30,000	40,000	10,000	3,000	7,000
	$60,000	$90,000	$30,000	$9,000	$21,000

(2)   Change in accounting principle — cumulative effect–type

(3)

Cumulative Effect of Change in Accounting Principle	21,000	
Taxes Payable	9,000	
Accumulated Depreciation		30,000

[Section 9.2]

9.3   Assume that in the previous problem the income from continuing operations for 19C and 19B was $200,000 and $250,000 respectively, that extraordinary gains (net of tax) were $20,000 and $15,000 respectively, and that there were 10,000 shares of common stock outstanding. Show partial comparative income statements for 19C and 19B.

SOLUTION

	19C	19B
Income from Continuing Operations	$200,000	$250,000
Extraordinary Items (net of tax)	20,000	15,000
Cumulative Effect of Change in Accounting Principle (net of tax)	(21,000)	—
Net Income	$199,000	$265,000

EARNINGS PER SHARE	**19C**	**19B**
Continuing Operations	$20.00	$25.00
Extraordinary Items	2.00	1.50
Cumulative Effect of Change in Accounting Principle (net of tax)	(2.10)	—
Total Earnings Per Share	$19.90	$26.50

[Section 9.2]

9.4 In the previous problem, prepare pro forma amounts assuming retroactive application of the new depreciation method.

SOLUTION

	19C	19B
Income from Continuing Operations	$200,000	$243,000*
Extraordinary Items	20,000	15,000
Net Income	$220,000	$258,000
Earnings Per Share	$22.00	$25.80

*Originally reported	$250,000
Extra depreciation (after taxes) due to change	(7,000)
	$243,000

[Section 9.2]

Cumulative Effect– and Retroactive Effect–Type Changes

9.5 The following table shows the net income for Corporation I computed under three different inventory methods:

	FIFO	Average Cost	LIFO
19A	$20,000	$18,000	$16,000
19B	25,000	20,000	18,000
	$45,000	$38,000	$34,000

(1) If in 19A and 19B Company I used FIFO, and then in 19C it decides to switch to average cost, prepare the required journal entry. What type of change is this? (Ignore taxes.)

(2) If in 19A and 19B Company I used LIFO and it now changes to FIFO, what is the journal entry? What type of change is this? (Ignore taxes.)

SOLUTION

(1) This is a change in accounting principle — cumulative effect–type. The entry is:

Cumulative Effect of Change in Accounting Principle	7,000	
Merchandise Inventory		7,000*

*$45,000 − $38,000

(2)   This is a change in accounting principle — retroactive effect–type. The entry is:

Merchandise Inventory	11,000	
Retained Earnings		11,000[†]

[†]$45,000 − $34,000   [Sections 9.2, 9.3]

9.6   For 19A and 19B, Company C used the percentage-of-completion method for its construction contracts. Early in 19C it decides to switch to the completed-contract method (for both book and tax purposes.) Its net income for 19A, 19B, and 19C under the percentage method was $400,000, $200,000, and $220,000, respectively; its net income under the completed-contract method for these years is $300,000, $180,000, and $190,000, respectively.

(1)   What type of change is this?

(2)   Prepare a table to indicate the effect of this change. (Ignore income taxes.)

(3)   Prepare the necessary journal entry.

SOLUTION

(1)   A change in accounting principle — retroactive effect–type

(2)

	Net Income		
	Percentage Method	**Completed-Contract Method**	**Difference**
19A	$400,000	$300,000	$100,000
19B	200,000	180,000	20,000
Total	$600,000	$480,000	$120,000
19C	$220,000	$190,000	$ 30,000

(3)

Retained Earnings	120,000	
Construction in Process		120,000	[Section 9.3]

9.7   For the previous problem, show comparative income statements for 19C and 19B. Assume there are 1,000 shares of common stock outstanding.

SOLUTION

	19C	**19B**
Net Income	$190,000	$180,000
Earnings Per Share	$190	$180	[Section 9.3]

9.8   In the previous problem, assume the beginning Retained Earnings balances for 19C and 19B were $900,000 and $950,000 respectively, and that dividends declared during these years were $10,000 and $15,000, respectively. Show comparative retained earnings statements for these years.

SOLUTION

	19C	**19B**
Beginning Balance, as previously reported	$ 900,000	$ 950,000
Less Adjustment Due to Change in Accounting for Construction	(120,000)	(100,000)
Beginning Balance, as adjusted	780,000	850,000
Net Income	190,000	180,000
Dividends Declared	(10,000)	(15,000)
Ending Balance	$ 960,000	$1,015,000	[Section 9.3]

Changes in Accounting Estimate

9.9   During 19A, GX Corporation had sales of $100,000 and estimated its bad debt expense at 5% of sales. In 19B, GX had sales of $150,000 and revised its estimate to 8%.

(1)   What type of change is this?

(2)   What correction entry for 19A should GX make in 19B?

(3)   What entry should GX make in 19B for its estimated 19B bad debts?

SOLUTION

(1)   A change in accounting estimate.

(2)   No correction entry. The revision only affects 19B and future years.

(3)   The 19B entry is based upon the new estimate of 8% multiplied by $150,000, as follows:

Bad Debt Expense	12,000		
Allowance for Doubtful Accounts		12,000	[Section 9.5]

9.10   Company M purchased a machine with an estimated life of 10 years and an estimated residual value of $10,000 for $110,000 on January 1, 19A. Early in 19E, the company realized that the *total* life of the machine is 15 years, and the residual value is $12,000.

(1)   What type of change is this?

(2)   Does this change require retroactive, current, or prospective treatment?

(3)   What is the book value of the machine at the beginning of 19E?

(4)   What should the new depreciation be for 19E and onward?

(5)   What entry is made at the end of 19E?

SOLUTION

(1)   A change in accounting estimate.

(2)   Prospective — no correction entries are made.

(3) $110,000 - 4($10,000^*) = $70,000

                             ————————————
                             *($110,000 - $10,000) ÷ 10

(4)   ($70,000 - $12,000) ÷ 11 remaining years = $5,273 (rounded)

(5)

Depreciation Expense	5,273		
Accumulated Depreciation		5,273	[Section 9.5]

Correction of Errors

9.11   In 19X1, Company I purchased a machine for $25,000 cash. The entry was a debit to *Land* and a credit to Cash. Depreciation was properly taken in 19X1 and 19X2.

(1)   If this error is discovered in 19X1, what correction entry should be made?

(2)   If this error is discovered in 19X2, would the correction entry be any different? Would assets or capital on the *19X1* balance sheet be incorrect?

SOLUTION

(1)

Machine	25,000	
Land		25,000

(2)   The same correction would be made. The total dollar value of assets and capital would be completely correct.

[Section 9.7]

9.12   In 19A, Company I made an error by debiting wages of $5,000 to Utility Expense. Cash was properly credited.

(1) If the error is discovered in 19A, what correction should be made?

(2) If the error is discovered in 19B, what correction should be made? Why? Would the net income figure on the *19A* income statement be wrong?

SOLUTION

(1)

Wages Expense	5,000	
Utility Expense		5,000

(2) No correction entry because both Wages Expense and Utilities Expense for 19A have been closed. The net income of 19A would be perfectly correct.   [Section 9.7]

9.13 Company I failed to record accrued salaries at the end of 19A, 19B, and 19C in the amounts of $3,000, $4,000, and $5,000, respectively. These salaries were recorded instead at the time of payment early during the next respective year. If these errors are not discovered until 19D (before closing), by how much will retained earnings be incorrect? Why? What correction should be made?

SOLUTION

The error in 19A is counterbalanced by the closing of 19B; the error of 19B is counterbalanced by the closing of 19C. The error of 19C has not yet been counterbalanced; thus retained earnings will be overstated by $5,000. The correction entry is:

Retained Earnings	5,000	
Salary Expense		5,000	[Section 9.7]

9.14 In 19A Company E failed to accrue utility expense of $3,000, but instead recorded it at the time of payment in 19B. What entry should be made to correct this error if (*a*) the error is discovered in 19B before closing or (*b*) the error is discovered in 19B after closing?

SOLUTION

(*a*)

Retained Earnings	3,000	
Utility Expense		3,000

(*b*) No correction entry — the error has counterbalanced.   [Section 9.7]

9.15 At the beginning of 19A, Company E purchased supplies for $8,000 and debited the entire amount to Supplies Expense. These supplies are expected to last for only 2 years. What correction entry should be made in 19B if (*a*) the error is discovered before closing; (*b*) the error is discovered after closing?

SOLUTION

(*a*)

Supplies Expense	4,000	
Retained Earnings		4,000

(*b*) No correction entry — the error has counterbalanced.   [Section 9.7]

9.16 During 19A, Company E made the following errors:

(1) On the last day of the year, it received a $50,000 prepayment of rent for a *19B* rental of a machine. The entry it made was a debit to Cash and a credit to Rent Revenue.

(2) On the last day of the year it failed to accrue interest expense of $20,000 on a note payable. The expense was recorded early in 19B when it was paid.

What corrective action must be taken in 19B if (*a*) the errors are discovered before closing, (*b*) the errors are discovered after closing?

SOLUTION

(*a*) For the first error:

Retained Earnings	50,000	
Rent Revenue		50,000

For the second error:

Retained Earnings	20,000	
Interest Expense		20,000

(*b*) No corrective action for either error because they have been counterbalanced.   [Section 9.7]

9.17 Silly Company made two errors at the end of 19X1. First, it overstated the ending inventory by $25,000 due to a mistake in counting. Second, it did not record an entry for goods it purchased in December on terms of FOB shipping point that did not arrive until January 2, 19B. The goods were *correctly* included in the ending 19A inventory, but the purchase was not recorded until arrival in 19B. The purchase price was $5,000.

(1) If these errors are discovered in 19B before closing, what corrections should be made?

(2) If these errors are discovered after the 19B closing, what corrections should be made?

SOLUTION

(1) Retained Earnings	25,000	
Merchandise Inventory		25,000
Retained Earnings	5,000	
Purchases		5,000

(2) No corrections need to be made because the errors have counterbalanced.   [Section 9.7]

9.18 For the following errors, use the table provided to indicate whether an overstatement or understatement has occurred. For an overstatement write "+"; for an understatement write "−". If neither has occurred, write "OK." Assume that all errors were discovered in 19B *before* closing.

(1) Failed to accrue wages end of 19A; recorded in 19B.

(2) Overstated 19A inventory.

(3) Recorded a purchase in 19A that belonged to 19B; the ending inventory of 19A was correct.

(4) Purchased a machine in 19A and debited Building.

(5) Failed to record interest on a notes receivable in 19A; recorded in 19B.

(6) Credited rent revenue in 19A to Sales.

(7) Bought a building with a 5-year life in 19A; debited Land.

(8) Purchased a 2-year insurance policy at the beginning of 19A; debited Insurance Expense.

(9) Received a prepayment of rent for 19B at the end of 19A; credited Rent Revenue.

(10) Expensed the purchase of a machine in 19A; the machine has a 5-year life.

	19A				19B			
	Net Income	Assets	Liabilities	Retained Earnings	Net Income	Assets	Liabilities	Retained Earnings
(1)								
(2)								
(3)								
(4)								
(5)								
(6)								
(7)								
(8)								
(9)								
(10)								

SOLUTION

	19A				19B			
	Net Income	Assets	Liabilities	Retained Earnings	Net Income	Assets	Liabilities	Retained Earnings
(1)	+	OK	—	+	OK	OK	OK	OK
(2)	+	+	OK	+	OK	OK	OK	OK
(3)	—	OK	+	—	OK	OK	OK	OK
(4)	OK	OK	OK	OK	OK	OK	OK	OK
(5)	—	—	OK	—	OK	OK	OK	OK
(6)	OK	OK	OK	OK	OK	OK	OK	OK
(7)	+	+	OK	+	OK	OK	OK	OK
(8)	—	—	OK	—	OK	OK	OK	OK
(9)	+	OK	—	+	OK	OK	OK	OK
(10)	—	—	OK	—	OK	OK	OK	OK

Note: Everything is OK in 19B since the errors were discovered in 19B and correction entries are presumed to have been made.　　　　　　　　　　　　　　　　　　　　　　　　[Section 9.7]

9.19 Use the same information as in the preceding problem to complete the table, but assume the errors were discovered in 19B *after* closing.

SOLUTION

	19A				19B			
	Net Income	Assets	Liabilities	Retained Earnings	Net Income	Assets	Liabilities	Retained Earnings
(1)	+	OK	—	+	—	OK	OK	OK
(2)	+	+	OK	+	—	OK	OK	OK
(3)	—	OK	+	—	+	OK	OK	OK
(4)	OK	OK	OK	OK	OK	OK	OK	OK
(5)	—	—	OK	—	+	OK	OK	OK
(6)	OK	OK	OK	OK	OK	OK	OK	OK
(7)	+	+	OK	+	+	+	OK	+
(8)	—	—	OK	—	+	OK	OK	OK
(9)	+	OK	—	+	—	OK	OK	OK
(10)	—	—	OK	—	+	—	OK	—

[Section 9.7]

9.20 Early in 19A Company E purchased a building for $50,000 with an estimated useful life of 10 years and no salvage value. The entry it made was:

Miscellaneous Expense	50,000	
Cash		50,000

(1) If the error is discovered in *19B before* closing, what entries must be made?

(2) If the error is discovered *after* the 19B closing, what entries must be made?

SOLUTION

(1)	Building	50,000	
	Accumulated Depreciation		5,000
	Retained Earnings		45,000
	Depreciation Expense	5,000	
	Accumulated Depreciation		5,000

(2)	Building	50,000		
	Accumulated Depreciation		10,000	
	Retained Earnings		40,000	
	Depreciation Expense	5,000		
	Accumulated Depreciation		5,000	[Section 9.7]

Supplementary Problems

9.21 During 19X1 and 19X2, Company A used straight-line depreciation for its assets, resulting in depreciation expense of $40,000 each year. During 19X3, the company decided to switch to the double-declining balance method. Had Company A used this method in 19X1 and 19X2, depreciation in these years would have been $60,000 and $50,000, respectively.

(*a*) What type of change is this?

(*b*) Does this change require cumulative effect, current, or prospective treatment?

(*c*) Prepare the necessary entry in 19X3. Assume the tax rate for all years is 30%.

9.22 During 19X1 and 19X2, Company B used the percentage-of-completion method of accounting for construction. At the beginning of 19X3 it decides to switch to the completed-contract method (for both book and tax purposes.) Under this method income before taxes would have been $100,000 lower for both years combined.

(*a*) What type of change is this?

(*b*) What type of approach does this change require: cumulative effect, retroactive, or prospective?

(*c*) Prepare the required entry for 19X3. Assume a tax rate for all years of 20%.

9.23 Company C changes to the LIFO inventory method in 19C. During 19A and 19B, it used FIFO. Had LIFO been used in those years, income before taxes would have been lower by $10,000 and $15,000, respectively. If we assume a tax rate of 30%, what entry is required in 19C? Why?

9.24 Company D acquired an asset in 19A for $100,000 and estimated it would have a life of 10 years and a salvage value of $10,000. At the beginning of 19E the company realized that the *total* life should only be 8 years, with a salvage value of $8,000.

(*a*) What type of change is this?

(*b*) What correction entry, if any, is needed in 19E? Why?

(*c*) How much depreciation should be taken annually from 19E onward?

9.25 In 19A Company E purchased a machine for $50,000 and erroneously debited the account Building. This error is discovered in 19B. What correction entry is needed in 19B? Assume a tax rate of 30% for all years.

9.26 In 19A the payment of a utility bill was erroneously debited to Telephone Expense. Prepare the required correction entries if:

(*a*) the error is discovered in 19A.

(*b*) the error is discovered in 19B.

9.27 On December 31, 19A, Company F failed to accrue a utility expense of $10,000. This expense was recognized in 19B when it was paid.

(*a*) What is the effect of this error on the 19A balance sheet and income statement?

(*b*) If this error is discovered in 19B before closing, what correction entry, if any, is needed? Ignore taxes.

(*c*) If the error is discovered in 19B after closing, what correction entry is needed?

9.28 At the beginning of 19A, Company G bought supplies for $4,000 and debited Supplies Expense. The supplies are expected to last 2 years. *No* adjusting entries regarding these supplies were made in 19A.

(*a*) What is the effect of this error on the 19A financial statements?

(*b*) If the error is discovered in 19B before closing, what correction should be made?

(*c*) If the error is discovered after closing, what correction should be made?

9.29 At the end of 19A, Company H failed to accrue interest of $300 on a note payable. It recognized this interest early in 19B when it was paid.

(*a*) What is the effect of this error on the 19A income statement and balance sheet?

(*b*) Show what entries should be made in 19B if (1) the error is discovered before closing, and (2) the error is discovered after closing.

9.30 On January 1, 19A, Company I purchased a machine with an estimated life of 5 years and no salvage value for $100,000. By mistake the company debited Machine Expense and credited Cash. The error was not discovered until 19B.

(*a*) Is this error counterbalancing or not? Why?

(*b*) What effect does the error have on the 19A income statement and balance sheet?

(*c*) If the error is discovered in 19B before closing, what correction entry should be made?

(*d*) If the error is discovered *after* closing in 19B, what correction entry, if any, should be made?

Examination III

Chapters 7, 8, 9

A. *True-False Questions.* **Place the letter T or F next to the question.**

1. _____ A lease that transfers a material ownership interest is an operating lease.

2. _____ For the lessor, if the lease term is *less* than 75% of the asset life, the lease is a capital lease.

3. _____ In a sales-type lease, the lessor makes a profit at the time of sale.

4. _____ The annual lease payment is determined by dividing the selling price by the future value of an annuity, at rate *i*, for *n* periods.

5. _____ If the lessee is aware of both his or her interest rate and the rate of the lessor, he or she should use the lower of the two rates.

6. _____ Executory costs should be capitalized.

7. _____ If the salvage value is guaranteed by the lessee, it should be capitalized as part of the asset cost.

8. _____ In the statement of cash flows, depreciation expense should be subtracted from the net income.

9. _____ To determine cash from operations, decreases in accounts receivable should be added to the net income.

10. _____ Cash received from the issuance of a company's own stock should be included in the investment activity section.

11. _____ Purchases of treasury stock should be included in the finance activity section.

12. _____ Payment of cash dividends should be included in the investment activity section.

13. _____ Significant noncash transactions should be disclosed in the *body* of the statement of cash flows.

14. _____ A change in accounting principle involves changing from an unacceptable accounting principle to an acceptable one.

15. _____ For cumulative effect–type changes, the statements of prior periods are not restated.

16. _____ Changes from LIFO to another method require the retroactive approach.

17. _____ Changes in accounting estimates affect the future but not the past.

18. _____ Corrections of careless estimates from previous periods are considered to be prior period adjustments.

19. _____ Counterbalancing errors self-correct over 3 years.

20. _____ Non-counterbalancing errors require a correction entry even if the error is discovered *after* closing.

B. *Completion Questions.* **Fill in the blanks.**

21. The two types of leases are _____ leases and _____ leases.

22. For capital leases, annual depreciation is recorded by the _____ .

23. Initial direct costs incurred by the lessor in consummating an operating lease should be debited to an _____ account.

24. If the present value of the rental annuity is greater than _____ % of the asset's fair market value, the lease is a(n) _____ lease.

25. In a _____ lease, the lessor does not make any profit at the inception of the lease.

26. A situation where the owner of an asset sells the asset and then immediately rents it back is called a _____ .

27. The two methods of determining cash flow from operations are the _____ method and the _____ method.

28. The three sections of the statement of cash flows are _____ , _____ , and _____ .

29. The collection of the principal on a loan would appear in the _____ section.

30. Decreases in the Investment in Subsidiary account (under the equity method) would be added to the _____ in the _____ section.

31. The direct method determines cash from _____ by directly analyzing the _____ .

32. The purchase of a bond would appear in the _____ section.

33. The total of all three sections of the statement of cash flows should equal the net change in _____ for the year.

34. Changing from the straight-line method of depreciation to an accelerated method is an example of a change in _____ .

35. Changes that require a "catch-up" entry are of the _____ effect type.

36. Changes in accounting for construction contracts require the _____ approach, and previous financial statements must be _____ .

37. Changes in accounting estimates are not retroactive but are instead _____ in nature.

38. If it is unclear as to whether an item is a change in principle or a change in estimate, it should be treated as a change in _____ .

39. A change to a presentation of consolidated statements versus separate statements is a change in _____ .

40. Prior period adjustments require the correction of the opening balance of _____ .

C. Problems

41. Lessor rents a building to Lessee for 4 years beginning on January 1, 19A. Both the cost and the selling price to Lessor are $60,000. There will be four lease payments, beginning on January 1, 19A. The building has a 4-year life with no salvage value. Lessor's target rate of return is 10%. Lessee is aware of this rate, but his own rate is 12%. There are no uncertainties regarding costs or collections.

   (a) What type of lease is this?

   (b) Determine the annual rental.

   (c) Prepare entries for both Lessor and Lessee for 19A.

42. Company Q had the following information regarding its operation for 19C:

Net income	($10,000)
Depreciation expense	5,000
Decrease in accounts receivable	1,000
Increase in merchandise	4,000
Decrease in prepaid items	3,000
Decrease in accounts payable	4,000
Increase in wages payable	2,000
Amortization of bond discount	500
Loss on sale of investment	3,000
Earnings from subsidiary (equity method)	5,000

Determine cash from operations under the indirect method.

43. Determine for each of the following items whether it belongs in the operating section, investments section, or finance section of the statement of cash flows:

(a) Issued 1,000 shares preferred stock.

(b) Paid a cash dividend.

(c) Sold shares it owned of another company's stock.

(d) Purchased a bond.

(e) Bought back treasury shares.

(f) Amortized a bond premium.

(g) Lent cash to another company.

(h) Purchased land for cash.

(i) Purchased a building by issuing stock.

(j) Amortized a patent.

44. Early in 19C, a company decided to change from the straight-line method of accounting to the double-declining method. Had it used this method during 19A and 19B, depreciation taken so far would have been $10,000 greater.

(a) What type of change is this?

(b) Prepare a journal entry for this change, if necessary. (Ignore taxes.)

45. In 19B Company E discovers that it failed to record utility expense of $8,000 for 19A. An entry was made in 19B at the time of payment.

(a) If this error is discovered before the 19B closings, what correction entry, if any, is required?

(b) If this error is discovered after the 19B closings, what correction entry is needed?

Answers to Examination III

A. True-False Questions

1. F   2. F   3. T   4. F   5. T   6. F   7. T   8. F   9. T   10. F   11. T   12. F   13. F

14. F   15. T   16. T   17. T   18. T   19. F   20. T

B. Completion Questions

21. capital; operating **22.** lessee **23.** expense **24.** 90%; capital **25.** finance-type **26.** sales-leaseback
27. direct; indirect **28.** operations, investments, finance **29.** investments **30.** net income; operating
31. operations; T-accounts **32.** investment **33.** cash **34.** accounting principle **35.** cumulative
36. retroactive; restated **37.** prospective **38.** estimate **39.** reporting entity **40.** retained earnings

C. Problems

41. (*a*) Capital lease

(*b*) $\dfrac{\$60,000}{3.16987} = \$18,928$ (rounded)

(*c*)	Lessor			Lessee		
Jan. 1	Lease Receivable	60,000		Building	60,000	
	Building		60,000	Lease Payable		60,000
	Cash	18,928		Lease Payable	18,928	
	Lease Receivable		18,928	Cash		18,928
Dec. 31	Lease Receivable	4,107		Interest Expense	4,107	
	Interest Revenue		4,107	Lease Payable		4,107
			(rounded)			
	No entry			Depreciation Expense	15,000	
				Accumulated Depreciation		15,000

42. $(10,000)   **43.** (*a*) Finance
       5,000   (*b*) Finance
       1,000   (*c*) Investments
      (4,000)   (*d*) Investments
       3,000   (*e*) Finance
      (4,000)   (*f*) Operating
       2,000   (*g*) Investments
         500   (*h*) Investments
       3,000   (*i*) None — footnote disclosure
      (5,000)   (*j*) Operating
    $ (8,500)

44. (*a*) Change in accounting principle

(*b*)

	Cumulative Effect of Change in Accounting Principle	10,000	
	Accumulated Depreciation		10,000

45. (*a*)

	Retained Earnings	8,000	
	Utility Expense		8,000

(*b*) No entry needed.

Chapter 10

Accounting for Pensions

10.1 INTRODUCTION

The basic purpose of all pension plans is the same — to provide benefits to employees upon retirement. In effect, a worker's total pay for a period consists of current pay, plus the right to receive additional pay upon retirement.

In 1987, the FASB issued Statement No. 87, "Employers' Accounting for Pensions." This statement changed significantly the way in which pension costs are accounted for by the employer. This chapter is based upon that statement.

There are two types of pension plans: defined contribution plans and defined benefit plans. In a *defined contribution plan,* periodic defined contributions are made by the employer into a trust fund administered by a third-party trustee. When an employee retires, the accumulated value in the fund determines how much is to be paid to the employee. If the fund has been invested wisely, the employee will receive a greater payout than if it was invested poorly. Thus the benefit to the employee is *undefined* and the employer's obligation extends only to making the specified *defined* contribution.

On the other hand, *defined benefit plans* guarantee the employee a specified retirement income related to the employee's average salary. The periodic contribution to the fund is based upon the expected future benefits to be paid. Thus the benefit is *defined,* while the contributions are *undefined,* and the employer is responsible to make sure the employee receives the defined benefits as specified in the plan.

Because the accounting for defined *contribution* plans is relatively easy (the periodic contribution is simply debited to Pension Expense), Statement No. 87 focuses on defined *benefit* plans. We will do the same in this chapter.

In order to make sure that the pension fund will contain enough money at retirement to pay the employees their defined benefits, Congress passed a law in 1974 known as the Employee Retirement Income Security Act (ERISA). This law requires companies to fund their pension plans in an orderly manner so that the employees are protected at retirement. The periodic amounts to be contributed to the fund are directly related to the future benefits expected to be paid. Most plans require contributions that will accumulate to the balance needed to pay the agreed-upon benefits at retirement. The contribution amounts are determined by actuaries and must be adjusted as estimates and assumptions are revised to reflect changing conditions.

In most cases, the employer contributes annually an amount equal to the present value of future benefits attributed to current services. If the employer contributes less than this amount, the plan is said to be *underfunded;* if the employer contributes more, the plan is *overfunded.*

10.2 THE PROJECTED BENEFIT OBLIGATION

A theme that runs through the entire topic of pension accounting is that of the *projected benefit obligation (PBO).* The PBO is the present value of the future benefits expected to be paid to employees based on their employment to date and taking into consideration expected increases in salaries that would affect their benefits. This measurement is based upon actuarial assumptions of employee turnover, life expectancy, and interest rates.

The PBO is increased and decreased by several items, thus leading to the following relationship:

> PBO, beginning year
> + Service cost
> + Interest cost
> − Benefits paid
> ± Changes in actuarial assumptions
> = PBO, year-end

Service costs and interest costs will be defined later on.

CHAP. 10] ACCOUNTING FOR PENSIONS 199

EXAMPLE 1

Company A had a beginning PBO of $100,000, service cost and interest cost were $10,000 and $9,000 respectively, changes in assumptions were −$4,000, and the ending PBO is $95,000. Using the above formula, benefits paid would be $20,000, determined as follows:

$$\$100,000 + \$10,000 + \$9,000 - X - \$4,000 = \$95,000$$
$$X = \$20,000$$

10.3 THE PENSION FUND

Under ERISA, companies must make periodic contributions to the pension fund, which is usually administered by an independent trustee. The trustee then invests these monies in stocks or interest-bearing securities. Thus the fund will increase through the earning of dividends and interest, or as a result of increases in the market value of these securities. Conversely, the fund will decrease if the market value of the securities falls. The relationship between the beginning fair value of the pension fund and its ending fair value may be expressed as follows:

> Pension fund value, beginning of year
> + Employer contributions
> + Actual return on fund assets
> − Benefits paid
> = Pension fund value, year-end

EXAMPLE 2

Company B had a beginning-of-year pension fund value of $200,000, and an end-of-year value of $300,000. This year its contributions to the fund were $150,000, while the fund paid benefits of $25,000. The actual return must have been a negative $25,000, calculated as follows:

$$\$200,000 + \$150,000 + X - \$25,000 = \$300,000$$
$$X = -\$25,000$$

10.4 PENSION EXPENSE; JOURNAL ENTRIES

A company's annual pension expense may consist of as many as six components. These components are:

1. Service cost
2. Interest cost
3. Expected return on pension fund
4. Amortization of unrecognized prior service cost
5. Effects of transition to Statement No. 87
6. Amortization of unrecognized gains or losses

The third item, expected return on the pension fund, would generally *decrease* rather than increase pension expense.

All of these items will be defined in later sections.

These six components are combined and their total is debited to Pension Expense. The actual contribution to the pension fund (which may or may not be exactly equal to this total) is credited to Cash. If the expense is greater than the contribution, the difference is a liability; if it is less, the excess contribution is an asset.

EXAMPLE 3

Company A has pension expense of $10,000 and contributes $10,000 to the pension fund. Company B also has pension expense of $10,000 but contributes only $8,000. Company C has pension expense of $10,000 and contributes $13,000. The entries for these companies are as follows:

Company A:		
Pension Expense	10,000	
Cash		10,000

Company B:		
Pension Expense	10,000	
Cash		8,000
Accrued Pension Liability		2,000
Company C:		
Pension Expense	10,000	
Prepaid Pension	3,000	
Cash		13,000

EXAMPLE 4

Company D had service cost, interest cost, and amortization of unrecognized prior service costs in the amounts of $20,000, $5,000, and $2,000, respectively. Its return on the pension fund was a *positive* $3,000 and it had no other elements of pension expense. The total pension expense is:

$$\$20,000 + \$5,000 + \$2,000 - \$3,000 = \$24,000.$$

If company D makes a $20,000 contribution to the pension fund, its entry is:

Pension Expense	24,000	
Cash		20,000
Accrued Pension Liability		4,000

10.5   SERVICE COST, INTEREST COST, RETURN ON PLAN ASSETS

The first element of pension expense is service cost. As employees perform services, they earn the right to receive future compensation for these services in the form of pension benefits. The present value of benefits earned for services performed *this* year is called *service cost.*

We've mentioned the concept of the PBO, which is the present value of future benefits to be paid. This PBO is increased every year by interest on the beginning balance of the PBO. The rate used, called the *settlement interest rate,* is the rate at which the pension liability could be effectively settled today. This interest is the second element of pension expense.

EXAMPLE 5

Company E had a beginning-of-year PBO of $100,000. Its settlement rate is 10%. Thus the interest component of pension expense is $10,000.

The pension fund generally increases from year to year due to interest, dividends, and increases in the market values of the securities comprising the fund. These increases are called *return on plan assets* and reduce pension expense. Conversely, any reduction in the market value would increase pension expense. We will assume throughout this chapter that the fund increases, rather than decreases as a result of market influences.

In computing the effect on pension expense of the return-on-plan assets, the accounting profession was faced with the issue of whether to use the *actual* return or the *expected* return. Because the actual return is a volatile short-term rate, the profession elected to use the more stable long-term expected rate. Thus it is the expected rate that currently is a component of pension expense, and any difference between this return and the actual return is deferred and recognized gradually ("amortized") over future periods. If the actual rate is greater than the expected rate, the difference is a deferred gain; if it is less, it is a deferred loss.

EXAMPLE 6

Company G had a beginning pension fund balance of $100,000. It had an actual rate of return of 10% ($10,000) and an expected rate of 8% ($8,000). This *expected* rate is used as a component of pension expense (as a reduction) while the remaining $2,000 is deferred as a *gain* to future periods.

EXAMPLE 7

Company H had a beginning pension fund balance of $100,000. Its actual rate of return was 10% ($10,000) but its expected rate was 12% ($12,000). Once again it is the expected rate which becomes a component of pension expense, and the remaining $2,000 is deferred as a loss to future periods.

As we have seen, the expected rate is multiplied by the fair market value of the plan assets at the beginning of the year. Another permissible approach is to multiply this rate by a weighted average value based on the market value of the pension plan assets over a period not to exceed 5 years.

10.6 AMORTIZATION OF UNRECOGNIZED PRIOR SERVICE COST

A company may decide to give pension benefits retroactively to employees who performed services prior to the initiation of the pension plan. For example, if the pension plan was created in 19X5, it may give pension credits to employees for their services prior to 19X5. Thus when these employees retire, say, in 19X9, they will be entitled to benefits both for services performed from 19X5 to 19X9 *and* for services performed before 19X5. These are called *prior service costs.*

Similarly, a company may decide to make retroactive amendments to its pension plan which increase the amount of benefits to be paid. These are also called prior service costs.

The question is: Should these prior service costs be recognized entirely in the year they are adopted? Or should they be recognized gradually (amortized) over several years? The accounting profession decided in favor of the latter option. Thus these costs must be amortized over the remaining service life of these employees. This can be done in two ways: either via straight-line amortization or by assigning to each remaining year of service an amortization fraction.

EXAMPLE 8

Company J has prior service costs of $60,000. It has four employees who are entitled to benefits for these prior services, with remaining expected service periods as follows:

Employee	Remaining Years
1	5
2	1
3	2
4	4

12 total service years

If we use straight-line amortization, we divide the $60,000 by the *average* number of years remaining. The average is determined by dividing the total remaining years (12) by the number of employees (4), yielding 3. We thus have:

$$\frac{\$60,000}{3} = \$20,000 \text{ per year}$$

EXAMPLE 9

Let's use the same information as in the previous example but assume each year is assigned its own amortization fraction. The fractions are computed as follows:

Employee	Remaining Years	Year 1	Year 2	Year 3	Year 4	Year 5
1	5	x	x	x	x	x
2	1	x				
3	2	x	x			
4	4	x	x	x	x	
	12	4	3	2	2	1

Year 1: 4/12 × $60,000 = $20,000
Year 2: 3/12 × $60,000 = $15,000
Year 3: 2/12 × $60,000 = $10,000
Year 4: 2/12 × $60,000 = $10,000
Year 5: 1/12 × $60,000 = $5,000

If the employees are going to retire according to a fixed pattern, a method similar to the sum-of-the-years'-digits method of depreciation can be used. Each year receives its own amortization fraction. The numerator is the number of employees who worked this year; the denominator (which represents the total service period) is determined under the following formula:

$$\text{Denominator} = \frac{n(n + 1)}{2} \times d$$

d represents the *decrease* in employees each year. *n* represents the *number* of *physical* years remaining from the point the prior service costs are created until the last of the employees affected by these service costs retires.

EXAMPLE 10

On January 1, 19X1, Company K amends its pension plan, resulting in prior service costs of $100,000. This amendment affects 100 employees. Twenty of these employees are expected to retire each year; thus by the end of 5 years, they will all be gone. Accordingly, $d = 20$ and $n = 5$. The denominator is:

$$\frac{n(n + 1)}{2} \times d = \frac{5(6)}{2} \times 20 = 300$$

The yearly computations are:

$$\text{Year 1: } \frac{100}{300} \times \$100,000 = \$33,333$$

$$\text{Year 2: } \frac{80}{300} \times \$100,000 = \$27,667$$

$$\text{Year 3: } \frac{60}{300} \times \$100,000 = \$20,000$$

$$\text{Year 4: } \frac{40}{300} \times \$100,000 = \$13,000 \text{ (rounded)}$$

$$\text{Year 5: } \frac{20}{300} \times \$100,000 = \$6,667 \text{ (rounded)}$$

10.7   AMORTIZATION OF TRANSITION GAIN OR LOSS

The *transition gain or loss* is the difference between the PBO and the fair market value of the pension fund at the time FASB No. 87 was adopted by the company. (For most companies, the changeover to FASB No. 87 took place in 1987). If at that time the PBO was greater, the difference is a loss; if it was smaller, the difference is a gain.

The total gain or loss is not recognized immediately, but is amortized gradually using straight-line amortization over the average remaining service life of the employees. If the life is less than 15 years, the company *may* choose 15 years as the life. Amortization of losses increases pension expense; amortization of gains decreases pension expense.

EXAMPLE 11

Company L had a PBO in 1987 of $100,000 and the market value of its pension fund was $80,000. It thus had a transition loss of $20,000. If the average remaining service life of its employees is 20 years, the amortization for 1987 would be $20,000 ÷ 20 = $1,000 and the *unrecognized* loss would be $19,000. In 1988, the amortization would again be $1,000 and the unrecognized loss would be $18,000. A similar pattern would exist for the remaining 18 years.

Because in this situation we are dealing with a loss, the annual amortization of $1,000 would *increase* pension expense.

EXAMPLE 12

Company M had a PBO in 1987 of $70,000 and the fair value of its pension fund was $100,000 at that time. It thus had a pension *gain* of $30,000. If the average service life of its employees is 10 years, the amortization would be $3,000 ($30,000 ÷ 10), which would decrease pension expense.

Alternatively, Company M may choose to use the minimum 15-year service period, thus resulting in annual amortization of $2,000.

10.8 AMORTIZATION OF UNRECOGNIZED GAINS OR LOSSES

We mentioned earlier that one of the six components of pension expense is the return on pension fund assets, and that the *expected* return, rather than the *actual* return, is to be used. Thus if the actual return was $10,000 but the expected return was only $7,000, the difference of $3,000 is *unrecognized* and deferred as a *gain* to future periods, to be amortized gradually over those periods. Conversely, if the actual return was $7,000 and the expected return was $10,000, the difference of $3,000 is an unrecognized and deferred *loss*.

There is one additional gain or loss that is currently unrecognized and deferred to future periods: a change in the PBO due to changes in actuarial estimates. As mentioned earlier, pension accounting relies heavily on estimates made by actuaries. If the actuaries revise their estimates and increase the PBO, the difference is a loss; if they decrease it, the difference is a gain. These losses or gains are unrecognized and deferred to later periods.

How should both of these gains and losses be amortized? The FASB has stated they should be amortized only if they accumulate to a value greater than the "corridor amount," and only the *excess* above this value should be amortized. The procedure is as follows:

1. Compare the PBO at the beginning of the year to the market value of the pension fund at that time and choose the larger figure.

2. Take 10% of this figure. This is the *corridor amount*.

3. Compare the unrecognized gain or loss at beginning of year to the corridor amount. If it is *greater* than the corridor amount, amortize the *excess* over the average remaining service years.

EXAMPLE 13

During 19X1, Company N had an expected rate of return of 10% on its beginning pension fund balance of $100,000. The actual return was 9%. Thus the difference of $1,000 is an unrecognized *loss*.

Also during 19X1, the company actuaries revised the PBO downward by $15,000. This is a *gain*. We thus have a *net* unrecognized pension gain of $14,000 ($15,000 − $1,000) which is to be deferred to future periods.

EXAMPLE 14

Let's use the same information given in the preceding example involving Company N. At the *beginning* of 19X2, the pension fund had a balance of $125,000 and the PBO was $135,000. Thus the corridor amount is $13,500 (10% of $135,000), and the excess above the corridor is $500 ($14,000 − $13,500). If the average remaining service period is 10 years, the amortization of the unrecognized gain is $50 ($500 ÷ 10). Thus the amount still *unrecognized* is $13,950 ($14,000 − $50).

EXAMPLE 15

Let's continue with Company N and go to 19X3. At the *beginning* of 19X3, the pension fund had a balance of $127,000 and the PBO balance was $123,000. The corridor is therefore 10% of $127,000 = $12,700.

During *19X2*, Company N had a *new* unrecognized net pension gain of $1,000. The *balance* of the unrecognized amount would be determined as follows, at January 1, 19X3:

Balance at January 1, 19X2	$14,000
Amortized during 19X2	(50)
New net gain	1,000
Balance, January 1, 19X3	$14,950

We now compare this balance to the corridor of $12,700, resulting in an excess of $2,250. Dividing this by the average service life of 10 years results in amortization of $225.

10.9 COMPREHENSIVE PROBLEM

Now that we have discussed the six components of pension expense, let's look at a problem containing all these components.

EXAMPLE 16

Company P had the following information regarding 19X2:

Pension fund market value, January 1	$100,000
PBO, January 1	$90,000
Pension fund market value, December 31	$110,000
PBO, December 31	$111,000
Service cost	$10,000
Interest rate (settlement rate)	10%
Retirement benefits paid	$5,000
Changes in actuarial assumptions (a loss)	$7,000
Actual rate of return on pension fund	11%
Expected rate of return on pension fund	9%
Contributions to fund	$4,000
Unamortized prior service costs, January 1	$10,000
Unamortized transition gain, January 1	$(5,000)
Unrecognized pension loss, January 1	$12,000
Average remaining service years	20

The ending PBO of $111,000 is confirmed as follows:

Beginning PBO	$ 90,000
+ Service cost	10,000
+ Interest cost (.10 × $90,000)	9,000
− Benefits paid	(5,000)
+ Change in actuarial assumptions	7,000
Ending PBO	$111,000

The ending fund value of $110,000 is confirmed as follows:

Beginning fund value	$100,000
+ Contributions	4,000
+ Actual return on fund (.11 × $100,000)	11,000
− Benefits paid	(5,000)
Ending fund value	$110,000

The six components of pension expense are determined as follows:

Service cost (given)	$10,000
Interest cost (.10 × $90,000)	9,000
Expected return on fund assets (9% × $100,000)	(9,000)
Amortization of prior service costs ($10,000 ÷ 20)	500
Amortization of transition gain ($5,000 ÷ 20)	(250)
Amortization of unrecognized pension loss*	100
	$10,350

---

*We compare the PBO of $100,000 at January 1 to the pension fund value at that time of $90,000 and choose the larger figure ($100,000). The corridor is 10% of this figure, yielding $10,000. Since the unrecognized pension loss at January 1 is $12,000, we amortize the excess of $2,000 over 20 years, yielding $100.

If the actual funding is only $9,000, the entry is:

Pension Expense	10,350	
Cash		9,000
Accrued Pension Liability		1,350

10.10　THE MINIMUM PENSION LIABILITY

We've seen in Section 10.4 that if the annual pension expense is greater than the annual funding, a liability (accrued pension liability) is recognized for the difference. We've also seen that there are certain items that are only recognized *piecemeal* through the process of amortization, such as prior service costs and unrecognized losses. The bulk of these items, however, remains unrecognized, and no liability is recorded or recognized for their existence.

The FASB was unhappy with this treatment. Accordingly they resolved that a minimum liability should be recognized. The *minimum liability* is the excess of the *ABO* (*accumulated benefit obligation*) at year-end over the fair value of the pension fund assets. The ABO is similar to the PBO in that it is the present value of the future benefits to be paid. However, there is one difference: The PBO is based upon future pension benefits determined according to salary levels in effect right before retirement; the ABO uses salaries that are *currently* in effect. Thus the ABO would usually be lower than the PBO.

If there already exists a balance in the Accrued Pension Liability account due to underfunding (i.e., current pension expense is greater than current funding) and this balance is greater than or equal to the minimum liability, no additional liability is recognized. If this balance is less than the minimum, an additional liability must be recognized for the difference.

EXAMPLE 17

Company R has an ABO of $100,000, the fair value of its pension fund is $80,000, and its accrued pension liability is $15,000. Since the minimum liability is $20,000 ($100,000 − $80,000) and the accrued pension liability is only $15,000, an additional liability of $5,000 must be recognized. This entry will be discussed in the next section.

EXAMPLE 18

Company S has the same balances as Company R except that its accrued pension liability is $25,000. Since this is at least equal to the minimum liability of $20,000, no additional liability need be recognized.

If the company has a prepaid pension asset rather than an accrued pension liability (because its funding exceeds its pension expense) and the ABO exceeds the fair market value of the pension fund (thus requiring the recognition of a minimum liability), an additional liability must be recognized in an amount equal to the minimum liability *plus* the prepaid asset. This combination of a plus and a minus will yield the desired minimum liability.

EXAMPLE 19

Company T has an ABO of $100,000 and the fair value of its pension fund is $80,000. Thus the minimum liability is $20,000. It also has a prepaid pension asset of $5,000. It must now recognize an *additional* liability of $25,000 ($20,000 + $5,000) because this liability minus the prepaid asset of $5,000 will yield the *minimum* liability of $20,000.

On its balance sheet, Company T will report a prepaid asset of $5,000 in the assets section, and a liability of $25,000 in the liabilities section. This results in a *net* liability of $20,000—the minimum liability.

In the situation just discussed, where the ABO is greater than the fair value of the fund, and a minimum liability must be recognized, the plan is said to be *underfunded*. In the opposite situation, where the fair value of the fund is greater than the ABO, the plan is said to be *overfunded*.

In this latter case, should a minimum asset be recognized for the difference? The FASB, in the interest of conservatism, said no.

10.11　RECORDING THE MINIMUM LIABILITY

If an additional pension liability has to be recognized in order to meet the minimum liability requirement, a journal entry should be made crediting an account called Additional Pension Liability and debiting an account called Deferred Pension Cost. This latter account is an intangible asset, and can only be debited up to a maximum value that equals the sum of unrecognized prior service costs and unamortized transition losses. If an additional debit is needed, it goes to another account called Excess of Additional Pension Liability over Unrecognized Prior Service Cost. This account is a contra-equity account and is deducted in the stockholders' equity section of the balance sheet.

Each year these accounts are adjusted upward or downward, as the need requires.

EXAMPLE 20

Company V had the following information relating to its pension plan on December 31, 19X1:

ABO	$170,000
Fair value of pension assets	100,000
Accrued pension liability	20,000
Unrecognized prior service cost	20,000
Unamortized transition loss	10,000

The minimum liability required is $70,000 ($170,000 − $100,000). Since the accrued pension liability is $20,000, an additional liability of $50,000 must be credited. Of this $50,000, the total of the prior service and transition costs ($20,000 + $10,000 = $30,000) is debited to Deferred Pension Cost, while the remainder of $20,000 is debited to the Excess of Additional Pension Liability over Unrecognized Prior Service Cost account. The entry would thus be:

Deferred Pension Cost	30,000	
Excess of Additional Pension Liability over		
Unrecognized Prior Service Cost	20,000	
Additional Pension Liability		50,000

On the balance sheet, the accrued pension liability of $20,000 may be combined with the additional pension liability of $50,000 to yield a total liability of $70,000.

EXAMPLE 21

Let's use the previous example and see what happens at December 31, 19X2. On this date, the relevant pension information is as follows:

ABO	$165,000
Fair value of pension assets	105,000
Accrued pension liability	22,000
Unrecognized prior service cost	17,000
Unamortized transition loss	8,000

The minimum liability has declined to $60,000 ($165,000 − $105,000), and the additional liability needed is now $38,000 ($60,000 − accrued pension liability of $22,000). Since the additional liability has a credit balance of $50,000, it must now be debited for $12,000 in order to bring it down to $38,000.

The unrecognized prior service cost and unamortized transition loss have declined by $3,000 and $2,000 respectively. Accordingly, the Deferred Pension Cost account must also be reduced (credited) for this total of $5,000. The remaining $7,000 (12,000 − 5,000) is credited to the excess of Additional Pension Liability over Unrecognized Prior Service Cost account. The entry thus is:

Additional Pension Liability	12,000	
Deferred Pension Cost		5,000
Excess of Additional Pension Liability over		
Unrecognized Prior Service Cost		7,000

We've stated earlier that the Deferred Pension Cost account is debited for the maximum sum of the unrecognized prior service cost and unamortized transition *loss*. If there is an unamortized transition *gain*, this would be deducted from the prior service cost in determining the debit to Deferred Pension Cost. If the transition gain is larger than the prior service cost, no deferred pension cost would be debited; the entire debit would go to the Excess of Additional Pension Liability over Unrecognized Prior Service Cost account.

EXAMPLE 22

Company W needs an additional pension liability of $40,000. It has unrecognized prior service cost of $30,000 and an unamortized transition *gain* of $15,000. The debit to Deferred Pension Cost would only be $15,000 ($30,000 − $15,000) and the entry is:

Deferred Pension Cost	15,000	
Excess of Additional Pension Liability over		
Unrecognized Prior Service Cost	25,000	
Additional Pension Liability		40,000

EXAMPLE 23

In the previous example, if the unamortized transition *gain* was $35,000, no deferred pension cost would be debited since the gain is larger than the prior service cost. The entry would thus be:

Excess of Additional Pension Liability over		
Unrecognized Prior Service Cost	40,000	
Additional Pension Liability		40,000

Summary

1. This chapter is based upon FASB No. 87, "Employers' Accounting for Pensions," which significantly changed the way in which pension costs are to be accounted for.

2. In a *defined contribution pension plan,* the employer makes periodic, *defined* contributions to a trust fund. The employee benefits at retirement, however, are *undefined* and depend on how well the fund was managed. In a *defined benefit pension plan,* the benefits are defined while the annual contributions are undefined. This chapter discussed the latter type of plan.

3. The *PBO* (*projected benefit obligation*) is the present value of the future benefits expected to be paid for services rendered to date, taking into consideration expected increases in salaries that would increase these benefits. The PBO uses assumptions made by actuaries regarding employee turnover, life expectancy, and interest rates.

4. The relationship between the beginning-of-period PBO and the end-of-period PBO is expressed as follows:

> PBO, beginning of year
> + Interest cost
> + Service cost
> − Benefits paid
> ± Changes in actuarial assumptions
> = PBO, year-end

5. Under ERISA, companies must make periodic contributions to the pension fund. The fund will increase as a result of dividends and interest earned on securities purchased from monies in the fund, and from increases in the market value of these securities. The fund can also decrease if these securities fall in market value. The relationship of the beginning and end-of-year balances in the fund is expressed as follows:

> Pension fund, beginning of year
> + Employer contributions
> + Actual return on fund assets
> − Benefits paid
> = Pension fund, year-end

6. A company's annual pension expense consists of six components: service cost, interest cost, expected return on the pension fund (a reduction of pension expense), amortization of unrecognized prior service cost, amortization of unrecognized gains and losses, and effects of the transition to Statement No. 87.

7. If the total pension expense is greater than the contribution to the fund, the difference is a liability; if it is less, the difference is a prepaid asset.

8. *Service cost* represents the present value of benefits earned for services performed this year. *Interest cost* represents the interest that accrues on the beginning-of-year PBO (using the settlement rate).

9. The return on the pension fund represents interest, dividends, and increases in the market value of the fund. It is the *expected* rate of return, rather than the *actual* rate, that is used for pension expense. Any difference is deferred and amortized over future periods. If the actual rate is greater, the difference is a deferred gain; if it is less, it is a deferred loss.

10. *Prior service costs* are retroactive benefits granted to employees for services performed before the initiation of the pension plan. Amendments to a plan also fall under this category. These costs are deferred and gradually amortized over the remaining service lives of the employees affected. Either straight-line amortization or a method similar to sum-of-the-years' digits depreciation may be used.

11. The *transition gain or loss* is the difference between the PBO and the fair value of the pension fund at the time the company changed over to the provisions of FASB No. 87. If at that time the PBO was greater, the difference is a loss; if it was smaller, the difference is a gain.

12. The gain or loss is not recognized immediately, but instead amortized over the remaining service period of the employees. If the service period is less than 15 years, the company *may* choose a 15-year minimum. Amortization of a loss increases pension expense; amortization of a gain decreases pension expense.

13. Unrecognized gains and losses are deferred and amortized over future periods. These include differences between the actual rate and expected rate of return, and changes in the PBO due to revisions in actuarial assumptions. If the PBO is revised upward, the change is an unrecognized loss; if it is revised downward, the change is an unrecognized gain.

14. The amount to amortize of these unrecognized items is determined according to the following procedure:
    (1) Compare the PBO at the beginning of the year to the market value of the pension fund at that time and choose the larger number.
    (2) Take 10% of this number. This is called the *corridor amount*.
    (3) If the unrecognized gain or loss at beginning of year is greater than the corridor, amortize the excess over the average remaining service period.

15. The *ABO* (*accumulated benefit obligation*) is similar to the PBO in that it is the present value of the future benefits to be paid. However, it is based upon salary levels *currently* in effect, rather than future salary levels.

16. The FASB requires recognition of a minimum pension liability. The minimum liability is the excess of the ABO at year-end over the fair value of the pension fund at that time. If the Accrued Pension Liability Account has a balance for less than this minimum, an additional liability must be recognized for the difference.

17. In this type of situation, where the ABO is greater than the fund fair value, the pension is said to be *underfunded*. In the opposite situation, where the ABO is less than the fund fair value, the pension is *overfunded*. A minimum *asset* would *not* be recognized in this case.

18. Where an additional pension liability has to be recorded in order to meet the requirement of the minimum liability, a journal entry is made that credits an account called Additional Pension Liability. The debit goes to Deferred Pension Cost. This account is an intangible asset and can only be debited up to a maxi-

mum value that equals the sum of the unrecognized prior service costs and unamortized transition losses. If an additional debit is needed, it goes to an account called Excess of Additional Pension Liability over Unrecognized Prior Service Cost. This is a contra-equity account.

19. If there is an unamortized transition gain, it would be deducted from the unrecognized prior service cost in determining the maximum to be debited to the Deferred Pension Cost Account.

Rapid Review

1. If the annual contributions are *undefined* and the retirement benefits are *defined,* this type of plan is called a _____ plan.

2. The present value of the future benefits to be paid, taking into consideration expected future increases in salaries, is the _____ .

3. An item that can either add to or subtract from the PBO is _____ .

4. Interest cost is based upon the beginning balance of the _____ and uses a rate called the _____ .

5. The six components of pension expense are _____ , _____ , _____ , _____ , _____ , and _____ .

6. If the total pension expense is greater than the contribution to the fund, the difference is a _____ .

7. The _____ rate of return, rather than the _____ rate of return, is used as a component of pension expense.

8. Retroactive benefits granted to employees for services performed before the initiation of the pension plan are called _____ .

9. The difference between the PBO and the fair value of the pension fund at the time the company changed over to FASB No. 87 is called the _____ .

10. If at that time the PBO was greater, the difference is a _____ ; if it was smaller, the difference is a _____ .

11. This difference may be amortized over a minimum period of _____ years.

12. If the PBO is revised downward due to changes in actuarial assumptions, this revision is an _____ gain.

13. Ten percent of the difference between the PBO at beginning of year and the value of the fund at that time is called the _____ amount.

14. The minimum liability is the excess of the _____ at year-end over the _____ at year-end.

15. When an additional pension liability has to be recorded, the credit goes to _____ , and the debit goes to _____ .

Answers: 1. defined benefit 2. PBO 3. changes in actuarial assumptions 4. PBO; settlement rate 5. interest cost, service cost, prior service cost, transition gains and losses, expected return, unrecognized gains or losses 6. liability 7. expected; actual 8. prior service costs 9. transition gain or loss 10. loss; gain 11. 15 12. unrecognized (or actuarial) 13. corridor 14. ABO; pension fund 15. additional pension liability; deferred pension cost

Solved Problems

The PBO

10.1 Company A had a beginning PBO of $50,000; service cost, interest cost, and benefits paid were $10,000, $20,000, and $30,000, respectively; and the ending PBO was $75,000. What factor is missing? How much is this factor?

SOLUTION

The missing factor is the change in actuarial assumptions of $25,000, computed as follows:

$$\begin{array}{ll} & \$50,000 \\ + & 10,000 \\ + & 20,000 \\ - & 30,000 \\ + & \underline{\quad X \quad} \\ & \$75,000 \qquad X = \$25,000 \end{array}$$

[Section 10.2]

10.2 Company B had a beginning PBO of $30,000, service cost was $10,000, and the ending PBO was $38,000. There were no actuarial changes and the settlement rate was 10%. What are the missing factors? How much are they?

SOLUTION

They are interest cost and benefits paid. Interest cost is 10% of $30,000 = $3,000. Benefits paid is calculated as follows:

$$\begin{array}{ll} & \$30,000 \\ + & 10,000 \\ + & 3,000 \\ - & \underline{\quad X \quad} \\ & \$38,000 \qquad X = \$5,000 \end{array}$$

[Sections 10.2, 10.5]

The Pension Fund

10.3 Company C had a pension fund balance of $150,000 at the beginning of 19A. It contributed $30,000 during the year and paid benefits of $20,000. Its expected rate of return was 10% while its actual rate was only 8%. What is the balance in the pension fund at the end of 19A?

SOLUTION

The actual return is 8% of $150,000 = $12,000. Thus:

$$\begin{array}{ll} & \$150,000 \\ + & 30,000 \\ + & 12,000 \\ - & \underline{\quad 20,000 \quad} \\ = & \quad X \qquad X = \$172,000 \end{array}$$

[Section 10.3]

10.4 Company D had pension expense of $200,000 during 19A. Prepare journal entries for the following three cases:

(1) Its contribution was $200,000.

(2) Its contribution was $180,000.

(3) Its contribution was $230,000.

SOLUTION

(1)	Pension Expense	200,000		
	Cash		200,000	
(2)	Pension Expense	200,000		
	Cash		180,000	
	Accrued Pension Liability		20,000	
(3)	Pension Expense	200,000		
	Prepaid Pension	30,000		
	Cash		230,000	[Section 10.4]

10.5   Company E had an opening balance of $300,000 in its pension fund at January 1, 19A. During 19A, its service cost and interest cost were $50,000 and $3,000, respectively. The expected return on the fund was 10% while the actual return was 12%. It had no prior service costs or unrecognized gains or losses, but it did have a transition gain whose amortization for this year amounted to $10,000. What is the amount of pension expense? If Company E made a contribution for $11,000, prepare the necessary journal entry.

SOLUTION

Pension expense is $13,000, as follows:

$$
\begin{array}{rl}
& \$50,000 \\
+ & 3,000 \\
- & 30,000 \quad (10\% \times 300,000) \\
- & 10,000 \\
\hline
& \$13,000
\end{array}
$$

Pension Expense	13,000		
Cash		11,000	
Accrued Pension Liability		2,000	[Sections 10.4, 10.5]

Amortization of Unrecognized Prior Service Cost

10.6   Company F has prior service costs of $100,000 and it has five employees entitled to benefits for these prior services. Their remaining service years are as follows:

Employee	Remaining Years
1	5
2	1
3	4
4	4
5	6

Determine the amortization using the straight-line method.

SOLUTION

The average number of years remaining is 20 divided by 5 which equals 4. Thus, $100,000 divided by 4 yields $25,000 (rounded).   [Section 10.6]

10.7   Determine the annual amortization for the previous problem using a separate amortization fraction for each year.

SOLUTION

	Remaining	Year					
Employee	Years	1	2	3	4	5	6
1	5	x	x	x	x	x	
2	1	x					
3	4	x	x	x	x		
4	4	x	x	x	x		
5	6	x	x	x	x	x	x
	20	5	4	4	4	2	1

Year 1: 5/20 × $100,000 = $25,000

Year 2: 4/20 × $100,000 = $20,000

Year 3: 4/20 × $100,000 = $20,000

Year 4: 4/20 × $100,000 = $20,000

Year 5: 2/20 × $100,000 = $10,000

Year 6: 1/20 × $100,000 = $5,000   [Section 10.6]

10.8   On January 1, 19X1, Company G amends its pension plan, resulting in prior service costs of $200,000. This amendment affects 50 employees. Ten of these employees are expected to retire each year over the next 5 years.

(1)   What is the denominator for each year's amortization fraction?

(2)   Calculate the amortization for each year.

SOLUTION

(1)
$$\text{Denominator} = \frac{n(n + 1)}{2} \times d$$

$$n = 5;$$
$$d = 10$$

$$\text{Denominator} = \frac{5(5 + 1)}{2} \times 10$$
$$= 150$$

(2)   Year 1: 50/150 × $200,000 = $66,667 (rounded)

Year 2: 40/150 × $200,000 = $54,333

Year 3: 30/150 × $200,000 = $40,000

Year 4: 20/150 × $200,000 = $26,667

Year 5: 10/150 × $200,000 = $13,333 (rounded)   [Section 10.6]

Amortization of Transition Gains and Losses

10.9   When Company H switched over to FASB No. 87 it had a pension fund whose fair value was $100,000 and a PBO of $150,000. The average remaining service years of its employees is 20.

(1)   Is this a transition gain or loss?

(2)   How much is amortized each year?

(3)   Would this increase or decrease pension expense?

SOLUTION

(1)   Transition loss

(2)
$$\frac{\$150,000 - \$100,000}{20} = \$2,500$$

(3)   Losses increase pension expense.   [Section 10.7]

10.10　Assume the same information as in the previous problem, except that the average remaining years is 12. What are two possible ways to amortize the gain or loss?

SOLUTION

One way is to amortize it over 12 years, yielding $4,167 per year.
Another way is to use the minimum 15-year period, yielding $3,333 per year.　　　　[Section 10.7]

Amortization of Unrecognized Gains or Losses

10.11　During 19X1, Company I had an expected rate of return of 10% on its pension fund balance of $400,000. Its actual rate of return, however, was 12%.

Also during 19X1, the company actuaries revised the PBO upward by $25,000.

(1)　Does this situation involve a net pension gain or loss?

(2)　Is this net gain or loss recognized this year?

SOLUTION

(1)　The first item is a gain:

$$.12(\$400,000) - .10(\$400,000) = \$8,000 \text{ gain}$$

The second item is a loss of $25,000.
We thus have a net loss of 17,000.

(2)　The net loss is unrecognized this year. In 19X2 we begin to gradually amortize it if it exceeds the corridor.
　　　　　　　　　　　　　　　　　　　　　　　　　　　　　　　　[Section 10.8]

10.12　At the *beginning* of 19A, Company J had an unrecognized net pension gain of $25,000. At that time its PBO was $200,000 and its pension fund balance was $210,000. The average remaining service life of its employees is 20 years.

(1)　What is the corridor amount?

(2)　How much should the amortization be this year?

(3)　How much of the net gain is still unrecognized after this year's amortization?

SOLUTION

(1)　10% of $210,000 = $21,000

(2)　$25,000 − $21,000 = $4,000;
　　　$4,000 ÷ 20 = $200

(3)　$24,800 ($25,000 − $200)　　　　　　　　　　　　　　　　[Section 10.8]

10.13　Let's use the same information as in the previous problem and go to 19B. At the *beginning* of 19B, the PBO was $215,000 and the fair market value of the pension fund was $214,000. During 19A, the expected rate of return on the pension fund balance of $210,000 was 10%; the actual rate, however, was only 9%. The average remaining service life is only 19 years.

(1)　Was this a pension gain or loss and what is the amount?

(2)　What is the total unrecognized net pension gain or loss at the end of 19B (before amortization for 19B)?

(3)　How much is the corridor amount?

(4)　How much is the 19B amortization?

(5)　How much of the net gain or loss is still unrecognized after the 19B amortization?

SOLUTION

(1)　$.10(\$210,000) - .09(\$210,000) = (\$2,100)$ loss

(2)　$24,800　　gain (from 19A)
　　　(2,100)　　loss (from 19B)
　　　———
　　　$22,700　　net gain

(3)   .10 × $215,000 = $21,500
(4) $22,700 − $21,500 = $1,200;
      $1,200 ÷ 19 = $63 (rounded)
(5) $22,700 − $63 = $22,637   [Section 10.8]

Comprehensive Problem

10.14 At the beginning of 19A, Company K had a PBO of $200,000 and a pension fund balance of $230,000. It also had an unrecognized net pension loss of $35,000, an unamortized transition gain of $7,000, and prior service costs of $24,000.

During 19A, service cost was $15,000 and the settlement rate was 10%. The actual rate of return on the pension fund was also 10%, but the expected rate was only 8%.

Also during 19A, the company contributed $25,000 to the fund and paid out benefits of $13,000. There were no changes in actuarial assumptions during the year, and the average remaining service years of the employees is 20.

(1)   Calculate the ending PBO.

(2)   Calculate the ending value of the pension fund.

(3)   Determine the amortization of transition costs and prior service costs.

(4)   Find the corridor amount.

(5)   Determine the amortization of the unrecognized net pension loss.

(6)   Determine pension expense and prepare a journal entry.

SOLUTION

(1)

$200,000	Beginning PBO
15,000	Service cost
20,000	Interest (.10 × $200,000)
(13,000)	Benefits paid
$222,000	Ending PBO

(2)

$230,000	Beginning pension fund
25,000	Contributions
23,000	Actual return (.10 × 230,000)
(13,000)	Benefits paid
$265,000	Ending pension fund

(3)   Transition costs: $7,000 ÷ 20 = $350 gain
      Prior service costs: $24,000 ÷ 20 = $1,200

(4)   .10 × $230,000 = $23,000

(5) $35,000 − $23,000 = $12,000;
      12,000 ÷ 20 years = $600

(6)

Service cost	$ 15,000	
Interest cost	20,000	(.10 × 200,000)
Expected return	(18,400)	(.08 × 230,000)
Amortization of prior service cost	1,200	
Amortization of transition cost	(350) gain	
Amortization of unrecognized pension loss	600	
Total pension expense	$ 18,050	

	Pension Expense	18,050	
(7)	Prepaid Pension	6,950	
	Cash		25,000

The Minimum Pension Liability

10.15 At December 31, 19A, Company L had a PBO of $70,000, an ABO of $50,000, and a pension fund with a value of $45,000. It also had an accrued pension liability of $3,000.

(1) What is the minimum pension liability?

(2) How much additional liability, if any, must be recorded?

(3) If the accrued pension liability had a balance of $8,000 instead of $3,000, how much additional liability, if any, need be recorded?

SOLUTION

(1) $5,000 ($50,000 − $45,000)

(2) $2,000 ($5,000 − $3,000)

(3) None   [Section 10.10]

10.16 Company M has a PBO of $100,000, an ABO of $90,000, and a pension fund with a market value of $95,000. It also had an accrued pension liability of $4,000.

(1) What is the minimum pension liability?

(2) Should any additional liability be recognized?

(3) Should a minimum pension asset be recognized? Why?

(4) Is the pension overfunded or underfunded?

SOLUTION

(1) None. (The pension fund is larger than the PBO.)

(2) No.

(3) No, because of the concept of conservatism.

(4) Overfunded by $5,000 ($95,000 − $90,000).   [Section 10.10]

10.17 On December 31, 19X1, Company L had a pension fund balance of $100,000 and an ABO of $130,000. It also had a prepaid pension asset of $7,000. Determine the additional liability needed, if any.

SOLUTION

The minimum liability is $30,000 ($130,000 − $100,000). The additional liability needed is $37,000 ($30,000 + $7,000).   [Section 10.10]

Recording the Minimum Liability

10.18 Company M had the following information relating to its pension plan on December 31, 19A:

ABO	$200,000
Fair value of pension assets	150,000
Accrued pension liability	25,000
Unrecognized prior service cost	7,000
Unamortized transition loss	8,000

(1) What is the minimum liability?

(2) How much additional liability is needed?

(3) How much of a debit should go to deferred pension cost? Why?

(4) Prepare the necessary journal entry.

SOLUTION

(1) $50,000 ($200,000 − $150,000)

(2) $25,000 (The accrued pension liability already shows 25,000.)

(3) $15,000 ($7,000 + $8,000)

(4)

Deferred Pension Cost	15,000		
Excess of Additional Pension Liability			
over Unrecognized Prior Service Cost	10,000		
Additional Pension Liability		25,000	[Section 10.11]

10.19   Company M needs an additional pension liability of $80,000. It has unrecognized prior service cost of $40,000 and an unamortized transition gain of $10,000. Prepare the necessary journal entry.

SOLUTION

Deferred Pension Cost	30,000*		
Excess of Additional Pension Liability			
over Unrecognized Prior Service Cost	50,000		
Additional Pension Liability		80,000	

————————
*$40,000 − $10,000   [Section 10.11]

10.20   Company N has the following pension information on December 31, 19A:

PBO	$90,000
ABO	80,000
Pension fund	30,000
Accrued pension liability	10,000
Unrecognized prior service cost	20,000
Unamortized transition *gain*	25,000

(1)   What is the minimum pension liability?

(2)   What additional liability, if any, must be recorded?

(3)   How much should be debited to deferred pension cost?

(4)   Show the necessary entry.

SOLUTION

(1) $50,000 ($80,000 − $30,000)

(2) $40,000 ($50,000 − $10,000)

(3)   Zero (because the prior service cost *minus* the transition gain is not a positive number)

(4)

Excess of Additional Pension Liability			
over Unrecognized Prior Service Cost	40,000		
Additional Pension Liability		40,000	[Section 10.11]

Supplementary Problems

10.21   Company A had a beginning PBO of $80,000; service cost and interest cost during the year were $8,000 and $7,000, respectively; changes in actuarial assumptions were −$3,000; and the ending PBO is $90,000. Determine benefits paid.

10.22 Company B had a balance of $100,000 in its pension fund at the beginning of 19A. During the year it contributed $12,000 into the fund, paid out benefits of $7,000, and had an actual return of 10%. The expected rate of return, however, was 8%. Determine the ending balance in the fund.

10.23 Company C had pension expense during 19B of $70,000. Prepare the necessary journal entry if:
(a) it contributed $70,000 into the fund.
(b) it contributed $60,000.
(c) it contributed $85,000.

10.24 Company D had service cost, interest cost, and amortization of prior service costs in the amounts of $19,000, $4,000, and $2,000, respectively. There were no transition gains or losses or unrecognized gains and losses, and the expected return on the fund was $5,000.
    If Company D contributed $24,000 into the fund, prepare the required journal entry.

10.25 Company E had a beginning-of-year pension fund balance of $70,000 and a beginning PBO of $50,000. The expected rate of return is 10%; the actual rate is 9%. The remaining expected service years of its employees is 18, and the settlement rate is 11%.
(a) Which rate should be used in determining interest cost? In determining the return on the fund?
(b) How should the difference between the expected rate of return and the actual rate of return be treated?

10.26 Company F has four employees whose expected remaining service years are as follows: No. 1, 6 years; No. 2, 2 years; No. 3, 3 years; No. 4, 5 years. If the unrecognized prior service cost is $160,000, determine the annual amortization under (a) the straight-line method and (b) the sum-of-the-years'-digits method.

10.27 In 1987, Company G switched over to the accounting rules prescribed by FASB No. 87 for pensions. At that time, it had a PBO of $90,000 and a pension fund of $70,000. The average remaining service life of its employees is 10 years.
(a) Was this a transition gain or loss?
(b) What should the annual amortization be?
(c) May Company G use an amount other than 10 in its denominator?

10.28 During 19X1 Company H had an expected rate of return of 10% on its beginning fund balance of $200,000. The actual rate of return, however, was 9%.
    Also during 19X1, the company actuaries revised the PBO downward by $28,000. Determine the *net* unrecognized gain or loss to be deferred to future periods.

10.29 Use the same information as in the previous question and assume that at the beginning of 19X2 the pension fund had a balance of $240,000 and the PBO was $250,000.
(a) Determine the corridor amount.
(b) If the average remaining service period is 10 years, determine the amortization for this year.
(c) How much of the gain or loss will still be unrecognized after this year's amortization?

10.30 Company I has an ABO of $150,000 and a pension fund of $125,000 at the end of 19A. Determine the additional liability to be recognized if:
(a) the balance in the Accrued Pension Liability account is $18,000.
(b) the balance in this account is $25,000.

Chapter 11

Net Operating Loss Carrybacks and Carryforwards; Deferred Income Taxes

11.1 NET OPERATING LOSS CARRYBACKS AND CARRYFORWARDS

Under current tax law, a company that incurs a net operating loss (NOL) may carry this loss back 3 years (to the earliest year first), reduce the reported income of these years, and receive a refund for the overpayment of taxes. This is called a *loss carryback*. If this loss is greater than the total income of the 3 previous years, the remainder may be carried forward to offset income of the next 15 years. This is called a *loss carryforward*. Thus the loss has a silver lining attached in that taxes of previous and future years are reduced.

If a company so wishes, it may elect to forgo the carryback and use the loss only as a carryforward. In this chapter, however, we will assume both carrybacks and carryforwards.

For carrybacks, an entry must be made to recognize a receivable for the tax refund, and a revenue item for the benefit of the carryback. This benefit reduces or "softens" the loss on the income statement.

EXAMPLE 1

Company L has the following information regarding its operations for the years 19A–19D:

	Income before Tax	Tax Rate	Tax Paid
19A	$ 100,000	20%	$20,000
19B	80,000	20%	16,000
19C	50,000	25%	12,500
19D	(280,000)	25%	0

Company L may now carry back the $280,000 loss in 19D and offset the total income of $230,000 ($100,000 + $80,000 + $50,000) for 19A, 19B, and 19C. It will thus receive a refund for the taxes paid of $48,500 ($20,000 + $16,000 + $12,500) and have $50,000 of the $280,000 left over to carry forward to future years. The entry is:

Tax Refund Receivable	48,500	
Tax Benefit of Loss Carryback		48,500

The income statement for 19D will show the following:

Loss from Operations	$(280,000)
Less Tax Benefit of Loss Carryback	48,500
Net Loss	$(231,500)

In the previous example, Company L has $50,000 left over to carry forward to future years after 19D. Should Company L make an entry in 19D to recognize the potential future benefits of this carryforward? The accounting profession has said no, since these benefits can only be realized if the company earns future income, and at the present time that likelihood is uncertain.

EXAMPLE 2

Let's go back to the previous example and assume that in 19E, Company L earns net income of $100,000 and the tax rate is 25%. The journal entry is:

Income Tax Expense	25,000	
Income Tax Payable		12,500
Tax Benefit of Loss Carryforward		12,500

Income Tax Expense is debited for what the tax *would have been* if there was no carryforward. This is $25,000 ($100,000 × 25%). The tax benefit of the $50,000 carryforward from last year is $12,500 ($50,000 × 25%). Thus the ac-

218

tual tax payable is only $12,500. The account Tax Benefit of Loss Carryforward is a contra to the Income Tax Expense account and it appears on the income statement as such.

The income statement for 19E would report the following:

Income before Taxes		$100,000
Income Tax Expense	(25,000)	
Less Tax Benefit of Loss Carryforward	12,500	
Net Income Tax Expense		(12,500)
Net Income		$ 87,500

11.2   DEFERRED INCOME TAXES—DEFERRED TAX LIABILITIES

Income for financial statement purposes is determined under generally accepted accounting principles as set forth by the accounting profession. Income for tax purposes is determined according to the rules of the Internal Revenue Service which are passed into law by Congress. These rules often do not follow generally accepted accounting principles. Accordingly, differences will arise between accounting income and taxable income.

These differences may be either temporary or permanent in nature. *Temporary differences* are referred to as *timing differences* because, with time, they reverse or "turn around." *Permanent differences* are forever — they do *not* reverse. Let's first discuss temporary differences.

Temporary differences involve the recognition of revenue or expense items in one year for tax purposes but in a different year for accounting purposes. Overall the *total* income is the same for both tax *and* accounting purposes; it is just the timing that is different. For example, under GAAP, revenue is recognized when earned, not when received. Thus if in year 1 a company earns revenue but does not receive it until year 2, it would recognize it as income in year 1. However, for tax purposes, revenue is usually recognized when received. Thus this item would not be reported on the tax return until year 2. Accordingly, in year 1, the income statement reports this revenue while the tax return does not; in year 2, the tax return reports it as revenue while the income statement does not. For both years together, however, the total income is the same — the difference is only in timing. Year 1 is called the *year of origination* of the difference; year 2 is the *year of reversal.*

Other examples of temporary differences would be as follows:

1. Unearned revenue received in 19A and recognized for tax purposes this year, but not recognized for accounting purposes until earned in 19B

2. Accrued expenses recognized in 19A for accounting purposes but not recognized for tax purposes until paid in 19B

3. Revenue from installment sales recognized totally in 19A for accounting purposes, but recognized gradually over several years under the installment method for tax purposes

4. Straight-line depreciation used for accounting purposes while an accelerated method is used for tax purposes

5. Warranty costs recognized in 19A for accounting purposes before they actually occur (using estimates), but not recognized until paid for tax purposes

6. Percentage-of-completion method for construction contracts used for accounting purposes while the completed-contract method is used for tax purposes

7. Expenditures for prepaid items in 19A deducted completely this year for tax purposes, but amortized gradually for accounting purposes

We've seen in the past that the standard entry to record income taxes has been:

Income Tax Expense	xxx	
Income Tax Payable		xxx

But now that we've become aware of temporary differences, this entry becomes more complex. The debit to Income Tax Expense is based upon what the tax should be according to *GAAP.* However, the credit to Income Tax Payable is based upon what is *physically* payable — and that is determined according to tax rules. The difference between the debit and credit goes to an account called Deferred Tax Liability or Deferred Tax Asset, depending upon the circumstances.

EXAMPLE 3

Company T has the following information regarding its income for 19A and 19B:

	19A		19B	
	Accounting Income	**Taxable Income**	**Accounting Income**	**Taxable Income**
Regular income	$100	$100	$100	$100
Temporary difference	10	0	0	10
Total	$110	$100	$100	$110
Tax rates	20%		20%	

By "regular" income we mean income recognized both for accounting and tax purposes. The temporary difference is due to revenue earned in 19A but not collected until 19B. Thus in 19A it is recognized for accounting purposes but not for tax purposes. Notice, however, that it reverses in 19B at the time of collection. At that time, it is recognized for tax purposes but not for accounting purposes.

The entry for 19A is:

Income Tax Expense	22	
Income Tax Payable		20
Deferred Tax Liability		2

Income tax expense is 20% of the accounting income of $110, which equals $22. Income tax payable is the amount that IRS demands we pay—20% of $100. The deferred tax liability of $2 is 20% of the $10 difference between accounting income and taxable income.

The reason why income tax expense is based upon accounting income is the matching principle. Under this principle, expenses relating to revenue must be matched against that revenue, and recognized in the same period. Since for accounting purposes we recognize the $10 revenue item this period, we must recognize the related $2 tax expense as well (even though the IRS isn't asking us for the money now!)

Thus income tax expense consists of two components—$20 payable now and $2 deferred until later. In this case, because the reversal takes place only 1 year from now, it is a *current* liability.

The entry for 19B is:

Income Tax Expense	20	
Deferred Tax Liability	2	
Income Tax Payable		22

Once again, income tax expense is based on accounting income and income tax payable on taxable income. The tax liability of $2 from last year which was deferred has now appeared, and it is being paid.

Let's take a look at a situation where the reversal takes more than 1 year.

EXAMPLE 4

Company T has the following information regarding its income for 19A, 19B, and 19C:

	19A		19B		19C	
	Accounting Income	**Taxable Income**	**Accounting Income**	**Taxable Income**	**Accounting Income**	**Taxable Income**
Regular income	$100	$100	$100	$100	$100	$100
Temporary difference	20	0	0	10	0	10
Total	$120	$100	$100	$110	$100	$110
Tax rates	20%		20%		20%	

The entry for 19A is:

Income Tax Expense	24*	
Income Tax Payable		20
Deferred Tax Liability		4

*Based upon accounting income

In 19B only one-half the deferred liability is paid. The entry is:

Income Tax Expense	20	
Deferred Tax Liability	2	
Income Tax Payable		22

This entry would also be made in 19C.

In 19A, only $2 of the $4 deferred liability is considered current. The other $2 is considered long-term since it requires more than 1 year to reverse.

In the situations discussed so far, the tax rates were the same for all years. If the tax rates are different, *and* they have already been passed by Congress and are known in the first year, then they should be taken into account in the journal entry.

EXAMPLE 5

Company T has the following information regarding years 19A and 19B:

	19A		19B	
	Accounting Income	**Taxable Income**	**Accounting Income**	**Taxable Income**
Regular income	$100	$100	$100	$100
Temporary difference	10	0	0	10
Total	$110	$100	$100	$110
Tax rates	20%		30%	

The 19B rate has already been passed by Congress in 19A. The 19A entry is:

Income Tax Expense	23	
Income Tax Payable		20
Deferred Tax Liability		3

Income tax payable is what we must physically pay the IRS — 20% of $100. The deferred tax liability of $3 is based upon the $10 temporary difference multiplied by the rate of 30%, which will be in effect in 19B when this difference reverses.

The entry for 19B is:

Income Tax Expense	30	
Deferred Tax Liability	3	
Income Tax Payable		33

EXAMPLE 6

Assume the same information as in the previous example except that the $10 difference in 19A will reverse $5 in 19B and $5 in 19C, and the tax rates for the 3 years are 20%, 30%, and 40%, respectively. The entry for 19A is:

Income Tax Expense	23.50	
Income Tax Payable		20
Deferred Tax Liability		3.50

The deferred tax liability consists of .30($5) + .40($5) = $3.50.

If in 19A a change in the rate has not yet been passed by Congress, then the 19A entry should use the 19A rate and not assume that any future changes will be made. This is true even if Congress is *discussing* the possibility of a change. Later on, if a rate change goes into effect, an adjusting entry should be made to account for the effect of this change.

EXAMPLE 7

Let's use the same information as in Example 5 but assume that the 30% rate for 19B has not yet been passed in 19A.

	19A		19B	
	Accounting Income	Taxable Income	Accounting Income	Taxable Income
Regular income	$100	$100	$100	$100
Temporary difference	10	0	0	10
Total	$110	$100	$100	$110
Tax rates	20%		30%	

The entry for 19A uses the 19A rate, as follows:

Income Tax Expense	22	
Income Tax Payable		20
Deferred Tax Liability (.20 × $10)		2

In 19B, when the new rate of 30% is passed and goes into effect, an adjusting entry must be made to recognize the additional $1 tax (10% of $10). The entry is:

Income Tax Expense	1	
Deferred Tax Liability		1

As a result, the Deferred Tax Liability now has a balance of $3 ($2 + $1).
The entry for 19B is:

Income Tax Expense	30	
Deferred Tax Liability	3	
Income Tax Payable		33

11.3 DEFERRED TAX ASSETS

In our previous discussion, accounting income was *greater* than taxable income in the year of origination, resulting in a deferred tax liability. If, however, accounting income is *less* than taxable income, a deferred tax asset results. Once again, income tax expense is based upon accounting income, income tax payable is based upon taxable income, and the difference is *debited* to a deferred tax asset account. However, the accounting profession has stated that a deferred tax asset may only be recognized to negate a deferred tax liability. If the deferred tax asset exceeds the deferred tax liability, the excess is not recognized.

EXAMPLE 8

Company T had the following information regarding its income for 19A and 19B:

	19A		19B	
	Accounting Income	Taxable Income	Accounting Income	Taxable Income
Regular income	$100	$100	$100	$100
Temporary difference no. 1	10	0	0	10
Temporary difference no. 2	0	8	8	0
Total	$110	$108	$108	$110
Tax rates	20%		20%	

Temporary difference no. 1 relates to income earned but not yet received, which is recognized for accounting purposes but not for tax purposes. Temporary difference no. 2 involves the opposite situation — income has been received but not earned.

The entry for 19A is:

Income Tax Expense	22.00*	
Deferred Tax Asset	1.60†	
Income Tax Payable		21.60‡
Deferred Tax Liability		2.00§

*$110 × 20%
†$8 × 20%
‡$108 × 20%
§$10 × 20%

Notice that the entire deferred tax asset of $1.60 has been recognized because it does not exceed the deferred tax liability of $2.00.

In 19B the entry is:

Income Tax Expense	21.60	
Deferred Tax Liability	2.00	
Income Tax Payable		22.00
Deferred Tax Asset		1.60

EXAMPLE 9

Assume the same information as in the previous example except that temporary difference no. 2 is $12 instead of $8. Since the deferred tax asset on $12 is $2.40 ($12 × 20%) and this exceeds the deferred tax liability of $2.00, we may only recognize $2.00. The entry for 19A would be:

Income Tax Expense	22.40	
Deferred Tax Asset	2.00	
Income Tax Payable		22.40
Deferred Tax Liability		2.00

The Deferred Tax Asset account represents a *prepayment* of taxes. For example, if accounting income is $200, taxable income is $220, and the tax rate is 20%, then, according to GAAP the tax should only be $40. Nevertheless, we are forced to pay $44 because IRS has a different set of accounting rules. Thus the extra $4 we are now paying is not an expense of this period (because in this period we only earned $200 under accounting rules), but rather a prepayment of next period's taxes.

11.4 PERMANENT DIFFERENCES

Thus far our discussion has centered around temporary differences — differences that reverse with time. However, some differences are permanent — they do not reverse. Some examples of these differences are:

1. Amortization of goodwill — this is permitted under GAAP but *permanently* prohibited under tax rules. It can neither be deducted this year nor in future years.

2. Proceeds from life insurance — this is considered a revenue item for accounting purposes but is permanently nontaxable.

3. Interest on municipal bonds — this is a revenue item for accounting purposes but is exempt for tax purposes.

For permanent differences, there is no deferred tax treatment. Neither deferred tax liabilities nor deferred tax assets are recognized. The debit to Income Tax Expense is exactly equal to the credit to Income Tax Payable and they are both based on what is physically payable.

Why is there no deferred tax treatment for permanent differences? The answer is simple: To defer means to postpone until later. In this case, there is no postponement; the difference is permanent and will never be recognized.

EXAMPLE 10

Company T has the following information regarding 19A and 19B:

	19A		19B	
	Accounting Income	Taxable Income	Accounting Income	Taxable Income
Regular income	$100	$100	$100	$100
Interest on municipal bonds	20	0	0	0
Total	$120	$100	$100	$100
Tax rates	20%		20%	

Notice that the $20 difference does *not* reverse. The entry for 19A is:

Income Tax Expense (.20 × 100)	20	
Income Tax Payable		20

The same entry will be made for 19B.

EXAMPLE 11

Company T has the following information regarding its income for 19A and 19B:

	19A		19B	
	Accounting Income	Taxable Income	Accounting Income	Taxable Income
Regular income	$100	$100	$100	$100
Amortization of goodwill	(20)	0	0	0
Total	$ 80	$100	$100	$100
Tax rates	20%		20%	

The entry for 19A and 19B is:

Income Tax Expense	20	
Income Tax Payable		20

Summary

1. Companies that incur losses may elect to carry these losses back 3 years (to the earliest year first) and forward 15 years to offset income. When losses are carried back, the company is entitled to a refund of taxes paid.

2. The entry to record a tax refund resulting from a carryback is:

Tax Refund Receivable	xxx	
Tax Benefit Due to Carryback		xxx

The entry to record a reduction in future taxes due to a carryforward is:

Income Tax Expense	xxx	
Income Tax Payable		xxx
Tax Benefit Due to Carryforward		xxx

3. The entry for carryforwards is made in the year the carryforward is actually used. It is not made in the year the carryforward is created since at that time it is uncertain whether there will be future income against which to use this carryforward.

4. Accounting income is based upon GAAP, whereas taxable income is based upon IRS rules. Accordingly, differences will arise between the two incomes. Some of these differences are *temporary* in nature — they reverse and turn around with time — while others are permanent. Because of this "turnaround" feature, temporary differences are also called *timing differences.*

5. Examples of temporary differences are revenue earned in one year but received in another, expenses incurred in one year but paid in another, and one method of depreciation used for accounting purposes while another is used for tax purposes. The year in which the difference is created is called the *year of origination;* the year in which it turns around is called the *year of reversal.*

6. For temporary differences, if accounting income is greater than taxable income, the following entry is made:

Income Tax Expense	xx	
Income Tax Payable		xx
Deferred Tax Liability		xx

Income tax expense is based upon accounting income; income tax payable is based upon what is physically payable to IRS; the deferred tax liability is determined by multiplying the difference by the tax rate to be in effect at the time of reversal.

7. If in the year of origination, the tax rates for the future years (the years of reversal) have already been passed by Congress, then these rates are used to determine the deferred tax liability. If not, even though Congress is *discussing* new rates, the old rate should be used. Should the rates change later on, an adjusting entry will have to be made to reflect the change.

8. For temporary differences, if accounting income is less than taxable income, a deferred tax asset is created. The entry is:

Income Tax Expense	xxx	
Deferred Tax Asset	xxx	
Income Tax Payable		xxx

Again, income tax expense is based upon accounting income and income tax payable is based upon what is physically payable to IRS.

9. Both deferred tax assets and deferred tax liabilities are considered current if the entire reversal will take place within 1 year. Otherwise, the portion that is due to reverse after 1 year is considered long-term.

10. The accounting profession has stated that deferred tax assets may only be recognized to negate deferred tax liabilities. If there are no deferred tax liabilities, or if the deferred tax asset exceeds the liability, the excess should not be recognized.

11. *Permanent differences* between accounting and taxable income do not turn around. Examples are interest on municipal bonds, proceeds from life insurance policies, and amortization of goodwill. Such differences do not require the creation of deferred tax assets or liabilities since the difference is not merely deferred but permanently cancelled. Thus the entry for these situations is simply a debit to Income Tax Expense and a credit to Income Tax Payable, and both of these are based upon what is physically payable to IRS.

Rapid Review

1. Operating losses may be carried back _____ years and forward _____ years.

2. The account Tax Benefit Due to Carryback is a _____ type of account.

3. The nature of the account Tax Benefit Due to Carryforward is that of a _____ account.

4. Accounting income is based upon _____ while taxable income is based upon _____ rules.

5. Differences that turn around with time are called _____ or _____ differences, while those that do not are _____ differences.

6. Revenue received in one year but earned in another is an example of a _____ difference.

7. Amortization of goodwill is a _____ difference.

8. The year in which a timing difference is created is the year of _____ .

9. Income tax expense is based upon _____ income, while income tax payable is based upon _____ income.

10. If accounting income is less than taxable income, the difference is a deferred tax _____ ; if it is more, the difference is a deferred tax _____ .

11. Deferred tax assets may only be recognized to _____ deferred tax liabilities.

12. For permanent differences, both income tax expense and income tax payable are based upon _____ income.

Answers: 1. 3; 15 2. revenue 3. contra-expense 4. GAAP; IRS 5. temporary, timing; permanent 6. temporary 7. permanent 8. origination 9. accounting; taxable 10. asset; liability 11. negate 12. taxable

Solved Problems

Net Operating Loss Carrybacks and Carryforwards

11.1   Company T had the following information for the years 19A–19E:

	Income before Tax	Tax Rate	Taxes Paid
19A	$ 50,000	20%	$10,000
19B	70,000	25%	17,500
19C	30,000	25%	7,500
19D	20,000	30%	6,000
19E	(90,000)	30%	–0–

(1)   Prepare journal entries for all years.
(2)   Show the income statement for 19E.

SOLUTION

(1)   The entry for years 19A through 19D involves a debit to Income Tax Expense and a credit to Income Tax Payable for the amounts of $10,000, $17,500, $7,500, and $6,000, respectively. The entry for 19E is:

Tax Refund Receivable	22,500	
Tax Benefit Due to Carryback		22,500*

*($70,000 × 25%) + ($20,000 × 25%)

The carryback negates all the 19B income and $20,000 of the 19C income.

(2)   The income statement for 19E shows:

Income before Taxes	$(90,000)
Less Tax Benefit Due to Carryback	22,500
Net Income	$(67,500)

[Section 11.1]

11.2   Company T has the following information regarding the years 19A–19C:

	Income before Tax	Tax Rate
19A	$(50,000)	20%
19B	20,000	25%
19C	40,000	30%

(1)   Prepare the necessary journal entries for all 3 years.
(2)   Show the income statement for 19C.
(3)   If the loss in 19A was sufficiently high, for how many years would Company T be able to carry it forward?

SOLUTION

(1)   19A   No entry.

19B	Income Tax Expense	5,000	
	Income Tax Payable		0
	Tax Benefit Due to Carryforward		5,000
19C	Income Tax Expense	12,000	
	Income Tax Payable		3,000*
	Tax Benefit Due to Carryforward		9,000

*($40,000 − $30,000) × 30%

(2)

Income before Tax		$40,000
Income Tax Expense	(12,000)	
Less Tax Benefit Due to Carryforward	9,000	
Net Income Tax Expense		(3,000)
Net Income		$37,000

(3)   For 13 years after 19C (15 years in total).   [Section 11.1]

11.3   Company T has the following information for the years 19A–19F:

	Income before Tax	Tax Rate	Taxes Paid
19A	$ 20,000	20%	$4,000
19B	30,000	25%	7,500
19C	10,000	20%	2,000
19D	(90,000)	30%	0
19E	10,000	20%	?
19F	40,000	30%	?

Prepare entries for all years.

SOLUTION

For 19A, 19B, and 19C the entry would be a debit to Income Tax Expense and a credit to Income Tax Payable for the amounts of $4,000, $7,500, and $2,000, respectively.

For 19D the entry is:

Tax Refund Receivable	13,500	
Tax Benefit Due to Carryback		13,500

For 19E:

Income Tax Expense	2,000	
Income Tax Payable		0
Tax Benefit Due to Carryforward		2,000

For 19F:

Income Tax Expense	12,000	
Income Tax Payable		6,000
Tax Benefit Due to Carryforward		6,000[†]

[†]$20,000 × 30%   [Section 11.1]

Deferred Tax Liabilities

11.4   For 19A and 19B, Company T had regular income of $50,000 and $70,000, respectively. During 19A it had additional income of $10,000 from services performed on account which it did not collect until 19B. Company T uses the accrual method of accounting for accounting purposes and the cash method for tax purposes. The tax rate for both years is 20%.

(1)   Is the $10,000 difference temporary or permanent?

(2)   What is accounting income and taxable income for each year?

(3)   Prepare journal entries for each year.

SOLUTION

(1)   Temporary.

(2)

19A:	Accounting income:	$60,000
	Taxable income:	50,000
19B:	Accounting income:	$70,000
	Taxable income:	80,000

(3) 19A:

Income Tax Expense	12,000	
Income Tax Payable		10,000
Deferred Tax Liability		2,000

19B:

Income Tax Expense	14,000	
Deferred Tax Liability	2,000	
Income Tax Payable		16,000

[Section 11.2]

11.5   Because Company T uses the straight-line method of depreciation for book purposes and an accelerated method for tax purposes, its 19A accounting income was greater than its taxable income by $60,000. Its 19B and 19C taxable incomes were greater than accounting income by the amounts of $20,000 and $40,000, respectively. The tax rate for all years is 20%.

(1)   Is this a temporary difference or a permanent difference? Why?

(2)   If it is temporary, does it give rise to a deferred tax asset or a deferred tax liability?

(3)   How much is this deferral?

SOLUTION

(1) Temporary — because it reverses with time.

(2) Deferred tax liability.

(3) $(20\% \times \$20,000) + (20\% \times \$40,000) = \$12,000$ [Section 11.2]

11.6 Company T has the following information for years 19A–19C:

	19A Accounting Income	19A Taxable Income	19B Accounting Income	19B Taxable Income	19C Accounting Income	19C Taxable Income
Regular income	$500	$500	$700	$700	$600	$600
Temporary difference	200	0	0	100	0	100
Tax rates	20%		30%		40%	

The temporary difference is due to different accounting methods used for a construction project. All tax rates have been passed by Congress in 19A. Prepare entries for each year.

SOLUTION

19A	Income Tax Expense	170	
	Income Tax Payable		100*
	Deferred Tax Liability		70†

_____

*20% of $500

†(30% of $100) + (40% of $100)

19B	Income Tax Expense	210	
	Deferred Tax Liability	30	
	Income Tax Payable		240
19C	Income Tax Expense	240	
	Deferred Tax Liability	40	
	Income Tax Payable		280

[Section 11.2]

11.7 Poor Company has the following information for 19A and 19B:

	19A Accounting Income	19A Taxable Income	19B Accounting Income	19B Taxable Income
Regular income	$100	$100	$100	$100
Temporary difference	60	0	0	60
Tax rates	20%		30%	

In 19A Congress is discussing a 30% tax rate for 19B, but this rate is not actually passed into law until 19B. Prepare all necessary entries for both years.

SOLUTION

19A			
	Income Tax Expense	32	
	Income Tax Payable		20*
	Deferred Tax Liability		12†

_____

*20% of $100

†20% of $60

19B

Adjustment entry:

Income Tax Expense	6	
Deferred Tax Liability		6

An additional 10% of $60

Income Tax Expense	30	
Deferred Tax Liability	18*	
Income Tax Payable		48†

————————

*12 + 6
†30% of $160   [Section 11.2]

Deferred Tax Assets

11.8   Bodner Corporation has the following information regarding 19A and 19B:

	19A		19B	
	Accounting Income	**Taxable Income**	**Accounting Income**	**Taxable Income**
Regular income	$500	$500	$600	$600
Temporary difference 1	0	100	100	0
Temporary difference 2	200	0	0	200
Tax rates		20%		20%

Temporary difference 1 is due to revenue received in 19A but not earned until 19B. Temporary difference 2 is due to a difference in depreciation methods.

(1)   Do these differences lead to the creation of deferred tax assets or liabilities?

(2)   Prepare entries for both years.

SOLUTION

(1)   Difference 1 creates a deferred tax asset; difference 2 creates a deferred tax liability.

(2)   For 19A:

Income Tax Expense	140	
Deferred Tax Asset	20*	
Income Tax Payable		120†
Deferred Tax Liability		40‡

————————

*20% of $100
†20% of $600
‡20% of $200

For 19B:

Income Tax Expense	140	
Deferred Tax Liability	40	
Income Tax Payable (.20 × $800)		160
Deferred Tax Asset		20	[Section 11.3]

11.9   Company T had the following information regarding 19A and 19B:

	19A		19B	
	Accounting Income	**Taxable Income**	**Accounting Income**	**Taxable Income**
Regular income	$400	$400	$500	$500
Temporary difference 1	0	100	100	0
Temporary difference 2	80	0	0	80
Total	$480	$500	$600	$580
Tax rates		20%		20%

(1) What type of tax deferral does difference 1 create? Difference 2?

(2) Would the deferred tax effect of difference 1 be totally recognized? Why?

(3) Prepare entries for 19A and 19B.

SOLUTION

(1) Deferred tax asset; deferred tax liability.

(2) No, because a deferred tax asset may only be recognized to negate a deferred tax liability. Since the deferred tax liability is $16 (20% of $80), the deferred tax asset may not exceed this amount.

(3) 19A:

Income Tax Expense	100	
Deferred Tax Asset	16	
Income Tax Payable		100
Deferred Tax Liability		16

19B:

Income Tax Expense	116	
Deferred Tax Liability	16	
Income Tax Payable		116
Deferred Tax Asset		16

[Section 11.3]

11.10 Company T has the following information:

	19A		19B	
	Accounting Income	**Taxable Income**	**Accounting Income**	**Taxable Income**
Regular income	$ 400	$400	$800	$800
Difference 1	200	0	0	0
Difference 2	(100)	0	0	0
Total	$ 500	$400	$800	$800
Tax rates	20%		20%	

Difference 1 represents proceeds from life insurance collected upon the death of a company executive; difference 2 represents the amortization of goodwill.

(1) What type of differences are these? Why?

(2) Prepare entries for both years.

SOLUTION

(1) Permanent — they do not turn around.

(2) 19A: 19B:

Income Tax Expense	80		Income Tax Expense	160	
Income Tax Payable		80	Income Tax Payable		160

[Section 11.4]

11.11 Company T had the following information for 19A and 19B:

	19A		19B	
	Accounting Income	**Taxable Income**	**Accounting Income**	**Taxable Income**
Regular income	$ 800	$800	$800	$800
Difference 1	100	0	0	100
Difference 2	200	0	0	0
Total	$1,100	$800	$800	$900
Tax rates	20%		20%	

Difference 1 was caused by a difference in depreciation methods; difference 2 represents interest on municipal bonds.

(1) What is the nature of difference 1? Difference 2? Why?

(2) Prepare entries for both years?

SOLUTION

(1) The first is temporary — it reverses. The second is permanent — it does not.

(2) For 19A:

Income Tax Expense	180	
Income Tax Payable (.20 × $800)		160
Deferred Tax Liability (.20 × $100)		20

For 19B:

Income Tax Expense	160	
Deferred Tax Liability	20	
Income Tax Payable		180

[Section 11.4]

Supplementary Problems

11.12 Company T has the following information regarding its operations for the years 19A–19D:

	Income before Tax	Tax Rate	Tax Paid
19A	$ 150,000	30%	$45,000
19B	75,000	30%	22,500
19C	50,000	25%	12,500
19D	(300,000)	25%	0

Prepare an entry for 19D to record the refund due for previous years.

11.13 In the previous problem assume that in 19E Company T earns $70,000 and the tax rate is 25%. Prepare the necessary entry, and show a partial income statement.

11.14 Identify the following as either temporary tax differences or permanent differences:

(a) Amortization of goodwill in 19A

(b) Revenue received in 19A but earned in 19B

(c) Expenses incurred in 19A but paid in 19B

(d) Life insurance proceeds collected in 19B

(e) Use of LIFO for tax purposes and FIFO for accounting purposes in 19A

(f) Interest earned from municipal bonds in 19B

11.15 Company T had "regular" income of $500 each in 19A and 19B for both accounting and tax purposes. It also had a $300 difference which is recognized in 19A for accounting purposes and in 19B for tax purposes. The rate for all years is 30%. Prepare the required journal entry for both years.

11.16 Assume the same information as in the previous problem except that the $300 difference is recognized for tax purposes partially in 19B ($200) and partially in 19C ($100). The rate for all years is 30%. Prepare the entries for 19A, 19B, and 19C. Assume that in 19C we once again have a "regular" income of $500 for both accounting and tax purposes.

11.17 Assume the same information as in Problem 11.16 except that the rate for 19C is 35%. Prepare entries for all years assuming that:

(*a*) the rates for all years have already been enacted by Congress in 19A.

(*b*) the 19C rate has not been enacted before 19C.

11.18 Company T has "regular" income of $800 for both accounting and tax purposes in each of 19A and 19B. It also has two temporary differences of $50 and $40, respectively. The $50 difference is recognized for accounting purposes in 19A and for tax purposes in 19B; the $40 difference is just the opposite — it is recognized for tax purposes in 19A and for accounting purposes in 19B. The rate for all years is 20%. Prepare entries for both years.

11.19 Assume the same information as in the previous problem except that the second difference is $60. Prepare entries for both years.

11.20 Company T has "regular" income of $600 in each of 19A and 19B. It also has amortization of goodwill in 19A of $100. The rate for each year is 20%. Prepare an entry for each year.

11.21 Company T has "regular" income of $500 in 19A and 19B for both accounting and tax purposes. It also has two differences. One involves the recognition of revenue of $100 in 19A for accounting purposes and in 19B for tax purposes. The other involves the recognition of $80 in municipal interest for accounting purposes just in 19B. The rate for all years is 20%. Prepare the entries for 19A and 19B.

Appendix: The Time Value of Money*

INTRODUCTION

The concept of the time value of money plays a very important role in accounting. According to generally accepted accounting principles, assets and liabilities must be presented on the balance sheet at their "present values." For example, long-term notes receivable and payable, leases, pensions, and amortization of bond premiums and discounts all must take into consideration the value of time. If they do not, then they are improperly presented on the balance sheet and violate GAAP.

What exactly do we mean by the "time value of money" and "present value"? This chapter answers these questions by presenting a detailed description of these concepts together with practical examples.

To begin with, the time value of money involves interest calculations. There are two types of interest: simple interest and compound interest. In *simple interest,* interest is earned only on the principal; in *compound interest,* interest is earned on the interest as well as on the principal. We will assume the use of compound interest throughout this book, since that is the way it is done in the "real world."

The actual computation of the interest is done through the use of complex formulas. We will not need to apply these formulas, since interest tables exist that quickly and easily provide the interest amount. These tables are presented at the end of this Appendix. The tables are:

Table 1. The Future Value of $1

Table 2. The Present Value of $1

Table 3. The Future Value of an Annuity of $1

Table 4. The Present Value of an Annuity of $1

Let us now proceed to examine each of these tables and study their underlying concepts.

THE FUTURE VALUE OF $1

Table 1 answers the following question: "If I deposit $1 today in the bank (or in some other investment), how much will it grow (i.e., be worth) in the future?" Naturally, it will be worth more than $1 because of the interest factor. But *exactly* how much will it be? Table 1 gives us the answer very quickly. The left-hand column specifies the number of periods involved, while the remaining columns specify the interest rate.

EXAMPLE 1

If I deposit $1 today for 6 years and the interest rate is 5% compounded annually, the table tells us that this will grow into 1.34010 (approximately $1.34) in 6 years.

Naturally, nobody makes deposits of just $1. Although this table deals only with $1 deposits, we can easily adapt it for any deposit by simply multiplying the table value by the amount of the deposit.

NOTE: The tables provide values with six decimal places. For simplification, we round these values to five decimal places.

EXAMPLE 2

If I deposit $1,000 for 10 years and the rate is 10% compounded *annually,* the table yields a value of 2.59374. Multiplying this by the deposit of $1,000 yields a future value of $2,593.74.

In the previous examples, the interest was compounded *annually.* However, if it is compounded *semiannually,* we must look up half the rate in the table and *double* the periods. Notice that the table does not use the word "years"; it uses "periods."

EXAMPLE 3

If I deposit $1,000 for 10 years and the rate is 10% compounded *semiannually,* I must look up 5% for *20* periods in the table; the table value is 2.65330. Multiplying this by 1,000 results in $2,653.30 for the future value.

If the compounding is *quarterly,* then look up *one-fourth* the rate in the table and quadruple the number of periods.

EXAMPLE 4

If a deposit of $1,000 for 10 years at the rate of 10% is compounded *quarterly,* find the table value at the $2\frac{1}{2}\%$ mark for *40* periods; the table value is 2.68506. Multiplying this by 1,000 yields $2,685.06.

*Reprinted from Schaum's Outline Series: Theory and Problems of Intermediate Accounting I, 2d ed. by Cashin, Feldman, Lerner, and England. McGraw-Hill Publishing Company, 1989.

Notice from the above examples that the rate is always given on an *annual* basis. This must then be converted to one-half or one-quarter if the compounding is not on an annual basis.

THE PRESENT VALUE OF $1

Table 2 answers the following question: "How much do I have to deposit today to receive $1 in the future?" This is the opposite side of the coin of the future value of $1. There the question was what will be the amount of the *future* withdrawal. Here the question is what is the amount of the present deposit.

EXAMPLE 5

If I wish to withdraw $8,000 seven years from now and the interest rate is 12% compounded *annually*, Table 2 yields a value of 0.45235. Multiplying this by 8,000 yields $3,618.80. This means that to receive the $8,000 seven years from now, I must deposit $3,618.80 today.

EXAMPLE 6

Using the same facts as in the previous example except that the 12% rate is compounded *quarterly* requires that we look up the table for 28 periods at 3% (from 12% ÷ 4). The table value is 0.43708, and multiplying this by $8,000 yields $3,496.64 for today's deposit.

The concepts of future amount of $1 and present amount of $1 can also be used to answer other questions, such as the number of periods needed to accumulate a certain sum, or what interest rate to invest at.

EXAMPLE 7

If I deposit $21,545 today, how many years will this take to grow into $90,000 assuming that the rate of interest is 10% compounded annually? This problem can be solved with either Table 1 or Table 2. Let's first use Table 1. We know that $21,545 multiplied by some table value (which we will call X) should yield $90,000. Thus,

$$\$21,545X = \$90,000$$
$$X = 4.17730$$

Looking at Table 1 in the 10% column, we find at the 15-period mark a value that is very close to 4.17730 (4.17725). Therefore, the answer is approximately 15 years.

We can also use Table 2 for this problem. But in this case, the equation has to be set up in reverse:

$$\$90,000X = \$21,545$$
$$x = 0.23939$$

Looking at Table 2 in the 10% column for 0.23939 yields the same answer of 15 years.

EXAMPLE 8

What rate of interest is needed for a deposit today of $42,241 to grow into $100,000 in 10 years assuming *annual* compounding?

Using Table 1:

$$\$42,241X = \$100,000$$
$$X = 2.36736$$

Searching horizontally across Table 1 at the 10-year mark yields a rate of 9%.

THE FUTURE VALUE OF AN ANNUITY OF $1

Table 3 answers the following question: "If I make a *series* of equal deposits of $1 each *over* several periods, how much will they accumulate to in the future?" Notice the key difference between this situation and the two previous situations. In the previous situations, I made just *one* deposit. Here I am making a *series* of deposits.

There are two types of annuities: an ordinary annuity and an annuity due. In the case of an *ordinary annuity,* the deposits are made at the *end* of each interest period; in the case of an *annuity due,* they are made at the *beginning* of each interest period.

EXAMPLE 9

If today is January 1, 19X7, and I plan to make a series of three deposits over the next 3 years with each deposit being made at the *end* of each year (December 31, 19X7, December 31, 19X8, December 31, 19X9), this is an example of an ordinary annuity.

However, if each deposit will be made at the beginning of each year (January 1, 19X7, January 1, 19X8, January 1, 19X9), then we are dealing with an annuity due.

In both cases the withdrawal takes place on December 31, 19X9. In the first case, therefore, the last deposit is made and withdrawn on the same day.

To find the future value of an *ordinary annuity,* we use Table 3. The left-hand column shows the number of deposits.

EXAMPLE 10

If I make a series of $5,000 deposits at the *end* of each of the next 5 years and the interest rate is 12% compounded annually, the future value of these deposits will be:

$$6.35285 \quad (5 \text{ deposits, } 12\%)$$
$$\times \quad \$5,000$$
$$\overline{\$31,764.25}$$

EXAMPLE 11

Assume that I plan to make a series of $1,000 deposits at the *end* of each 6-month period for the next 5 years and interest is 12% compounded semiannually. In this case, the total number of deposits will be 10 (two per year for 5 years), and each interest period is 6% ($12\% \times 1/2$).

The table value at 10 deposits and 6% is 13.18079. Multiplying this by $1,000 yields a future value of $13,180.79.

Using some elementary algebra, the table can also be used to calculate the value of each deposit, or the number of deposits that need to be made.

EXAMPLE 12

If I wish to accumulate $20,000 five years from now (in order to make a down payment on a Mercedes) by making a series of deposits at the *end* of every 3 months, and the interest rate is 12% compounded quarterly, the amount of *each* deposit can be computed as follows:

The rate per period is 3%, and the number of deposits is 20 (four deposits per year for 5 years). Looking at Table 3 at 20 periods and 3% yields a value of 26.87037. Let's call the amount of each deposit X. Then

$$26.87037X = \$20,000$$
$$X = \$744.31$$

Therefore, if $744.31 is deposited every 3 months for 5 years, the result will be a total of $20,000.

EXAMPLE 13

Suppose that the future desired value if $117,332, the annual deposits are $20,000 each at the end of each year, and interest is compounded annually at 8%. How many deposits have to be made?

Let X = table value. Therefore,

$$\$20,000X = \$117,332$$
$$X = 5.8666$$

Looking at the table in the 8% column for 5.8666 yields five deposits.

Table 3 will work only for an *ordinary annuity.* It cannot be used *directly* for an *annuity due.* However, by using a conversion formula, we can adapt the table value and then use it for an annuity due. The formula involves two steps:

Step 1.   Look up the table for one additional deposit.

Step 2.   Take this value, subtract 1 from it, and then proceed as if you were calculating an ordinary annuity.

EXAMPLE 14

To find the future value of an *annuity due* of 10 deposits of $1,000 each, with a 10% rate compounded annually, we would look up the table for 11 deposits and find:

		18.53117
Subtract 1	−	1.00000
		17.53117
Multiply by $1,000	×	$1,000
Yielding a future value of		$17,531.17

THE PRESENT VALUE OF AN ANNUITY OF $1

Table 4 answers the following question: "How much do I have to deposit today to be able to make several equal withdrawals of $1 each in the future?" Note carefully the difference between this and the future value of an annuity. In that situation, there were several deposits and one withdrawal. In this situation, there is one deposit and several withdrawals.

Once again, we have two types of annuities: an ordinary annuity and an annuity due. In the former case, the first withdrawal is made *one period after* the deposit, while in the latter it is made *immediately* (i.e., right after the deposit is made).

EXAMPLE 15

If today, January 1, 19X7, I make one big deposit with the intention of making three withdrawals starting one period after today (December 31, 19X7, December 31, 19X8, December 31, 19X9), then it is an *ordinary annuity* situation.

However, if the first withdrawal takes place immediately (i.e., the withdrawal dates are January 1, 19X7, January 1, 19X8, January 1, 19X9), then it is an *annuity due* situation.

For the ordinary annuity situation, we use Table 4. For the annuity due situation, however, we must adapt Table 4 by the following conversion formula:

Step 1.   Look up the table for one *less* withdrawal.

Step 2.   Add 1 to that value, and then proceed as if you were calculating an ordinary annuity.

EXAMPLE 16

How much must one deposit now to be able to withdraw $1,000 per year at the end of each of the next 5 years if the interest rate is 15%? Since the first withdrawal does not take place immediately, this is an ordinary annuity. Table 4 shows a value of

$$
\begin{array}{ll}
3.35216 & \text{for 5 periods, 15\%} \\
\times \quad \$1,000 & \\
\hline
\$3,352.16 & \text{the deposit today}
\end{array}
$$

EXAMPLE 17

Assume the same facts as in the previous example except that the first withdrawal takes place immediately. This is an annuity due situation. Looking up four withdrawals in the table yields:

$$
\begin{array}{lr}
 & 2.85498 \\
\text{Add 1} & 1.00000 \\
\hline
 & 3.85498 \\
\times & \$1,000 \\
\hline
 & \$3,854.98 \quad \text{is the present value}
\end{array}
$$

Table 4 can also be used to determine the interest rate.

EXAMPLE 18

Assume that you owe $634.52 on your credit card and you have a choice of either paying it now or paying $60 a month for 12 months, starting at the *end* of the first month. You wish to determine the interest rate involved. The calculation is:

$$
60X = \$634.52
$$
$$
X = \$10.57533
$$

Searching through Table 4 for this amount brings you to the 2% column. This is the rate per month. On a yearly basis the rate is 24% (2% × 12).

INTERPOLATION OF INTEREST TABLES

Thus far, when we used an algebraic equation to help us find a table value, we were lucky to be able to find precisely that value in the table. But this is not always the case. Sometimes the "result" will be between two table values, and a technique called *interpolation* must be used to calculate the exact value.

EXAMPLE 19

Assume that we deposit $1,000 today and it accumulates to $2,900 after 20 years. We wish to know the annual rate of interest being earned. Using the method discussed previously, we have

$$\$1,000X = \$2,900$$
$$X = 2.900$$

Searching through Table 1 at the 20-period mark, we do not find precisely 2.900. However, we find 2.65330 at the 5% mark and 3.20714 at the 6% mark. We therefore conclude that the rate is between 5% and 6%. But if we want more precision, we must *interpolate,* and that works as follows:

Let's call the actual rate i.

Let's call the difference between i and 5%, d.

Now we set up a table showing all these relationships:

Rate	Table Value
5%	2.65330
i	2.90000
6%	3.20714

The difference between 5% and 6% is 1%.

The difference between 5% and i is d.

The difference between 2.65330 and 3.20714 is 0.55384.

The difference between 2.65330 and 2.90000 is 0.2467.

We now express these differences as a proportion:

$$\frac{1\%}{d} = \frac{0.55384}{0.2467}$$

Cross-multiplication yields

$$0.55384d = 0.002467$$
$$d = 0.00445$$

Since $i = 5\% + d$, by substitution we get:

$$i = 5\% + 0.00445$$
$$= 0.05445$$
$$= 5.45\%$$

Rapid Review

1. If I make one deposit today and wish to know how much it will accumulate to in the future, that value is called _____ .

2. If I want to know how much to deposit today in order to be able to make a one-time withdrawal in the future, today's deposit is called _____ .

3. The concept of making a *series* of deposits for the purpose of making one withdrawal at the end is called _____ .

4. Making one deposit today in order to be able to make several withdrawals later is called _____ .

5. If the interest rate is 10% compounded semiannually and deposits will be made for 10 years, then the table should be looked up at the _____ rate and at the _____ period mark.

6. If the rate is 16% compounded quarterly and deposits will be made for 5 years, the table rate is _____ and the number of periods is _____ .

7. If the first deposit of an annuity is made *after* one period goes by, it is called an _____ .

8. If the first deposit of an annuity is made immediately, it is called an _____ .

9. The conversion formula for Table 3 requires looking up the table for _____ period(s) and then _____ 1.000.

10. The process of finding a precise value that lies between two table values is called _____ .

Answers: 1. the future value of 1 2. the present value of 1 3. the future value of an annuity of 1 4. the present value of an annuity of 1 5. 5%, 20 6. 4%, 20 7. ordinary annuity 8. annuity due 9. one extra, subtracting 10. interpolation

Solved Problems

A.1 For each of the following cases, indicate what interest rate and number of periods should be looked up in a table of the future value of 1:
(*a*) 10%, 10 years, compounded annually
(*b*) 12%, 10 years, compounded semiannually
(*c*) 16%, 8 years, compounded quarterly

SOLUTION

(*a*) 10%, 10 periods
(*b*) 6%, 20 periods
(*c*) 4%, 32 periods

A.2 Buck Greenfield deposited $13,000 in a money market account that provides interest at 8% compounded quarterly. How much will he have after 3 years?

SOLUTION

Since we want to know the future value of $1, we use Table 1.

At 2%, 12 periods	1.26824
×	$13,000
Future value	$16,487.12

A.3 If I invest $2,000 at 10% compounded annually, how much will I have after 10 years?

SOLUTION

Again referring to Table 1, we get

At 10%, 10 periods	2.59374
×	$2,000
Future value	$5,187.48

A.4 Esther Englard will receive $20,000 four years from now from a trust fund established by her rich uncle. Assuming that the rate is 10% compounded semiannually, how much must her uncle deposit today?

SOLUTION

We want to find out the present value of $1 and therefore use Table 2.

At 5%, 8 periods	0.67684
×	$20,000
Present value	$13,536.80

A.5   What is the present value of $3,000 due in 6 periods, discounted at 11%?

SOLUTION

The word "discounted" is often used in accounting and simply means "at an interest rate." Using Table 2, we get:

At 11%, 6 periods	0.53464
×	$3,000
Present value	$1,603.92

A.6   If a series of deposits of $8,000 each is made at the end of each period for the next 10 periods at 8%, what will be the total accumulated?

SOLUTION

Since we are dealing with a *series,* this is an annuity situation. Because this question involves the future, and the deposits are made at the *end* of each period, we use Table 3 (future value of an ordinary annuity). According to the table:

8%, 10 periods	14.48656
×	$8,000
Future value	$115,892.48

A.7   What is the future value of 10 deposits of $2,000 each made at the *beginning* of each period, if the rate is 10%?

SOLUTION

This, again, involves determining the future value of an annuity. However, since the deposits are made at the *beginning* of each period, it is an annuity due and we must use the conversion formula on the value listed in Table 3. In the table, we look up the value for *11* deposits and 10%.

	18.53117
Subtract 1	− 1.00000
	17.53117
×	$2,000
Future value	$35,062.34

A.8   What is the future value of $3,000 deposited quarterly for the next 9 years, if the interest rate is 10% compounded quarterly? Assume that the deposits are made at the *beginning* of each quarter.

SOLUTION

This again is a future value of annuity due situation, with a rate of 2½% and 36 deposits. We check the table for *37* deposits:

	59.73395
−	1.00000
	58.73395
×	$3,000
Future value	$176,201.85

A.9   What is the present value of $4,000 to be received at the *end* of each of the next 25 periods and discounted at 12%?

SOLUTION

This is a present value of ordinary annuity situation; hence, we use Table 4.

	7.84314
×	$4,000
Present value	$31,372.56

A.10   Assume the same information as in the previous problem, except that the withdrawals will be made at the *beginning* of each period. What is the present value?

SOLUTION

Since this is an annuity due, we must apply the conversion formula to Table 4, by looking at one *less* period and *adding* 1.

At 24 periods and 12%	7.7843
+	1.0000
	8.7843
×	$4,000
Present value	$35,137.20

A.11   If I deposit $1,845 today at 10% interest compounded annually, how many years will it take for it to accumulate to $20,000?

SOLUTION

Using Table 1 and letting X = the table values:

$$\$1,845X = 20,000$$
$$X = 10.8401$$

Searching through the table at 10% yields approximately 25 years.

A.12   If I deposit $25,331 at annual compounding for 6 years, and this results in $50,000, what is the interest rate?

SOLUTION

Using the value listed in Table 1, we get:

$$\$25,331X = \$50,000$$
$$X = 1.97386$$

This yields 12% in the row for 6 years.

A.13   If a deposit of $18,000 results in $36,000 after 6 periods, what is the rate?

SOLUTION

Again, we use Table 1:

$$\$18,000X = \$36,000$$
$$X = 2.0$$

We must interpolate:

12%	1.97382
i	2.0000
15%	2.31306

i is the rate, d is the difference between 12% and i, 3% is the difference between 12% and 15%, and 0.33924 is the difference between the table values at 12% and 15%.

$$\frac{3\%}{d} = \frac{0.33924}{0.02618}$$
$$0.33924d = 0.000785$$
$$d = 0.002299$$
$$i = 12\% + d$$
$$= .122299$$
$$= 12.22\%$$

A.14   How much do I have to deposit *each* year for the next 7 years if the rate is 8%, the deposits are made at the end of each year, and I wish to accumulate $200,000?

SOLUTION

Here we have several deposits and one withdrawal, making this a future value of annuity case. Since the deposits are at the end of each year, it is an ordinary annuity and we use Table 3:

$$8.92280X = 200,000$$
$$X = \$22,414.49 \qquad \text{deposited each year}$$

A.15 Assume the same facts as in the previous problem except that it is an annuity due. How much must be deposited each year?

SOLUTION

Using the conversion formula and *8* years, we refer to Table 3:

$$10.63663$$
$$- \quad 1.0000$$
$$9.63663$$
$$9.63663X = \$200,000$$
$$X = \$20,754.14 \qquad \text{deposited each year}$$

A.16 If a bank lends me \$62,065 today and I have to pay back \$10,000 at the end of each year for the next 11 years, what interest rate am I paying?

SOLUTION

This is a present value of annuity (ordinary) situation, because the bank is making one "deposit" (by lending me \$62,065) and several "withdrawals" (by my paying the bank \$10,000 each year). We use the values listed in Table 4 to calculate the interest rate:

$$\$10,000X = \$62,065$$
$$X = 6.2065$$

Searching the table for 6.2065 at the 11-period mark yields 11%.

A.17 Abraham Englard owes \$600,000. He has a choice of paying the \$600,000 now or paying \$100,000 at the end of each of the next 10 years; the interest rate is 9%. Which method of payment should he use?

SOLUTION

We must compare the present value of each method and choose the *lower* one. Using Table 4, the present value of an ordinary annuity at 10 years and 9% is \$641,766 (from 6.41766 × \$100,000).

The present value of paying \$600,000 now is, naturally, \$600,000.

Therefore the company should pay \$600,000 now.

A.18 On June 1, 19X8, Lisa Grade borrowed \$50,000 from her boyfriend, promising to pay him back in ten equal annual installments of \$6,000, starting on June 1, 19X9. What is the rate of interest?

SOLUTION

Here we have one big deposit (\$50,000) and several withdrawals (\$6000 each), making this a present value of annuity situation. Since the payments are being made at the end of each period, it is an ordinary annuity, and we use Table 4:

$$\$6000X = \$50,000$$
$$X = 8.33333$$

We must interpolate:

$$
\begin{array}{ll}
3\% & 8.53020 \\
i & 8.33333 \\
4\% & 8.11090
\end{array}
$$

$$\frac{1\%}{d} = \frac{0.4193}{0.1969}$$

$$0.4913d = 0.001969$$

$$d = 0.00469$$

$$i = 3\% + d$$

$$= 3\% + 0.00469$$

$$= 0.03469$$

$$= 3.47\%$$

Compound Interest Tables*

Table 1 Future Amount of 1 at Compound Interest Due in n Periods: $a_{\overline{n}|i} = (1 + i)^n$

n \ i	½%	1%	1½%	2%	2½%	3%
1	1.005000	1.010000	1.015000	1.020000	1.025000	1.030000
2	1.010025	1.020100	1.030225	1.040400	1.050625	1.060900
3	1.015075	1.030301	1.045678	1.061208	1.076891	1.092727
4	1.020151	1.040604	1.061364	1.082432	1.103813	1.125509
5	1.025251	1.051010	1.077284	1.104081	1.131408	1.159274
6	1.030378	1.061520	1.093443	1.126162	1.159693	1.194052
7	1.035529	1.072135	1.109845	1.148686	1.188686	1.229874
8	1.040707	1.082857	1.126493	1.171659	1.218403	1.266770
9	1.045911	1.093685	1.143390	1.195093	1.248863	1.304773
10	1.051140	1.104622	1.160541	1.218994	1.280085	1.343916
11	1.056396	1.115668	1.177949	1.243374	1.312087	1.384234
12	1.061678	1.126825	1.195618	1.268242	1.344889	1.425761
13	1.066986	1.138093	1.213552	1.293607	1.378511	1.468534
14	1.072321	1.149474	1.231756	1.319479	1.412974	1.512590
15	1.077683	1.160969	1.250232	1.345868	1.448298	1.557967
16	1.083071	1.172579	1.268986	1.372786	1.484506	1.604706
17	1.088487	1.184304	1.288020	1.400241	1.521618	1.652848
18	1.093929	1.196147	1.307341	1.428246	1.559659	1.702433
19	1.099399	1.208109	1.326951	1.456811	1.598650	1.753506
20	1.104896	1.220190	1.346855	1.485947	1.638616	1.806111
21	1.110420	1.232392	1.367058	1.515666	1.679582	1.860295
22	1.115972	1.244716	1.387564	1.545980	1.721571	1.916103
23	1.121552	1.257163	1.408377	1.576899	1.764611	1.973587
24	1.127160	1.269735	1.429503	1.608437	1.808726	2.032794
25	1.132796	1.282432	1.450945	1.640606	1.853944	2.093778
26	1.138460	1.295256	1.472710	1.673418	1.900293	2.156591
27	1.144152	1.308209	1.494800	1.706886	1.947800	2.221289
28	1.149873	1.321291	1.517222	1.741024	1.996495	2.287928
29	1.155622	1.334504	1.539981	1.775845	2.046407	2.356566
30	1.161400	1.347849	1.563080	1.811362	2.097568	2.427262
31	1.167207	1.361327	1.586526	1.847589	2.150007	2.500080
32	1.173043	1.374941	1.610324	1.884541	2.203757	2.575083
33	1.178908	1.388690	1.634479	1.922231	2.258851	2.652335
34	1.184803	1.402577	1.658996	1.960676	2.315322	2.731905
35	1.190727	1.416603	1.683881	1.999890	2.373205	2.813862
36	1.196681	1.430769	1.709140	2.039887	2.432535	2.898278
37	1.202664	1.445076	1.734777	2.080685	2.493349	2.985227
38	1.208677	1.459527	1.760798	2.122299	2.555682	3.074783
39	1.214721	1.474123	1.787210	2.164745	2.619574	3.167027
40	1.220794	1.488864	1.814018	2.208040	2.685064	3.262038

*These tables are adapted from A. N. Mosich, *Intermediate Accounting,* Revised Sixth Edition, McGraw-Hill, 1989. Used with permission of McGraw-Hill Book Company, © 1989.

Table 1   **Future Amount of 1** (*continued*)

n	3½%	4%	4½%	5%	5½%	6%
1	1.035000	1.040000	1.045000	1.050000	1.055000	1.060000
2	1.071225	1.081600	1.092025	1.102500	1.113025	1.123600
3	1.108718	1.124864	1.141166	1.157625	1.174241	1.191016
4	1.147523	1.169859	1.192519	1.215506	1.238825	1.262477
5	1.187686	1.216653	1.246182	1.276282	1.306960	1.338226
6	1.229255	1.265319	1.302260	1.340096	1.378843	1.418519
7	1.272279	1.315932	1.360862	1.407100	1.454679	1.503630
8	1.316809	1.368569	1.422101	1.477455	1.534687	1.593848
9	1.362897	1.423312	1.486095	1.551328	1.619094	1.689479
10	1.410599	1.480244	1.552969	1.628895	1.708144	1.790848
11	1.459970	1.539454	1.622853	1.710339	1.802092	1.898299
12	1.511069	1.601032	1.695881	1.795856	1.901207	2.012196
13	1.563956	1.665074	1.772196	1.885649	2.005774	2.132928
14	1.618695	1.731676	1.851945	1.979932	2.116091	2.260904
15	1.675349	1.800944	1.935282	2.078928	2.232476	2.396558
16	1.733986	1.872981	2.022370	2.182875	2.355263	2.540352
17	1.794676	1.947901	2.113377	2.292018	2.484802	2.692773
18	1.857489	2.025817	2.208479	2.406619	2.621466	2.854339
19	1.922501	2.106849	2.307860	2.526950	2.765647	3.025600
20	1.989789	2.191123	2.411714	2.653298	2.917757	3.207135
21	2.059431	2.278768	2.520241	2.785963	3.078234	3.399564
22	2.131512	2.369919	2.633652	2.925261	3.247537	3.603537
23	2.206114	2.464716	2.752166	3.071524	3.426152	3.819750
24	2.283328	2.563304	2.876014	3.225100	3.614590	4.048935
25	2.363245	2.665836	3.005434	3.386355	3.813392	4.291871
26	2.445959	2.772470	3.140679	3.555673	4.023129	4.549383
27	2.531567	2.883369	3.282010	3.733456	4.244401	4.822346
28	2.620172	2.998703	3.429700	3.920129	4.477843	5.111687
29	2.711878	3.118651	3.584036	4.116136	4.724124	5.418388
30	2.806794	3.243398	3.745318	4.321942	4.983951	5.743491
31	2.905031	3.373133	3.913857	4.538039	5.258069	6.088101
32	3.006708	3.508059	4.089981	4.764941	5.547262	6.453387
33	3.111942	3.648381	4.274030	5.003189	5.852362	6.840590
34	3.220860	3.794316	4.466362	5.253348	6.174242	7.251025
35	3.333590	3.946089	4.667348	5.516015	6.513825	7.686087
36	3.450266	4.103933	4.877378	5.791816	6.872085	8.147252
37	3.571025	4.268090	5.096860	6.081407	7.250050	8.636087
38	3.696011	4.438813	5.326219	6.385274	7.648803	9.154252
39	3.825372	4.616366	5.565899	6.704751	8.069487	9.703507
40	3.959260	4.801021	5.816365	7.039989	8.513309	10.285718

Table 1 Future Amount of 1 (*continued*)

n \ i	7%	8%	9%	10%	12%	15%
1	1.070000	1.080000	1.090000	1.100000	1.120000	1.150000
2	1.144900	1.166400	1.188100	1.210000	1.254400	1.322500
3	1.225043	1.259712	1.295029	1.331000	1.404928	1.520875
4	1.310796	1.360489	1.411582	1.464100	1.573519	1.749006
5	1.402552	1.469328	1.538624	1.610510	1.762342	2.011357
6	1.500730	1.586874	1.677100	1.771561	1.973823	2.313061
7	1.605781	1.713824	1.828039	1.948717	2.210681	2.660020
8	1.718186	1.850930	1.992563	2.143589	2.475963	3.059023
9	1.838459	1.999005	2.171893	2.357948	2.773079	3.517876
10	1.967151	2.158925	2.367364	2.593742	3.105848	4.045558
11	2.104852	2.331639	2.580426	2.853117	3.478550	4.652391
12	2.252192	2.518170	2.812665	3.138428	3.895976	5.350250
13	2.409845	2.719624	3.065805	3.452271	4.363493	6.152788
14	2.578534	2.937194	3.341727	3.797498	4.887112	7.075706
15	2.759032	3.172169	3.642482	4.177248	5.473566	8.137062
16	2.952164	3.425943	3.970306	4.594973	6.130394	9.357621
17	3.158815	3.700018	4.327633	5.054470	6.866041	10.761264
18	3.379932	3.996019	4.717120	5.559917	7.689966	12.375454
19	3.616528	4.315701	5.141661	6.115909	8.612762	14.231772
20	3.869684	4.660957	5.604411	6.727500	9.646293	16.366537
21	4.140562	5.033834	6.108808	7.400250	10.803848	18.821518
22	4.430402	5.436540	6.658600	8.140275	12.100310	21.644746
23	4.740530	5.871464	7.257874	8.954302	13.552347	24.891458
24	5.072367	6.341181	7.911083	9.849733	15.178629	28.625176
25	5.427433	6.848475	8.623081	10.834706	17.000064	32.918953
26	5.807353	7.396353	9.399158	11.918177	19.040072	37.856796
27	6.213868	7.988061	10.245082	13.109994	21.324881	43.535315
28	6.648838	8.627106	11.167140	14.420994	23.883866	50.065612
29	7.114257	9.317275	12.172182	15.863093	26.749930	57.575454
30	7.612255	10.062657	13.267678	17.449402	29.959922	66.211772
31	8.145113	10.867669	14.461770	19.194342	33.555113	76.143538
32	8.715271	11.737083	15.763329	21.113777	37.581726	87.565068
33	9.325340	12.676050	17.182028	23.225154	42.091533	100.699829
34	9.978114	13.690134	18.728411	25.547670	47.142517	115.804803
35	10.676581	14.785344	20.413968	28.102437	52.799620	133.175523
36	11.423942	15.968172	22.251225	30.912681	59.135574	153.151852
37	12.223618	17.245626	24.253835	34.003949	66.231843	176.124630
38	13.079271	18.625276	26.436680	37.404343	74.179664	202.543324
39	13.994820	20.115298	28.815982	41.144778	83.081224	232.924823
40	14.974458	21.724521	31.409420	45.259256	93.050970	267.863546

Table 2 Present Value of 1 at Compound Interest Due in n Periods: $p_{\overline{n}|i} = \dfrac{1}{(1+i)^n}$

n \ i	½%	1%	1½%	2%	2½%	3%
1	0.995025	0.990099	0.985222	0.980392	0.975610	0.970874
2	0.990075	0.980296	0.970662	0.961169	0.951814	0.942596
3	0.985149	0.970590	0.956317	0.942322	0.928599	0.915142
4	0.980248	0.960980	0.942184	0.923845	0.905951	0.888487
5	0.975371	0.951466	0.928260	0.905731	0.883854	0.862609
6	0.970518	0.942045	0.914542	0.887971	0.862297	0.837484
7	0.965690	0.932718	0.901027	0.870560	0.841265	0.813092
8	0.960885	0.923483	0.887711	0.853490	0.820747	0.789409
9	0.956105	0.914340	0.874592	0.836755	0.800728	0.766417
10	0.951348	0.905287	0.861667	0.820348	0.781198	0.744094
11	0.946615	0.896324	0.848933	0.804263	0.762145	0.722421
12	0.941905	0.887449	0.836387	0.788493	0.743556	0.701380
13	0.937219	0.878663	0.824027	0.773033	0.725420	0.680951
14	0.932556	0.869963	0.811849	0.757875	0.707727	0.661118
15	0.927917	0.861349	0.799852	0.743015	0.690466	0.641862
16	0.923300	0.852821	0.788031	0.728446	0.673625	0.623167
17	0.918707	0.844377	0.776385	0.714163	0.657195	0.605016
18	0.914136	0.836017	0.764912	0.700159	0.641166	0.587395
19	0.909588	0.827740	0.753607	0.686431	0.625528	0.570286
20	0.905063	0.819544	0.742470	0.672971	0.610271	0.553676
21	0.900560	0.811430	0.731498	0.659776	0.595386	0.537549
22	0.896080	0.803396	0.720688	0.646839	0.580865	0.521893
23	0.891622	0.795442	0.710037	0.634156	0.566697	0.506692
24	0.887186	0.787566	0.699544	0.621721	0.552875	0.491934
25	0.882772	0.779768	0.689206	0.609531	0.539391	0.477606
26	0.878380	0.772048	0.679021	0.597579	0.526235	0.463695
27	0.874010	0.764404	0.668986	0.585862	0.513400	0.450189
28	0.869662	0.756836	0.659099	0.574375	0.500878	0.437077
29	0.865335	0.749342	0.649359	0.563112	0.488661	0.424346
30	0.861030	0.741923	0.639762	0.552071	0.476743	0.411987
31	0.856746	0.734577	0.630308	0.541246	0.465115	0.399987
32	0.852484	0.727304	0.620993	0.530633	0.453771	0.388337
33	0.848242	0.720103	0.611816	0.520229	0.442703	0.377026
34	0.844022	0.712973	0.602774	0.510028	0.431905	0.366045
35	0.839823	0.705914	0.593866	0.500028	0.421371	0.355383
36	0.835645	0.698925	0.585090	0.490223	0.411094	0.345032
37	0.831487	0.692005	0.576443	0.480611	0.401067	0.334983
38	0.827351	0.685153	0.567924	0.471187	0.391285	0.325226
39	0.823235	0.678370	0.559531	0.461948	0.381741	0.315754
40	0.819139	0.671653	0.551262	0.452890	0.372431	0.306557

Table 2   Present Value of 1 (*continued*)

n	3½%	4%	4½%	5%	5½%	6%
1	0.966184	0.961538	0.956938	0.952381	0.947867	0.943396
2	0.933511	0.924556	0.915730	0.907029	0.898452	0.889996
3	0.901943	0.888996	0.876297	0.863838	0.851614	0.839619
4	0.871442	0.854804	0.838561	0.822702	0.807217	0.792094
5	0.841973	0.821927	0.802451	0.783526	0.765134	0.747258
6	0.813501	0.790315	0.767896	0.746215	0.725246	0.704961
7	0.785991	0.759918	0.734828	0.710681	0.687437	0.665057
8	0.759412	0.730690	0.703185	0.676839	0.651599	0.627412
9	0.733731	0.702587	0.672904	0.644609	0.617629	0.591898
10	0.708919	0.675564	0.643928	0.613913	0.585431	0.558395
11	0.684946	0.649581	0.616199	0.584679	0.554911	0.526788
12	0.661783	0.624597	0.589664	0.556837	0.525982	0.496969
13	0.639404	0.600574	0.564272	0.530321	0.498561	0.468839
14	0.617782	0.577475	0.539973	0.505068	0.472569	0.442301
15	0.596891	0.555265	0.516720	0.481017	0.447933	0.417265
16	0.576706	0.533908	0.494469	0.458112	0.424581	0.393646
17	0.557204	0.513373	0.473176	0.436297	0.402447	0.371364
18	0.538361	0.493628	0.452800	0.415521	0.381466	0.350344
19	0.520156	0.474642	0.433302	0.395734	0.361579	0.330513
20	0.502566	0.456387	0.414643	0.376889	0.342729	0.311805
21	0.485571	0.438834	0.396787	0.358942	0.324862	0.294155
22	0.469151	0.421955	0.379701	0.341850	0.307926	0.277505
23	0.453286	0.405726	0.363350	0.325571	0.291873	0.261797
24	0.437957	0.390121	0.347703	0.310068	0.276657	0.246979
25	0.423147	0.375117	0.332731	0.295303	0.262234	0.232999
26	0.408838	0.360689	0.318402	0.281241	0.248563	0.219810
27	0.395012	0.346817	0.304691	0.267848	0.235605	0.207368
28	0.381654	0.333477	0.291571	0.255094	0.223322	0.195630
29	0.368748	0.320651	0.279015	0.242946	0.211679	0.184557
30	0.356278	0.308319	0.267000	0.231377	0.200644	0.174110
31	0.344230	0.296460	0.255502	0.220359	0.190184	0.164255
32	0.332590	0.285058	0.244500	0.209866	0.180269	0.154957
33	0.321343	0.274094	0.233971	0.199873	0.170871	0.146186
34	0.310476	0.263552	0.223896	0.190355	0.161963	0.137912
35	0.299977	0.253415	0.214254	0.181290	0.153520	0.130105
36	0.289833	0.243669	0.205028	0.172657	0.145516	0.122741
37	0.280032	0.234297	0.196199	0.164436	0.137930	0.115793
38	0.270562	0.225285	0.187750	0.156605	0.130739	0.109239
39	0.261413	0.216621	0.179665	0.149148	0.123924	0.103056
40	0.252572	0.208289	0.171929	0.142046	0.117463	0.097222

Table 2   Present Value of 1 (*continued*)

n \ i	7%	8%	9%	10%	12%	15%
1	0.934580	0.925926	0.917431	0.909091	0.892857	0.869565
2	0.873439	0.857339	0.841680	0.826446	0.797194	0.756144
3	0.816298	0.793832	0.772183	0.751315	0.711780	0.657516
4	0.762895	0.735030	0.708425	0.683013	0.635518	0.571753
5	0.712986	0.680583	0.649931	0.620921	0.567427	0.497177
6	0.666342	0.630170	0.596267	0.564474	0.506631	0.432328
7	0.622750	0.583490	0.547034	0.513158	0.452349	0.375937
8	0.582009	0.540269	0.501866	0.466507	0.403883	0.326902
9	0.543934	0.500249	0.460428	0.424098	0.360610	0.284262
10	0.508349	0.463193	0.422411	0.385543	0.321973	0.247185
11	0.475093	0.428883	0.387533	0.350494	0.287476	0.214943
12	0.444012	0.397114	0.355535	0.318631	0.256675	0.186907
13	0.414964	0.367698	0.326179	0.289664	0.229174	0.162528
14	0.387817	0.340461	0.299246	0.263331	0.204620	0.141329
15	0.362446	0.315242	0.274538	0.239392	0.182696	0.122894
16	0.338735	0.291890	0.251870	0.217629	0.163122	0.106865
17	0.316574	0.270269	0.231073	0.197845	0.145644	0.092926
18	0.295864	0.250249	0.211994	0.179859	0.130040	0.080805
19	0.276508	0.231712	0.194490	0.163508	0.116107	0.070265
20	0.258419	0.214548	0.178431	0.148644	0.103667	0.061100
21	0.241513	0.198656	0.163698	0.135131	0.092560	0.053131
22	0.225713	0.183941	0.150182	0.122846	0.082643	0.046201
23	0.210947	0.170315	0.137781	0.111678	0.073788	0.040174
24	0.197147	0.157699	0.126405	0.101526	0.065882	0.034934
25	0.184249	0.146018	0.115968	0.092296	0.058823	0.030378
26	0.172195	0.135202	0.106393	0.083905	0.052521	0.026415
27	0.160930	0.125187	0.097608	0.076278	0.046894	0.022970
28	0.150402	0.115914	0.089548	0.069343	0.041869	0.019974
29	0.140563	0.107328	0.082155	0.063039	0.037383	0.017369
30	0.131367	0.099377	0.075371	0.057309	0.033378	0.015103
31	0.122773	0.092016	0.069148	0.052099	0.029802	0.013133
32	0.114741	0.085200	0.063438	0.047362	0.026609	0.011420
33	0.107235	0.078889	0.058200	0.043057	0.023758	0.009931
34	0.100219	0.073045	0.053395	0.039143	0.021212	0.008635
35	0.093663	0.067635	0.048986	0.035584	0.018940	0.007509
36	0.087535	0.062625	0.044941	0.032349	0.016910	0.006529
37	0.081809	0.057986	0.041231	0.029408	0.015098	0.005678
38	0.076457	0.053690	0.037826	0.026735	0.013481	0.004937
39	0.071455	0.049713	0.034703	0.024304	0.012036	0.004293
40	0.066780	0.046031	0.031838	0.022095	0.010747	0.003733

APPENDIX: COMPOUND INTEREST TABLES

Table 3 Future Amount of Ordinary Annuity of 1 per Period: $A_{\overline{n}|i} = \dfrac{(1+i)^n - 1}{i}$

n \ i	½%	1%	1½%	2%	2½%	3%
1	1.000000	1.000000	1.000000	1.000000	1.000000	1.000000
2	2.005000	2.010000	2.015000	2.020000	2.025000	2.030000
3	3.015025	3.030100	3.045225	3.060400	3.075625	3.090900
4	4.030100	4.060401	4.090903	4.121608	4.152516	4.183627
5	5.050251	5.101005	5.152267	5.204040	5.256329	5.309136
6	6.075502	6.152015	6.229551	6.308121	6.387737	6.468410
7	7.105879	7.213535	7.322994	7.434283	7.547430	7.662462
8	8.141409	8.285671	8.432839	8.582969	8.736116	8.892336
9	9.182116	9.368527	9.559332	9.754628	9.954519	10.159106
10	10.228026	10.462213	10.702722	10.949721	11.203382	11.463879
11	11.279167	11.566835	11.863262	12.168715	12.483466	12.807796
12	12.335562	12.682503	13.041211	13.412090	13.795553	14.192030
13	13.397240	13.809328	14.236830	14.680332	15.140442	15.617790
14	14.464226	14.947421	15.450382	15.973938	16.518953	17.086324
15	15.536548	16.096896	16.682138	17.293417	17.931927	18.598914
16	16.614230	17.257864	17.932370	18.639285	19.380225	20.156881
17	17.697301	18.430443	19.201355	20.012071	20.864730	21.761588
18	18.785788	19.614748	20.489376	21.412312	22.386349	23.414435
19	19.879717	20.810895	21.796716	22.840559	23.946007	25.116868
20	20.979115	22.019004	23.123667	24.297370	25.544658	26.870374
21	22.084011	23.239194	24.470522	25.783317	27.183274	28.676486
22	23.194431	24.471586	25.837580	27.298984	28.862856	30.536780
23	24.310403	25.716302	27.225144	28.844963	30.584427	32.452884
24	25.431955	26.973465	28.633521	30.421862	32.349038	34.426470
25	26.559115	28.243200	30.063024	32.030300	34.157764	36.459264
26	27.691911	29.525632	31.513969	33.670906	36.011708	38.553042
27	28.830370	30.820888	32.986679	35.344324	37.912001	40.709634
28	29.974522	32.129097	34.481479	37.051210	39.859801	42.930923
29	31.124395	33.450388	35.998701	38.792235	41.856296	45.218850
30	32.280017	34.784892	37.538681	40.568079	43.902703	47.575416
31	33.441417	36.132740	39.101762	42.379441	46.000271	50.002678
32	34.608624	37.494068	40.688288	44.227030	48.150278	52.502759
33	35.781667	38.869009	42.298612	46.111570	50.354034	55.077841
34	36.960575	40.257699	43.933092	48.033802	52.612885	57.730177
35	38.145378	41.660276	45.592088	49.994478	54.928207	60.462082
36	39.336105	43.076878	47.275969	51.994367	57.301413	63.275944
37	40.532785	44.507647	48.985109	54.034255	59.733948	66.174223
38	41.735449	45.952724	50.719885	56.114940	62.227297	69.159449
39	42.944127	47.412251	52.480684	58.237238	64.782979	72.234233
40	44.158847	48.886373	54.267894	60.401983	67.402554	75.401260

Table 3   Future Amount of Ordinary Annuity of 1 (*continued*)

n \ i	3½%	4%	4½%	5%	5½%	6%
1	1.000000	1.000000	1.000000	1.000000	1.000000	1.000000
2	2.035000	2.040000	2.045000	2.050000	2.055000	2.060000
3	3.106225	3.121600	3.137025	3.152500	3.168025	3.183600
4	4.214943	4.246464	4.278191	4.310125	4.342266	4.374616
5	5.362466	5.416323	5.470710	5.525631	5.581091	5.637093
6	6.550152	6.632975	6.716892	6.801913	6.888051	6.975319
7	7.779408	7.898294	8.019152	8.142008	8.266894	8.393838
8	9.051687	9.214226	9.380014	9.549109	9.721573	9.897468
9	10.368496	10.582795	10.802114	11.026564	11.256260	11.491316
10	11.731393	12.006107	12.288209	12.577893	12.875354	13.180795
11	13.141992	13.486351	13.841179	14.206787	14.583498	14.971643
12	14.601962	15.025805	15.464032	15.917127	16.385591	16.869941
13	16.113030	16.626838	17.159913	17.712983	18.286798	18.882138
14	17.676986	18.291911	18.932109	19.598632	20.292572	21.015066
15	19.295681	20.023588	20.784054	21.578564	22.408664	23.275970
16	20.971030	21.824531	22.719337	23.657492	24.641140	25.672528
17	22.705016	23.697512	24.741707	25.840366	26.996403	28.212880
18	24.499691	25.645413	26.855084	28.132385	29.481205	30.905653
19	26.357181	27.671229	29.063562	30.539004	32.102671	33.759992
20	28.279682	29.778079	31.371423	33.065954	34.868318	36.785591
21	30.269471	31.969202	33.783137	35.719252	37.786076	39.992727
22	32.328902	34.247970	36.303378	38.505214	40.864310	43.392290
23	34.460414	36.617889	38.937030	41.430475	44.111847	46.995828
24	36.666528	39.082604	41.689196	44.501999	47.537998	50.815577
25	38.949857	41.645908	44.565210	47.727099	51.152588	54.864512
26	41.313102	44.311745	47.570645	51.113454	54.965981	59.156383
27	43.759060	47.084214	50.711324	54.669126	58.989109	63.705766
28	46.290627	49.967583	53.993333	58.402583	63.233510	68.528112
29	48.910799	52.966286	57.423033	62.322712	67.711354	73.629798
30	51.622677	56.084938	61.007070	66.438848	72.435478	79.058186
31	54.429471	59.328335	64.752388	70.760790	77.419429	84.801677
32	57.334502	62.701469	68.666245	75.298829	82.677498	90.889778
33	60.341210	66.209527	72.756226	80.063771	88.224760	97.343165
34	63.453152	69.857909	77.030256	85.066959	94.077122	104.183755
35	66.674013	73.652225	81.496618	90.320307	100.251364	111.434780
36	70.007603	77.598314	86.163966	95.836323	106.765189	119.120867
37	73.457869	81.702246	91.041344	101.628139	113.637274	127.268119
38	77.028895	85.970336	96.138205	107.709546	120.887324	135.904206
39	80.724906	90.409150	101.464424	114.095023	128.536127	145.058458
40	84.550278	95.025516	107.030323	120.799774	136.605614	154.761966

Table 3   Future Amount of Ordinary Annuity of 1 (*continued*)

n \ i	7%	8%	9%	10%	12%	15%
1	1.000000	1.000000	1.000000	1.000000	1.000000	1.000000
2	2.070000	2.080000	2.090000	2.100000	2.120000	2.150000
3	3.214900	3.246400	3.278100	3.310000	3.374400	3.472500
4	4.439943	4.506112	4.573129	4.641000	4.779328	4.993375
5	5.750740	5.866601	5.984711	6.105100	6.352847	6.742381
6	7.153291	7.335929	7.523335	7.715610	8.115189	8.753738
7	8.654021	8.922803	9.200435	9.487171	10.089012	11.066799
8	10.259803	10.636628	11.028474	11.435888	12.299693	13.726819
9	11.977989	12.487558	13.021036	13.579477	14.775656	16.785842
10	13.816448	14.486562	15.192930	15.937425	17.548735	20.303718
11	15.783599	16.645487	17.560293	18.531167	20.654583	24.349276
12	17.888451	18.977126	20.140720	21.384284	24.133133	29.001667
13	20.140643	21.495297	22.953385	24.522712	28.029109	34.351917
14	22.550488	24.214920	26.019189	27.974983	32.392602	40.504705
15	25.129022	27.152114	29.360916	31.772482	37.279715	47.580411
16	27.888054	30.324283	33.003399	35.949730	42.753280	55.717472
17	30.840217	33.750226	36.973705	40.544703	48.883674	65.075093
18	33.999033	37.450244	41.301338	45.599173	55.749715	75.836357
19	37.378965	41.446263	46.018458	51.159090	63.439681	88.211811
20	40.995492	45.761964	51.160120	57.274999	72.052442	102.443583
21	44.865177	50.422921	56.764530	64.002499	81.698736	118.810120
22	49.005739	55.456755	62.873338	71.402749	92.502584	137.631638
23	53.436141	60.893296	69.531939	79.543024	104.602894	159.276384
24	58.176671	66.764759	76.789813	88.497327	118.155241	184.167841
25	63.249038	73.105940	84.700896	98.347059	133.333870	212.793017
26	68.676470	79.954415	93.323977	109.181765	150.333934	245.711970
27	74.483823	87.350768	102.723135	121.099942	169.374007	283.568766
28	80.697691	95.338830	112.968217	134.209936	190.698887	327.104080
29	87.346529	103.965936	124.135356	148.630930	214.582754	377.169693
30	94.460786	113.283211	136.307539	164.494023	241.332684	434.745146
31	102.073041	123.345868	149.575217	181.943425	271.292606	500.956918
32	110.218154	134.213537	164.036987	201.137767	304.847719	577.100456
33	118.933425	145.950620	179.800315	222.251544	342.429446	644.665525
34	128.258765	158.626670	196.982344	245.476699	384.520979	765.365353
35	138.236878	172.316804	215.710755	271.024368	431.663496	881.170156
36	148.913460	187.102148	236.124723	299.126805	484.463116	1014.345680
37	160.337402	203.070320	258.375948	330.039486	543.598690	1167.497532
38	172.561020	220.315945	282.629783	364.043434	609.830533	1343.622161
39	185.640292	238.941221	309.066463	401.447778	684.010197	1546.165485
40	199.635112	259.056519	337.882445	442.592556	767.091420	1779.090308

Table 4 Present Value of Ordinary Annuity of 1 per Period: $P_{\overline{n}|i} = \dfrac{1 - \dfrac{1}{(1+i)^n}}{i}$

n \ i	½%	1%	1½%	2%	2½%	3%
1	0.995025	0.990099	0.985222	0.980392	0.975610	0.970874
2	1.985099	1.970395	1.955883	1.941561	1.927424	1.913470
3	2.970248	2.940985	2.912200	2.883883	2.856024	2.828611
4	3.950496	3.901966	3.854385	3.807729	3.761974	3.717098
5	4.925866	4.853431	4.782645	4.713460	4.645829	4.579707
6	5.896384	5.795476	5.697187	5.601431	5.508125	5.417191
7	6.862074	6.728195	6.598214	6.471991	6.349391	6.230283
8	7.822959	7.651678	7.485925	7.325481	7.170137	7.019692
9	8.779064	8.566018	8.360517	8.162237	7.970866	7.786109
10	9.730412	9.471305	9.222185	8.982585	8.752064	8.530203
11	10.677027	10.367628	10.071118	9.786848	9.514209	9.252624
12	11.618932	11.255077	10.907505	10.575341	10.257765	9.954004
13	12.556151	12.133740	11.731532	11.348374	10.983185	10.634955
14	13.488708	13.003703	12.543382	12.106249	11.690912	11.296073
15	14.416625	13.865053	13.343233	12.849264	12.381378	11.937935
16	15.339925	14.717874	14.131264	13.577709	13.055003	12.561102
17	16.258632	15.562251	14.907649	14.291872	13.712198	13.166118
18	17.172768	16.398269	15.672561	14.992031	14.353364	13.753513
19	18.082356	17.226009	16.426168	15.678462	14.978891	14.323799
20	18.987419	18.045553	17.168639	16.351433	15.589162	14.877475
21	19.887979	18.856983	17.900137	17.011209	16.184549	15.415024
22	20.784059	19.660379	18.620824	17.658048	16.765413	15.936917
23	21.675681	20.455821	19.330861	18.292204	17.332110	16.443608
24	22.562866	21.243387	20.030405	18.913926	17.884986	16.935542
25	23.445638	22.023156	20.719611	19.523456	18.424376	17.413148
26	24.324018	22.795204	21.398632	20.121036	18.950611	17.876842
27	25.198028	23.559608	22.067617	20.706898	19.464011	18.327031
28	26.067689	24.316443	22.726717	21.281272	19.964889	18.764108
29	26.933024	25.065785	23.376076	21.844385	20.453550	19.188455
30	27.794054	25.807708	24.015838	22.396456	20.930293	19.600441
31	28.650800	26.542285	24.646146	22.937702	21.395407	20.000428
32	29.503284	27.269589	25.267139	23.468335	21.849178	20.388766
33	30.351526	27.989693	25.878954	23.988564	22.291881	20.765792
34	31.195548	28.702666	26.481728	24.498592	22.723786	21.131837
35	32.035371	29.408580	27.075595	24.998619	23.145157	21.487220
36	32.871016	30.107505	27.660684	25.488842	23.556251	21.832253
37	33.702504	30.799510	28.237127	25.969453	23.957318	22.167235
38	34.529854	31.484663	28.805052	26.440641	24.348603	22.492462
39	35.353089	32.163033	29.364583	26.902589	24.730344	22.808215
40	36.172228	32.834686	29.915845	27.355479	25.102775	23.114772

Table 4　Present Value of Ordinary Annuity of 1 (*continued*)

n	3½%	4%	4½%	5%	5½%	6%
1	0.966184	0.961538	0.956938	0.952381	0.947867	0.943396
2	1.899694	1.886095	1.872668	1.859410	1.846320	1.833393
3	2.801637	2.775091	2.748964	2.723248	2.697933	2.673012
4	3.673079	3.629895	3.587526	3.545951	3.505150	3.465106
5	4.515052	4.451822	4.389977	4.329477	4.270284	4.212364
6	5.328553	5.242137	5.157872	5.075692	4.995530	4.917324
7	6.114544	6.002055	5.892701	5.786373	5.682967	5.582381
8	6.873956	6.732745	6.595886	6.463213	6.334566	6.209794
9	7.607687	7.435332	7.268791	7.107822	6.952195	6.801692
10	8.316605	8.110896	7.912718	7.721735	7.537626	7.360087
11	9.001551	8.760477	8.528917	8.306414	8.092536	7.886875
12	9.663334	9.385074	9.118581	8.863252	8.618518	8.383844
13	10.302738	9.985648	9.682852	9.393573	9.117079	8.852683
14	10.920520	10.563123	10.222825	9.898641	9.589648	9.294984
15	11.517411	11.118387	10.739546	10.379658	10.037581	9.712249
16	12.094117	11.652296	11.234015	10.837770	10.462162	10.105895
17	12.651321	12.165669	11.707191	11.274066	10.864609	10.477260
18	13.189682	12.659297	12.159992	11.689587	11.246074	10.827603
19	13.709837	13.133939	12.593294	12.085321	11.607654	11.158116
20	14.212403	13.590326	13.007936	12.462210	11.950382	11.469921
21	14.697974	14.029160	13.404724	12.821153	12.275244	11.764077
22	15.167125	14.451115	13.784425	13.163003	12.583170	12.041582
23	15.620410	14.856842	14.147775	13.488574	12.875042	12.303379
24	16.058368	15.246963	14.495478	13.798642	13.151699	12.550358
25	16.481515	15.622080	14.828209	14.093945	13.413933	12.783356
26	16.890352	15.982769	15.146611	14.375185	13.662495	13.003166
27	17.285365	16.329586	15.451303	14.643034	13.898100	13.210534
28	17.667019	16.663063	15.742874	14.898127	14.121422	13.406164
29	18.035767	16.983715	16.021889	15.141074	14.333101	13.590721
30	18.392045	17.292033	16.288889	15.372451	14.533745	13.764831
31	18.736276	17.588494	16.544391	15.592811	14.723929	13.929086
32	19.068865	17.873552	16.788891	15.802677	14.904198	14.084043
33	19.390208	18.147646	17.022862	16.002549	15.075069	14.230230
34	19.700684	18.411198	17.246758	16.192904	15.237033	14.368141
35	20.000661	18.664613	17.461012	16.374194	15.390552	14.498246
36	20.290494	18.908282	17.666041	16.546852	15.536068	14.620987
37	20.570525	19.142579	17.862240	16.711287	15.673999	14.736780
38	20.841087	19.367864	18.049990	16.867893	15.804738	14.846019
39	21.102500	19.584485	18.229656	17.017041	15.928662	14.949075
40	21.355072	19.792774	18.401584	17.159086	16.046125	15.046297

Table 4   Present Value of Ordinary Annuity of 1 (*continued*)

n	7%	8%	9%	10%	12%	15%
1	0.934579	0.925926	0.917431	0.909091	0.892857	0.869565
2	1.808018	1.783265	1.759111	1.735537	1.690051	1.625709
3	2.624316	2.577097	2.531295	2.486852	2.401831	2.283225
4	3.387211	3.312127	3.239720	3.169865	3.037349	2.854978
5	4.100197	3.992710	3.889651	3.790787	3.604776	3.352155
6	4.766540	4.622880	4.485919	4.355261	4.111407	3.784483
7	5.389289	5.206370	5.032953	4.868419	4.563757	4.160420
8	5.971299	5.746639	5.534819	5.334926	4.967640	4.487322
9	6.515232	6.246888	5.995247	5.759024	5.328250	4.771584
10	7.023582	6.710081	6.417658	6.144567	5.650223	5.018769
11	7.498674	7.138964	6.805191	6.495061	5.937699	5.233712
12	7.942686	7.536078	7.160725	6.813692	6.194374	5.420619
13	8.357651	7.903776	7.486904	7.103356	6.423548	5.583147
14	8.745468	8.244237	7.786150	7.366687	6.628168	5.724476
15	9.107914	8.559479	8.060688	7.606080	6.810864	5.847370
16	9.446649	8.851369	8.312558	7.823709	6.973986	5.954235
17	9.763223	9.121638	8.543631	8.021553	7.119630	6.047161
18	10.059087	9.371887	8.755625	8.201412	7.249670	6.127966
19	10.335595	9.603599	8.950115	8.364920	7.365777	6.198231
20	10.594014	9.818147	9.128546	8.513564	7.469444	6.259331
21	10.835527	10.016803	9.292244	8.648694	7.562003	6.312462
22	11.061241	10.200744	9.442425	8.771540	7.644646	6.358663
23	11.272187	10.371059	9.580207	8.883218	7.718434	6.398837
24	11.469334	10.528758	9.706612	8.984744	7.784316	6.433771
25	11.653583	10.674776	9.822580	9.077040	7.843139	6.464149
26	11.825779	10.809978	9.928972	9.160945	7.895660	6.490564
27	11.986709	10.935165	10.026580	9.237223	7.942554	6.513534
28	12.137111	11.051078	10.116128	9.306567	7.984423	6.533508
29	12.277674	11.158406	10.198283	9.369606	8.021806	6.550877
30	12.409041	11.257783	10.273654	9.426914	8.055184	6.565980
31	12.531814	11.349799	10.342802	9.479013	8.084986	6.579113
32	12.646555	11.434999	10.406240	9.526376	8.111594	6.590533
33	12.753790	11.513888	10.464441	9.569432	8.135352	6.600463
34	12.854009	11.586934	10.517835	9.608575	8.156564	6.609099
35	12.947672	11.654568	10.566821	9.644159	8.175504	6.616607
36	13.035208	11.717193	10.611763	9.676508	8.192414	6.623137
37	13.117017	11.775179	10.652993	9.705917	8.207513	6.628815
38	13.193473	11.828869	10.690820	9.732651	8.220993	6.633752
39	13.264928	11.878582	10.725523	9.756956	8.233030	6.638045
40	13.331709	11.924613	10.757360	9.779051	8.243777	6.641778

Note: This table is for the present value of an *ordinary* annuity. To find the present value of *annuity due,* look up the table for one *less* payment, and then add 1.00 to the table value. For example, to find the present value of annuity due of 5 payments at a rate of 10%, look up the table at 4 payments, 10% (3.169865), add 1.00, resulting in 4.169865.

Index

Index